T0388254

'Cor's analysis [gives] us insights of what is happening at a macro-economic level worldwide level, at the same time bringing us at arm's length of what is happening both at the customer's side and the business side so close by.'

Dr. Sofie Geeroms, *Managing Director, BeCommerce, Belgium*

'In the retail arena where my business is competing, changes are rapid and disruptive and this calls for connecting with communities in new ways. Digitisation, technology and data management all play a critical role in this transformation. This book will show you how you can use it to create a competitive edge!'

Giovanni Colauto, *CEO, de Bijenkorf department stores, The Netherlands*

Demand-Driven Business Strategy

Demand-Driven Business Strategy explains the ways of transforming business models from supply driven to demand driven through digital technologies and big data analytics.

The book covers important topics such as digital leadership, the role of artificial intelligence, and platform firms and their role in business model transformation. Students are walked through the nature of supply- and demand-driven models and how organizations transform from one to the other. Theoretical insights are combined with real-world application through global case studies and examples from Amazon, Google, Uber, Volvo and Picnic. Chapter objectives and summaries provide consistent structure and aid learning, whilst reflective questions encourage further thought and discussion.

Comprehensive and practical, this is an essential text for advanced undergraduate and postgraduate students studying strategic management, marketing, business innovation, consumer behavior, digital transformation and entrepreneurship.

Cor Molenaar is Professor at Rotterdam School of Management, Erasmus University, The Netherlands.

Business and Digital Transformation

Digital technologies are transforming societies across the globe, the effects of which are yet to be fully understood. In the business world, technological disruption brings an array of challenges and opportunities for organizations, management and the workplace.

This series of textbooks provides a student-centred library to analyse, explore and critique the evolutionary effects of technology on the business world. Each book in the series takes the perspective of a key business discipline and examines the transformational potential of digital technology, aided by real-world cases and examples.

With contributions from expert scholars across the globe, the books in this series enable critical thinking students to excel in their studies of the new digital business environment.

Strategic Digital Transformation
A Results-Driven Approach
Edited by Alex Fenton, Gordon Fletcher and Marie Griffiths

Hospitality Management and Digital Transformation
Balancing Efficiency, Agility and Guest Experience in the Era of Disruption
Richard Busulwa, Nina Evans, Aaron Oh and Moon Kang

Digital Transformation in Accounting
Richard Busulwa and Nina Evans

Demand-Driven Business Strategy
Digital Transformation and Business Model Innovation
Cor Molenaar

For more information about this series, please visit www.routledge.com/ Routledge-New-Directions-in-Public-Relations-Communication-Research/ book-series/BAD

Demand-Driven Business Strategy
Digital Transformation and Business Model Innovation

Cor Molenaar

Routledge
Taylor & Francis Group

LONDON AND NEW YORK

Cover image: © Getty Images

First published 2022
by Routledge
4 Park Square, Milton Park, Abingdon, Oxon OX14 4RN

and by Routledge
605 Third Avenue, New York, NY 10158

Routledge is an imprint of the Taylor & Francis Group, an informa business

© 2022 Cor Molenaar

British Library Cataloguing-in-Publication Data
A catalogue record for this book is available from the British Library

Library of Congress Cataloging-in-Publication Data
Names: Molenaar, Cor, author.
Title: Demand-driven business strategy : digital transformation and business model innovation / Cor Molenaar.
Description: Milton Park, Abingdon, Oxon ; New York, NY : Routledge, 2022. | Includes bibliographical references and index.
Identifiers: LCCN 2021039301 (print) | LCCN 2021039302 (ebook) | ISBN 9781032127651 (hardback) | ISBN 9781032127668 (paperback) | ISBN 9781003226161 (ebook)
Subjects: LCSH: Organizational change. | Management--Technological innovations. | Business planning.
Classification: LCC HD58.8 .M626 2022 (print) | LCC HD58.8 (ebook) | DDC 658.4/06--dc23
LC record available at https://lccn.loc.gov/2021039301
LC ebook record available at https://lccn.loc.gov/2021039302

ISBN: 978-1-032-12765-1 (hbk)
ISBN: 978-1-032-12766-8 (pbk)
ISBN: 978-1-003-22616-1 (ebk)

DOI: 10.4324/9781003226161

Typeset in Bembo
by Taylor & Francis Books

Contents

Figures

Preface

The rapid development of a new focus in economy, changing the supply focus to a demand focus, leads to the implication that to remain competitive in today's world, businesses need to build upon what customers want, rather than what suppliers have. This fast-approaching development requires an entire shift in business models. Consequently, the book examines the question of *how a company needs to reimagine its business to succeed in the new demand-driven economy*. The literature and practical research show that the most important ingredient to become demand-driven is implementing a digital leadership strategy to lead the creation of a demand-driven business model. Additionally, new tools such as *demand profit pooling* and the *demand value chain model* can be used to create a demand-driven business. Specifically, this book explores how firms can create value in a demand-driven economy by implementing a product-as-a-service business model. The analysis of the subscription-based model, Care by Volvo, underlined the possibility for a legacy business to adapt to the realities of shifting consumer habits and use this information to develop a competitive advantage understanding of demand, as well as rebuild their value chain into one that is fit to survive the demand-driven economy. However, it must be taken into consideration that a shift in mindset and strategy should not be underestimated and takes a long time to be profoundly accepted and implemented. New entrants to the market use also new business models and will grow aggressively. Booking.com, Alibaba, Airbnb and Uber are just a few new companies using new business models, using new technologies and having a focus on customers' behavior. Machine learning is just one of the new supportive technologies and fundamental for these companies. Networking, cloud computing and platforms are new concepts disrupting the present market conditions. It is evident that existing companies have to change to survive these disruptors and new market circumstances.

Digitalization is not enough. Digitalization only transfers existing processes into digital processes. The concept is the same, the tools are different.

New Business Models

A transformation from supply-driven to demand-driven is a fundamental change. It has an effect on the structure of an organization, the marketing strategy, the IT tools and, of course, the business model. No longer is the focus on transactions, but on value creation for customers, the network and eventually also for the companies involved. This change started with multi-sided platforms like Uber and Airbnb, matching platforms based on customer needs and supply. The original focus of companies was on products, but this focus changed to customer needs. A matching of customer needs with supply needed an integration of analyses and a change of the buying process. Companies like Amazon and Alibaba started as a selling platform and attracted brands, but also other web shops start selling through these platforms. They are aggregators of supply; "everything stores" as Amazon was once called. But because of the immense range in supply and diversity it was also a non-stop store with search tools for products. They implemented analyses and later on machine learning tools to detect similar buying patterns between customers. That way they formed clusters based on buying preferences. This was a new world for marketing. A new form of clustering based on customer behavior. Comparison within the cluster was used to predict future sales and to predict loyalty. Marketing changed in marketing intelligence.

Data as Strategic Marketing Tool

This matching for products and looking for causalities became a competitive edge for companies. In the last few years the focus changed based on the data generated. Personal data, browsing data, social media data and "need" detection. Data became the most essential asset of a company. Based on the data, predictive modelling became possible and the alignment of the supply (chain), or imploding, was a logical consequence. The focus shifted to the buying needs and therefore a stronger focus on the added value of a company. This was the start of value networks and a new ecosystem. Collaboration, interaction and communication are supported by the internet, smartphones and apps. The communication is based on algorithms, predefined triggers and responses. Human beings need communication, which is a clear lesson from the lockdowns of Covid-19. This book will outline the changes, transformation of companies and disruption in markets. Threats and opportunities, but above all the changes in marketing and organizations that are needed for a sustainable future. Times have changed, people have changed, so strategy and focus have to change. Data will guide us in this strategic change for companies.

Research

Students from RSM/Erasmus University have conducted intense research based on topics, literature and discussions. The findings of the research teams are included in this book and are a mix of solid research, but also the views of a new generation looking ahead to possibilities and an exciting future. This generation are the leaders of the future. The future is a fundament for their success and the success of companies. This book will highlight the changes and disruption, and form an academic basis for teaching this new generation. A mix of causality, correlation and research from the past. We, as academics, have to work together, share knowledge and insights to help our students to be ready for an unpredicted future. Some research teams I like to highlight specially: Sarah Maier and Luciana Mordoh for their research about business models in a demand-driven economy was of a high standard, as was the research of Valeria Kapleva, Clara Siersema and Isabella Severinio about the impact of technology on competitive relationships.

But, although I used some specific research findings, all students have participated one way or another in various discussions and briefings. I see this book as a nice example of student participation in the focus of teaching.

And of course, I thank Patricia for her patience once again.

Cor Molenaar
Oosterbeek, The Netherlands

1 Introduction

The rapid development away from supply- towards a demand-driven economy leads to the implication that to remain competitive in today's world, businesses need to build upon what customers want, rather than what suppliers already have. New tools such as demand profit pooling and the demand chain model can be used to create a demand-driven business. Specifically, how firms can create value in a demand-driven economy by implementing a product-as-a-service business model. However, it must be taken into consideration that a shift in mindset and strategy should not be underestimated and takes a long time to be profoundly accepted and implemented. This chapter will outline the change in attitude and the consequences of a demand-driven strategy.

> Just how did McDonalds know that it was time to introduce salads and to keep their stores open twenty-four hours per day? How did Apple know that consumers wanted to bring the best mobile phones and PCs together into a device that might ultimately reinvent both industries?
>
> (Kash & Calhoun, 2010, p. 28)

And how can Amazon predict the sales four weeks ahead? The answer to these questions is that each of these companies had a deeper understanding of their consumers and used this information to change the way in which they operated business (Gupta, 2018, p. 21). In addition, these companies not just asked what their customers really wanted, but they recognized patterns and saw trends to develop a hypothesis about what their customers *will* want in the future (Kash & Calhoun, 2010, p. 28).

Airbnb, Uber, Google, Alibaba, Facebook are seen as the new market leaders, disruptive because they changed the processes from analogue to digital, from selling goods to connecting people and business. This is the base of disrupting processes and markets which will shape our lives and our businesses in the coming years. A change in budget spending, a different business model and new forms of collaboration between people, people and companies, and between institutions. An interactive network. Especially companies where information and services are the core business or where access of information is part of the sales process, customer needs and preferences will be the main focus

DOI: 10.4324/9781003226161-1

point. Collaboration in a platform or a network to fulfill the demand of customers will be the fundament of business in the near future. From supply to demand, supported by data, machine learning and algorithms.

A platform and a value network are value creating interactions, demand-driven between external producers and customers it provides an open, participative infrastructure.

Shift in Mindset

Because of a digitalizing world, the urge toward "being digital" and part of the new platform world is more relevant than ever. There is a shift in mindset needed to manage this new world. This shift concerns the shift in business principles and business models while acknowledging that value creation is not based on supply of goods and services but on customer needs. A mind shift, from supply to demand. Customers specify their needs and will search for the right products or services. This is a mind shift, because no longer are product values dominant, rather they need criteria, and matching values will offer the right product or service.

The vast majority of traditional media, television, radio and newspapers act like pipelines, pushing content to consumers. YouTube, podcasts, search engines like Google and social media use interactive platform models. These platforms continue to encourage content producers and consumers to communicate with each other. The democratization of content production and the transformation of media capabilities from journalists to user producers have led to a shift from traditional media to social media (Choudary, 2015). Like other shifts to platform scale, emerging media platforms rely less on the ownership of resources (content) and rely more on their ability to coordinate the interaction between content producers and consumers. Interaction and need specifications will lead to a demand-driven supply. Knowledge of the need of a buyer will be the most important value of organization in the digital world. Because of a more connected world, it gives companies the opportunity to leverage on a new source of scale. This is an external ecosystem of users and partners who are connected over the internet to the businesses (Choudary, 2015). The ecosystem-based view of value creation is completely different from the traditional resource-based view of value creation. Control of resources isn't an important source of competitive advantage anymore. In fact, this community creates value for itself.

What Do Customers Want?

These developments underline the fundamental shift in the relationship between supply and demand in the global economy. It is a shift away from the supply-driven economy (companies *push* goods to the market) to a demand-driven economy (the customer *pulls* goods from the market), which requires a new set of tools, skills and strategies (Bursa, 2015, pp. 1–2). This shift has been fast approaching since the beginning of the 21st century, due to an oversupply and technological developments, which changed the way in which consumers engage with business and vice versa (Kash & Calhoun, 2010, p. 28). To remain competitive in today's world, businesses need to build upon what customers want, rather than what the suppliers already have, and this requires leveraging technology to analyze, predict and develop a supreme understanding of demand. However, although it may sound very simple to become demand-driven, it can be a difficult concept to execute (Gupta, 2018, p. 28). In order to survive, an entire shift in the business model is required. The major question for every boardroom looking at future success should be: *How should a company reimagine their business model in order to succeed in the new demand-driven economy, and what tools are needed to predict the behavior of customers?*

The introduction of digital technology has presented customers with transparency and new ways to search for information about products. Consumers are increasingly relying on online reviews on the internet or "word of mouth" from friends. The change in consumer behavior has likewise presented firms with a new way to connect with its customer base. Firms that are the most effective at connecting information regarding the customer's path to purchase (supporting the buying process) are able to position themselves strongly in the future market. Large organizations such as Amazon and Uber realized that competitive advantage is no longer derived from low cost or product differentiation. Instead, competitive advantage is gained and sustained through a platform offering a system of connected and complementary products that raise consumer's switching costs through strong network effects, meaning the value of the platform increases, the more people use it (Gupta, 2018). Network effects and knowledge of customer behavior and needs, provide the driving force behind any successful organization and platform, together with a demand-driven approach (what will customers want and why?).

Changing Organizations

Additionally, traditional companies (supply-driven) are facing new challenges as a growing proportion of their customer base are becoming increasingly impatient and standards for demand rise. As a result, customers are incrementally shifting towards digital firms, putting pipeline companies without similar digital capabilities at risk (McKinsey & Company, 2019). This presents a compelling case for firms that wish to remain prosperous to become more consumer centered. An illustration showing the shift in the digital age of business is the realization that today, seven of the world's twelve largest corporations are platform businesses. However, despite these figures only a marginal percentage (2%) of companies have adopted a demand-driven platform strategy. Therefore, it appears that most pipeline business managers still believe that their product is valuable by itself and that users will interact with it because of this.

Customer-driven sounds similar to demand-driven; however, that is not the case. In case of customer centered, the interaction is still based on the supply of products. The communication is based on a single customer. Customer centricity was established in direct marketing in the 1980s and was adopted by organization. Customer relationship management (CRM) was a kind of customer file with contact history. Based on the contact history a direct communication was possible using the new digital tools. Loyalty became a key variable and was based on repeat sales and later on the level of contact with an organization, as we will see later (see discussion of RFM in Chapter 5).

Despite these moderate numbers of organizations which used customer demand as an energetic policy, there is enough evidence to suggest that more organizations will have to adapt to a demand-driven business model eventually. Thomas Cook, a former English travel agency, recently filed for administration due to unendurable debt and insufficient revenues. Thomas Cook followed a pipeline business structure and was successful for over a century; however, as the digital age emerged and customer preferences changed, they failed to adapt. The last decade has seen a rise in online bookings as customers prefer to book their own travels independently. The shift in consumer preferences directly negatively affected the sales of Thomas Cook. Despite this, limited action was taken to prevent continued loss. While Thomas Cook struggled, online platforms such as online travel agents Booking.com and Expedia were able to take advantage of a gaping hole in the market. Booking.com and Expedia could both offer customers a convenience and facilitate a demand-based platform that contained information about customers, behavior and buying preferences, and the availability of thousands of hotels, and offers a service to book direct.

Thomas Cook is not the only company to suffer as a result of lack of adaptability, agility. Worldwide the taxi industry has experienced a major disruption with the introduction of Uber and Lyft. Uber and Lyft revolutionized transportation by creating a completely new supply of cars and drivers by connecting drivers and reducing the transaction cost of finding a driver or rider. Taxi companies have as a result lost their market share by ignoring the changing needs of their consumers.

From Products to Services

As consumer interests are shifting from products towards experiences, companies must adapt in a similar fashion by creating unique customer experiences that complement their products, and by using data about customer needs and preferences. Companies such as Sephora allow consumers to scan a QR code next to products which takes them to a website with information, reviews and video-tutorials (Gupta, 2018). This has seen Sephora increase its sales by creating unique experience, as well as providing other firms with ideas of how to remain competitive in a pipeline business. On top of it, they gathered the customer information based on behavior and preferences. Demand-driven businesses have led to the adoption of disruptive digital strategies such as platforms and ecosystems. A platform is a business model that aims to facilitate value-creating interactions between external producers and consumers.

Platforms are able to create value by providing an open interface for active participation. In contrast to pipeline businesses, which will be discussed later, the community and the resources of the platform's members are the platform's most valuable asset. As a result, the focus of matching platforms shifts towards facilitating interactions and increasing customer satisfaction (Parker et al., 2018).

The Power of Platforms

Platforms provide greater value to consumers than pipelines by offering greater convenience and variety of products, as shown by Uber and Airbnb. Furthermore, platforms possess the ability to open new areas of demand and supply that were previously unheard off. Previous barriers to entry, such as geography, which remains a costly obstacle for pipeline business, are vastly reduced by platforms that are able to extend their reach to both buyers and suppliers around the world. This is a major advantage concerning platforms. Also, a platform is not based on transaction but on matching of needs and supply. Therefore, customers will buy more frequently, as we will see later on. These processes of demand-driven structure (platforms) need to go from outside in, which means that market-facing processes will change to supplier-facing processes.

Lastly, demand-driven companies keep their focus on the outcome/results. Because of the implementation of demand-driven value networks, the focus shifts from selling to the channel, to selling through the channel. Besides that, the focus can also shift from product-based focus to a more value-based focus, in which service is more important. These shifts can make big differences in the organization. From customer demand to product supply and not the other way round.

Interactive platforms allow parties such as consumers and developers or the buyer and seller to connect. For example, Apple's App Store connects app developers to iPhone users and Alibaba connects buyers and sellers through their online marketplace. Developing a platform provides firms with increased access to suppliers and sellers through aggregating the dispersed supply and demand within a market (Gupta, 2018). Platforms use technology to connect people, organizations and resources in an interactive ecosystem in which an amazing amount of value can be created and exchanged. As a result, platforms are transforming business strategies and the economy. Platforms are designed with the intention to enable value-creating interaction between external producers and consumers, based on needs and preferences. Platforms accomplish this by providing an open interactive infrastructure for participation, yet equally providing necessary governance. Furthermore, this kind of platforms can be referred to as a matchmaker, as its aim is to create value for its participants by matching users–needs and facilitate their subsequent exchange of goods and interactions (Parker et al., 2018). Platforms are often able to unlock spare capacity and harness contributions from a wider community which previously had only been used as a source of demand. A great example is Uber, who were able to unlock a brand-new supply of drivers who were previously viewed as just customers to traditional taxi companies just by connecting them with customers based on an app.

Disruption

This is a disruption, as the traditional markets are disrupted by new companies with a new approach to the market, the new network structure and the demand approach instead of a sales approach. The value of a platform is often created by its community of users, and thus, in order to become or remain successful, it needs to shift its model from internal to external activities. This entails shifting focus towards people, information and resources existing outside of the platform (Gupta, 2018).

There are several different strategies that matching platform businesses may choose to implement. A key decision early on is whether to operate with or without physical capital. Operating with physical capital is referred to as an inventory-based model, often found in pipeline businesses. An inventory-based model has several benefits for firms who are able to control the production and delivery process and therefore have greater supervision over quality and customer service (supply-driven). This permits companies to exert larger control on customers' experience. In the demand-driven approach, data is always needed. Not only historical data but behavioral data is the basis for predictive analysis.

Ecosystems in a Demand-Driven Economy

An ecosystem enables users to fulfill an assortment of needs by utilizing an interconnected network of services. According to a 2019 McKinsey report, ecosystems have three defining characteristics (McKinsey & Company, 2019):

- First of all, ecosystems reduce friction or transaction costs for customers wishing to switch between products or services. Amazon.com, one of the world's largest ecosystems, allows its users to purchase products, watch movies or even publish their own books.
- Second, ecosystems are able to take advantage of scale provided by network effects. Due to the large size of platforms, consumers can easily compare products or services, making the purchasing process more customer friendly. Another scale advantage is the security for both parties. When taking Alibaba as an example, suppliers are not exposed to a risk of not getting paid while customers are sure of a refund if the quality is not similar to what was promised. But the large scale of these platforms leads also to big databases with behavioral and buying data of customers. With machine learning, clusters can be made based on similar behavior, as we will see later on. The advantage is more precise forecasting on an individual level.
- Finally, ecosystems possess the ability to provide a superior experience for customers, through collection of integrated data that facilitates the production of value for customers. According to McKinsey & Company (2019) ecosystems allow for companies to reduce customer acquisition costs, exploit network effects, and enhance customer relationships and retention. As a result, they predict that in six years' time around 30% of

the global economy activity will be mediated through the use of demand-driven digital platforms.

Just as platforms, ecosystem firms focus on optimizing customer experience by focusing on the multidimensional consumer demands (McKinsey & Company, 2019), demand-driven economies follow strategies that minimize stock and just-in-time inventory management. This implies that products or services will only enter the supply chain if a customer demands a particular product or service. As a result, companies are able to save immense costs otherwise spent on inventory and storage work.

Conclusion

Demand-driven business strategies are distinguishable through five main characteristics (Cecere, 2011):

- Firstly, a demand-driven business needs to illuminate the concept of demand sensing—the process of anticipating and correctly reacting to demand fluctuations.
- Additionally, to maximize profitability, it is critical to shape the demand by aligning all functions through demand orchestration. This arranging process is horizontal and includes functional departments within a company, such as delivery, production and sales, to facilitate market-to-market corrections to stimulate or decelerate demand (Cecere, 2011). This can be done in several ways, such as marketing campaigns, launching new products, price management and selling old and outmoded products.
- The third characteristic of demand-driven business models is that the value networks are designed instead of inherited. There are several value networks, each having unique traits such as throughput times and production flows. Traits concerning demand flows are recognized and integrated into the design of value networks. The variability in demand for products ultimately effects the goal of a firm's supply chain. Networks that contain little demand variability are able to have push-based supply chain that focuses on minimizing the cost per unit through increased efficiency (Cecere, 2011). On the contrary, networks that contain a lot of variability or are seasonal dependent (such as ice-cream stores) must be designed to be flexible and responsive. The lowest costs are sacrificed, in order for the value network to be able to react as quickly as possible. High variability networks need to be designed for agility, in which the quality, cost and service will remain the same on every level of demand.
- The fourth characteristic contains the nimbleness through demand translation, so the flexibility of influencing demand. The orchestration of demand, consisting of how it is sensed, shaped and eventually translated to maximize the profitability, should be coordinated through a couple of horizontal processes (Cecere, 2011). These processes need to go from the

outside in, which means from the market-facing processes to the supplier-facing processes.

- Lastly, demand-driven companies keep their focus on the outcomes. Because of the implementation of demand-driven value networks, the focus shifts from selling to the channel, to selling through the channel. Besides that, the focus can also shift from product-based focus to a more value-based focus, in which service is more important. These shifts can make big differences in the organization. It is evident that customer data and analytics are the core of demand-driven organization. It is no longer an add-on function, but it is the reason for their existence.

Student's Mind

1. What is the major difference between a pipeline company and a platform company?
2. A platform has a focus on two markets, suppliers and buyers. What does this mean for the marketing strategy?
3. How can a brand be built based on a network or platform approach?
4. A supply-driven company has a narrow focus whereas a demand-driven company has a wider focus. Please explain.
5. How will this difference show in the contact with the final buyer?

Discussion Point

How can classical media companies survive the demand-based approach of social media?

References

Bursa, K. (2015). The Impact of Becoming Demand-Driven. *The European Business Review*. Retrieved September 25, 2020 from www.europeanbusinessreview.com/the-impact-of-becoming-demand-driven-2/#

Cecere, L. (2011). What Happened to the Concept of Demand-Driven? Retrieved from www.supplychainshaman.com/demand/demanddriven/what-happened-to-the-concept-of-demand-driven

Choudary, S. P. (2015). *Platform Scale: How a New Breed of Startups Is Building Large Empires with Minimum Investment*. London: Platform Thinking Labs.

Gupta, S. (2018). *Driving Digital Strategy: A Guide to Reimagining Your Business*. Boston, MA: Harvard Business Review Press.

Kash, R. & Calhoun, D. (2010). *How Companies Win: Profiting from Demand-Driven Business Models No Matter What Business You're in*. London: HarperCollins.

McKinsey & Company. (2019). Technology, Media & Telecommunications. Retrieved from www.mckinsey.com/industries/technology-media-and-telecommunications/our-insights/thinking-inside-the-subscription-box-new-research-on-ecommerce-consumers#

Parker, G., Alstyne, M. v. & Evans, P. (2018). How Platform Strategies Continue to Create Value. *MITSloan*, September, p. 5.

2 Demand-Driven versus Supply-Driven

The shift from supply-driven to demand-driven is only possible with the use of technology. Ever since the start of the century, scientists predicted the impact of technology on our daily lives and on business. Not only would transparency lead to involvement of all participants in decision making, but also the use of advanced communication technology would lead to more democratic processes. It should be the start of social capitalism where every stakeholder would demand an equal place. Over the last few years, the knowledge of customers and buying process disrupted markets with new start-ups and new business models of the start-ups. Classical pipeline concepts and supply-driven marketing would change in knowledge-based concepts. This shift is a major change in our daily lives and for organizations. What is happening and how will it change organizations and marketing?

In order to understand the topic regarding demand-driven economy versus supply-driven economy, we have to define the difference. In this book we will talk about supply chains when demand- and/or supply-driven. A supply chain is in principle a chain composed of a set of sequentially connected production or distribution units, giving rise to information and material flow between its members (Cao et al., 2017). The function of a supply chain is the same; however, the links, partners, in a supply chain will differ. It could be a set of independent

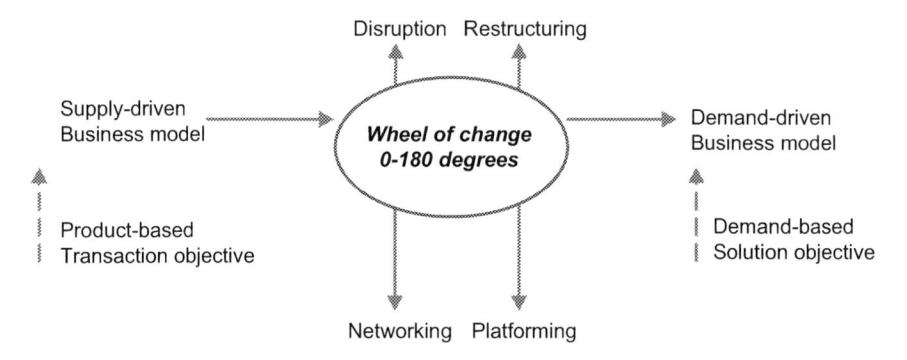

Figure 2.1 An interactive change model from supply to demand.

DOI: 10.4324/9781003226161-2

companies with their own value in the process from factory (supplier) to buyer, but it can also be a platform connecting all the parties as a middleman, as seen in most demand-driven organizations.

A Supply-Driven Business Model

A supply-driven economy was common in the last 70 years (after the Second World War). With the rise of technology in the mid-20th century businesses started to integrate their downstream units. This was to cut the costs and make the flow of the product and information more efficient. At the end of the 20th century this process was called supply chain management. The traditional supply chain is a supply chain where the supplier activates the flow; this is called supply-driven. This means that the information flows in the same direction as the product (Hull, 2005).

Hull (2005) describes four themes that are common in supply-driven supply chains:

- The first is, as mentioned above, supply activates flow. The flow of production does not await the demand of the customers. (Every supply will create its own demand.)
- The second theme is resilience. Normally when demand drops, the supply also reacts. A supply-driven supply chain is responsible to keep the capacity at full flow. It needs to be resilient when the demand drops to keep the supply at the same level.
- Third is the need to sell the product in different markets. Since most of the products are commodity-like, selling too much in one market may decrease the price.
- The last theme has to do with the customer service. Since customers can disrupt the supplier and may cause a reversed bullwhip effect (see below), keeping the customers satisfied is needed. A way to regulate demand and keep the customers on the good side is with adjusting prices when needed. A strong focus of supply-driven companies is price, as focus of demand-driven companies is customer needs.

The bullwhip effect is a supply chain phenomenon describing how small fluctuations in demand at the retail level can cause progressively larger fluctuations in demand at the wholesale, distributor, manufacturer and raw material supplier levels. The effect is named after the physics involved in cracking a whip. When the person holding the whip snaps their wrist, the relatively small movement causes the whip's wave patterns to increasingly amplify in a chain reaction.

In supply chain management, customers, suppliers, manufacturers and salespeople all have only partial understanding of demand and direct control over only part of the supply chain, but each influences the entire chain with their forecasting inaccuracies (ordering too much or too little). A change in any link along the supply chain can have a profound effect on the rest of the supply chain. Given that, there are many contributors and causes of the bullwhip effect in supply chain management.

In a demand-driven approach this effect is not existing, because the relationship with a supplier should be a kind of partnership which might lead to an implosion of the supply chain.

As stated above, the rise of technological innovation pathed the way to integrate all individual units into one big chain. But the technological innovation did not stop, on the contrary it got bigger. Not only the flow of production got bigger, but more important, the flow of information got bigger, more detailed and most important more accessible. The impact of technology can be seen in three phases: efficiency, optimalization and disruption.

- The first phase is cost driven as we have seen above;
- the second phase is optimalization but based on existing processes, supply-driven; but
- as a side effect, information and data was gathered and is the basis for a demand-driven approach (disruption).

Especially the greater flow of information, and transparency, make it possible to change the way the whole supply chain works, from a supply focus to a demand focus. Technology in a supply chain will optimize the flow of data and processes, although the principle of a supply chain will stay the same. New business concepts like online propositions and internet-based processes are still built upon the existing supply chain. Data transfer was a big issue, because links between the different, independent partners in a supply chain means also matching of data and infrastructure. Technology was used in every company individually based on their criteria and their own IT systems (hardware and software). These interfaces were a

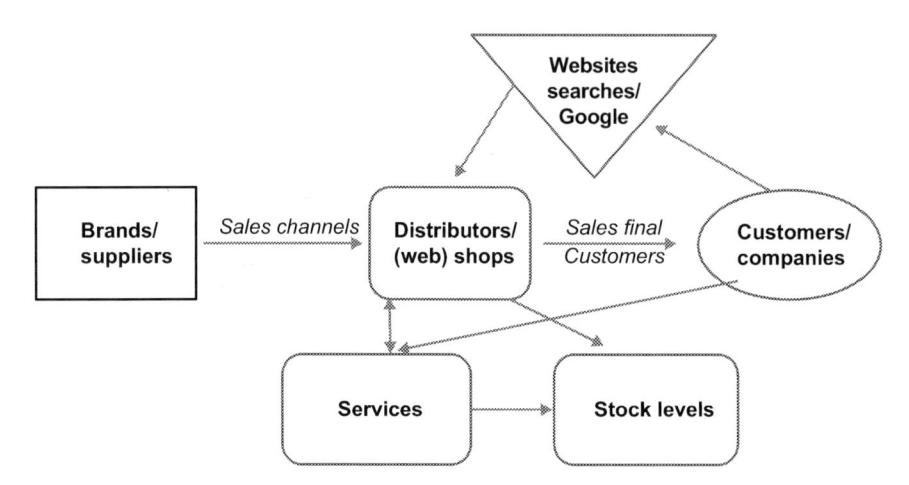

Figure 2.2 A supply-driven business model.

major roadblock for integration in a supply chain, also the development of internet-based websites was based upon the classical business structures: supply and delivery. Even in this day and age IT infrastructures are not based on connections and sharing, but on optimizing existing business processes. However, this will lead to a loss of competitive advantages because:

- Price is no longer the main issue of sales due to a change in customer preference, service, sustainability, availability next to price (consumer and business customers).
- Increased competition based on internet access, more inside knowledge in the total market offerings, international competition (like Amazon and Alibaba in most countries).
- New business-model-based collaborations (sales platforms like Amazon and eBay; multi-sided matching platforms like Uber, Airbnb; communication platforms/social media like LinkedIn, Tik-Tok, Facebook) are powerful because of their number of users and big data.
- Available technology based on agility, like scrum technology, low coding, cloud-based interfaces and APIs for interfaces.

Successful new start-ups will not only innovate but disrupt markets because they change the rules and the competitive weapons. Changes in the business model are needed because the market is more volatile than ever, and technology will offer new possibilities.

A Demand-Driven Approach

A supply chain where demand activates the flow of production instead of the supplier is called a demand-driven supply chain. A demand-driven supply chain is

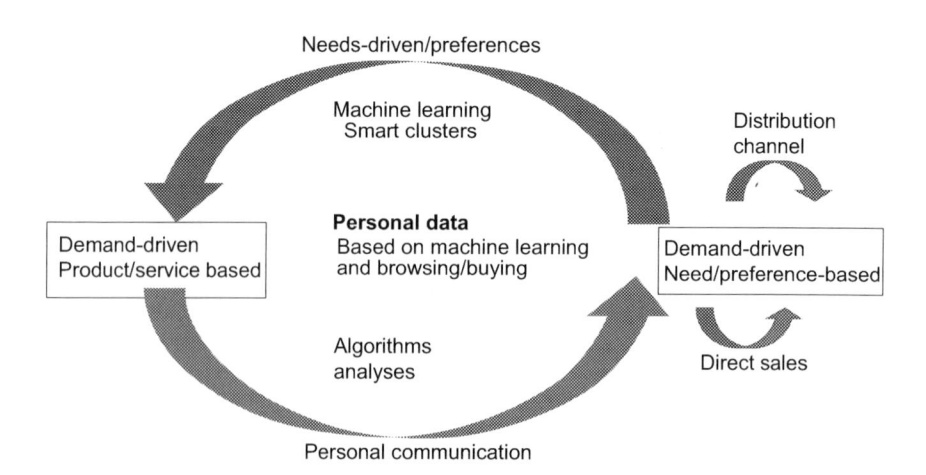

Figure 2.3 Aspects of a demand chain.

a system of coordinated technologies and processes that senses and reacts to real-time demand signals across a network of customers, suppliers and employees (Budd et al., 2012). In other words, this means that when the demand (needs) changes, the supply has to be matched through adjusting various points in the supply chain.

As Budd et al. (2012) mention: "Despite the advances in technology and the growing willingness among supply chain players to share information, creating a demand chain is far from a plug-and-play exercise." A typical supply chain is not transformed into a demand chain overnight. In order for a supply chain to be demand-driven a few key features need to be realized.

- At first a right form of technology infrastructure is necessary. A key part of the demand chain is the fact that the flow of information is enormous, so all the data need to be processed the right way and transformed into information for the right unit, in order to keep the supply matched to the demand. When there is not a right infrastructure a change in demand cannot be reacted adequately to match the supply.
- Second, rethink the chain. Objects that hinder the supply chain to be agile should be removed, such as slow transportation or certain rules and decisions. If the supply chain cannot react fast to changes and so be agile, a demand chain cannot be realized efficiently.
- Also, align the whole supply chain. Incentives and targets in the whole supply chain need to be clear so everyone knows where to go. Not only the measurable objectives but also the behavior of the supply chain and its employees need to be the same.
- Partnership within the demand chain is needed to fulfill the needs of the buyers. A network infrastructure (and ecosystem) will facilitate the partnership. A platform will be the best infrastructure facilitator.
- Finally, to monitor behavior and to implement new processes like algorithms and machine learning techniques (marketing intelligences) are needed.

Now that it is clear what a supply-driven supply chain and a demand-driven supply chain is, it will be made clear what the differences are between the two. The most distinct difference between the two is the way the flow of orders goes through the supply chain. The flow of orders in a demand chain starts where the demand is detected and from there on specified to the supplier. Whereas in a supply-driven demand chain it starts at the ready-made product of a supplier and from there on goes on to the customers (no share of information). It is a process of need detection, profile of demand, clustering based on demand and finally the right supply.

Not only the flow of orders follows this path, also the flow of information follows this path in their respective supply chain. For both supply-driven demand as well as demand chains this has a negative effect. For supply-driven it is called the bullwhip effect, as described above. The bullwhip effect leads to the mismatch between market demand and production, because of order variability, which results in lowering the supply chain performance, as we have seen before. The overstock will lead to lower prices and therefore to lower margins for all players in the supply chain.

For a demand chain, information sharing and close cooperation are key factors in dampening the bullwhip effect. Because opening up the infrastructure so the information will flow direct to suppliers and sharing the information faster, shortens the lag between the demand side and the supplier. The supply chain will implode because of this direct interaction between supplier and buyer based on demand and behavior. For supply-driven supply chains, secrecy (no real partnership between the links) the direct opposite, is necessary. Because when a supplier has trouble selling his total production, customers can use this information to ask for more price concessions, and on and on. A closer relationship between seller and producer is needed, sometimes even a direct relationship between buyer and producer. The effect will be an implosion of the supply chain. Some links will lose their value. This might be the case for wholesalers. On the other hand, wholesalers might be a buffer for inventory (stocks), as a middleman between the volatility of demand and the supply. A redesign of the supply chain is needed in the case of a demand-driven business model.

Role of Technology and Organization

Improvements and changes in the IT departments have been crucial in developing an effective demand chain, developing a platform or organization where the information can flow in real time to all the players of the supply chain and being able to properly leverage the data collected are the first step towards a supply chain driven by demand. In that case a focus on online behavior, browsing and analyzing searches are needed to specify needs and buying preferences. Also, the information should be accurate, recent and relevant. Following the new digital infrastructure firms and network structure to effectively put in practice a demand chain, the firms have to adapt their operations as well for them to be as flexible as possible.

Flexible elements of manufacturing such as access to temporary workforce and external capacity and ability to produce cost-effectively on demand, small batches are key for success using the demand chain (Budd et al., 2012). Technology should facilitate this change from supply to demand, from internal information flows and reporting, analysis to external connections and control and analytics for predictions. As seen in Figure 2.1 the steps of digitalization will lead to a demand chain based on the present supply chain and organization (efficiency). By using the new opportunities and tools in the existing business model (supply based) leads to innovation but is not enough for a sustainable competitive advantage. It is not a matter of applying new tools in an existing business model but to adapt a new business model based on digital techniques and application. This is the basis for a demand-based supply chain.

Marketing plays a crucial role as demand defines the supply chain target, while supply-side capabilities support and sustain demand. The focus of supply chain is on supply of materials, while the focus of demand chain is on market demand (Madhani, 2013).

The functions in a supply chain include product development, marketing, operations, distribution, finance and customer service. Marketing is based on target groups products and generic services. The functions in a demand chain are collecting and analyzing data, machine learning demand prediction. Marketing intelligence will be the main marketing driver of a demand-based business model.

Platforms are the Basis of a Demand-Driven Supply Chain

However, the rise of technology and software didn't only change the approach of businesses to supply chains but had them reconsider their entire core business models. Platform business models are becoming more and more popular because of their characteristic of creating value by enabling interactions (supply and demand) inside an ecosystem (Choudary, 2015). Giants such as Uber, Facebook and Amazon managed to scale very successfully; thanks to their platform approach they succeeded in creating ecosystems where users can interact and create value while they take care of making the infrastructure available, cultivate the community and leverage the data obtained (Choudary, 2015). In an ever more demand-driven economy, platforms enable businesses to better understand customers and better match demand and supply by leveraging data. Data also plays a crucial role in the long-term development of the platform, most of the data keep their value and in time can be used to improve or expand the structure and the community layer of the platform. Because of this, today many firms are focusing more on creating ecosystems where more value can be created than in improving the effectiveness of their supply chain (Molenaar, 2020). Businesses today do not need to own resources, transform them and channel the products to consumers to be successful. Using a platform strategy, firms create value through enabling interactions between potential consumers and producers, in this way competitive advantage comes not from owning the resources, but from coordinating and managing the value exchanges in the ecosystem. The basis of a demand-driven strategy is a strong network and machine learning application as part of marketing intelligence.

These shifts towards new business models (platforms) and agile demand-driven supply chains have been constantly happening in the last 20 to 30 years with an obvious acceleration in recent years due to availability of new technology (Budd et al., 2012).

However, the pandemic of Covid-19 at the start of 2020 created a shock that is forcing many firms to rethink themselves, based on the possible implications of this current crisis on business models and the shifts in supply chains.

Conclusion

The impact of a demand-driven approach cannot be neglected. Not only will it change the relationship with customers and the position in the market, but it will also have consequences of the role of data. Data is needed to facilitate the change, but an organization has to adapt in every aspect, especially in the speed of change (agility). The difference between supply-driven and demand-driven is a change in focus where no longer the product is the central focus, but the need of customers.

Student's Mind

1   What is the key denominator of the change from a supply-driven focus to a demand-driven focus?
2   Fast movers are normally supply-driven. How can they implement also some demand-based decisions?
3   What is the role of marketing in this transformation process?
4   Why will the present supply chain implode?
5   What can be the future role of a wholesaler?

Discussion Point

The travel industry is suffering from online suppliers/platforms. Low prices and self-service are key business drivers. What can the existing supplier do to challenge these new players?

References

Budd, J., Knizek, C. & Tevelson, B. (2012). *The Demand-Driven Supply Chain: Making it Work and Delivering Results*. Boston, MA: Boston Consulting Group.

Cao, B.-B., Xiao, Z.-D. & Sun, J.-N. (2017). A Study of the Bullwhip Effect in Supply- and Demand-Driven Supply Chain. *Journal of Industrial and Production Engineering*, 34(2): 124–134.

Choudary, P. S. (2015). *Platform Scale: How an Emerging Business Model Helps Startups Build Large Empires with Minimum Investment*. London: Platform Thinking Labs.

Hull, B. Z. (2005). Are Supply (Driven) Chains Forgotten? *The International Journal of Logistics Management*, 16(2): 218–236.

Madhani P. M. (2013). Marketing Firms vs. SCM-led Firms: DCM Comparatistics. *SCMS Journal of Indian Management*, 10(2): 5–19.

Molenaar, C. (2020). *The End of Competition: The Impact of the Network Economy*. New York: World Scientific.

3 Shifting from a Supply-Driven to a Demand-Driven Economy

Digitalization

The change to a demand-driven approach starts with the existing supply focus. This supply focus will change in various steps. From optimalization (lower costs) to innovation, applying technology in existing processes to changing process and consequently organizations. It is a matter of using digital possibilities. A change from being digital, using digital possibilities in existing process and structures to doing digital where technology is the basis for an organization. This process change is a major disruption for every organization, but also for competition and markets.

Being Digital or Doing Digital?

The world is in the midst of the Fourth Industrial Revolution and the main catalyst of this shift to a demand-driven economy is continuous technological development.

On the supply side, technological development has led to an unparalleled increase in productivity and output. The benefits of using technology on the supply side of business to reduce costs, improve efficiency and output are evident. However, due to the changed economic landscape of oversupply, where there is simply not enough demand to fill supply, technology needs to be leveraged to capture and enhance the demand side of your business. In addition, in the last few

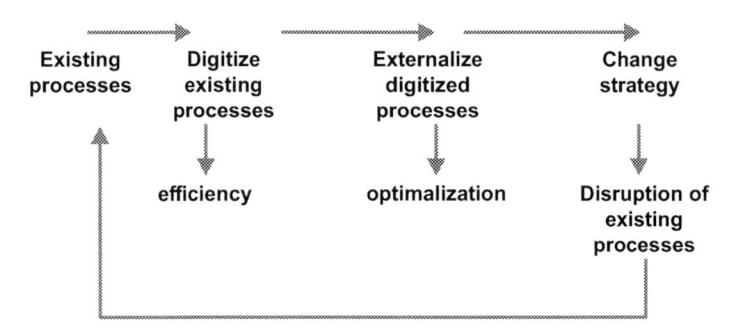

Figure 3.1 Steps of transformation, from efficiency to optimalization to disruption.

DOI: 10.4324/9781003226161-3

years people are realizing the power of utilizing technology on the demand side of businesses. Increased access to technology has fundamentally changed the way in which consumers engage with businesses, since they are better informed and consequently more assertive. Consumers now expect more. If a company does not have exactly what we are looking for or offer the experience we seek, we have the power to switch to a different business at the click of a mouse (Kash & Calhoun, 2010, pp. 28–31).

Consequently, in order to survive, businesses need a deeper understanding of their consumers and the behavior of their customers. Technology can be leveraged to analyze, predict and develop this competitively advantaged understanding of demand and use this information to change the way in which their business functions across all areas of their value chain while still remaining agile in this fast-paced new landscape (Kash & Calhoun, 2010, pp. 28–31). Firms are required to switch from making processes more efficient through technology ("doing digital") to "being digital" and using technology to capture information about demand and use this to create value.

In addition, for companies to survive in a world where the consumers determine who will succeed and who will fail, it is imperative that you construct a framework in your company that encompasses and aligns everyone toward meeting, not just the current, but the latent and emerging demand of your highest-profit customers and consumers (Gupta, 2018, pp. 6–7). It is important to keep in mind that in comparison to a supply-driven economy, "the demand-driven company not only thinks about today and tomorrow, but next year and the next five years" (Kash & Calhoun, 2010, p. 28). Often this shift from a supply- to a demand-driven company requires an entire shift in the business model to acquire, convert and retain consumers (Gupta, 2018, p. 31). This shift can only take place when the data is available but also structured and usable.

The reality is, that at many companies today most data is not up to standard, organized and structured. A quality check is needed and sometimes even formatting. Transformation almost certainly involves understanding new types of unstructured data, like images, telephone data, video data and massive quantities of data external to your company. All this data has to specified, uniformed and analyzed and integrated all together. Most companies know data is important and they know quality is bad, yet they waste enormous resources by failing to put the proper roles and responsibilities in place. They often blame their IT functions for all these failures.

Digitalization

Technology, data, process, and organizational change capability are all part of the digitalization process. Quite often these domains operate as if they existed in isolation, which they don't. Rather, they are part of a larger whole; digitalization involves the total organization from marketing to production, from logistics to finance. Technology is the engine of digital transformation, data is the fuel, process and ecosystems are the guidance system, and organizational change capability is the landing gear. All the parts work together to be successful. An individual approach will lack optimalization success, it leads to enormous process inefficiencies and therefore the motivation for change.

This non-integrated approach stems from a lack of solid data architecture, and it may involve organizational structure and politics issues that are difficult to change. The best solution is working together from an integral view of change. Optimization of existing processes and functions to innovation. Optimalization is only making existing functions and processes more efficient, not changing the function of processes; that will be the next step. Optimalization changes can be implemented to improve processes and functions and finally disrupt them. In all cases data is leading together with new applications like machine learning, connections like API and block chain technology for external contacts.

The steps of digitalization are based on the existing functions and processes and the available data. In many cases, process improvement or reengineering must come first, to create an overall planning of change. Start with your end goals, then develop the sequence of steps best suited to achieving them. Digital transformation can and should be focused on problems of greatest need to the company. If the focus is on transforming customer relationships, for example, the change team should have particular expertise in customer data, the process talent on sales and marketing processes. More important, however, is that the team has knowledge or experts of all four focus points: technology, data, process and organizational change.

Companies need to establish management practices to govern these complex transformations. An important approach is to formulate a digital transformation strategy, a kind of blueprint of all changes and the end goal to integrate the entire coordination, prioritization and implementation of digital transformations within a company.

The exploitation and integration of digital technologies often influence large parts of companies and even go beyond their borders (in case of a network), by impacting products, business processes, sales channels and supply chains. Potential benefits of digitization are manifold and include increases in sales or productivity, innovations in value creation, as well as novel forms of interaction with customers, among others. As a result, entire business models can be reshaped or replaced (Downes & Nunes, 2013). Owing to this wide scope and the far-reaching consequences, digital transformation strategies seek to coordinate and prioritize the many independent threads of digital transformation. To account for their company characteristics, digital transformation strategies cut across other business strategies and should be aligned with them. Hence, IT strategies usually focus on the management of the IT infrastructure within a firm, with rather limited impact on driving innovations in business development. Therefore, the main focus is on optimalization, transforming the present business functions and processes in digital function and processes. To some degree, this restricts the product-centric and customer-centric opportunities that arise from new digital technologies, which often cross firms' borders.

Optimizing is not changing a business model but will make it more efficient. This focus will not lead to defendable competitive advantage, because it is easy to copy. Competition on prices will be fierce because of lower cost; also competition will copy the changes after they proved to be successful but will use the latest insights and technologies. This way a kind of *leapfrogging* in competition will be the result. Leapfrogging is the notion that areas which have poorly-developed technology or economic bases can move themselves forward rapidly through the adoption of modern systems without going through intermediary steps.

IT strategies present system-centric road maps to the future uses of technologies in a firm, but they do not necessarily account for the transformation of products, processes and structural aspects that go along with the integration of technologies; this will be the next step: innovation. Beyond the process paradigm, and include changes to and implications for products, services and business models as a whole. It will prove that community-based digital business models can create profitable revenue streams with new business models (like platforms and networks). Drnevich and Croson (2013) show how IT can impact on a firm's business-level strategies and its capabilities. Therefore, while digital business strategies often describe desired future business opportunities, the fundament is data based and should interpret the data, as we will see in the next chapter. In contrast, a digital transformation strategy is a blueprint that supports companies in governing the transformations that arise owing to the integration of digital technologies, as well as in their operations after a transformation. This blueprint has an internal focus on all four aspects, but also an external focus on the supply chain, networks and community-based business propositions.

Dimensions of Digital Strategies

Christian Matt et al. (2015) specify four dimensions of digital strategies:

- use of technologies;
- changes in value creation;
- structural changes; and
- financial aspects.

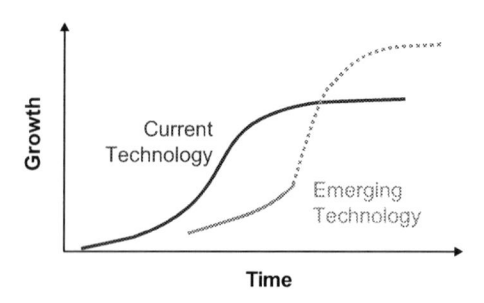

Figure 3.2 Innovation life cycle.

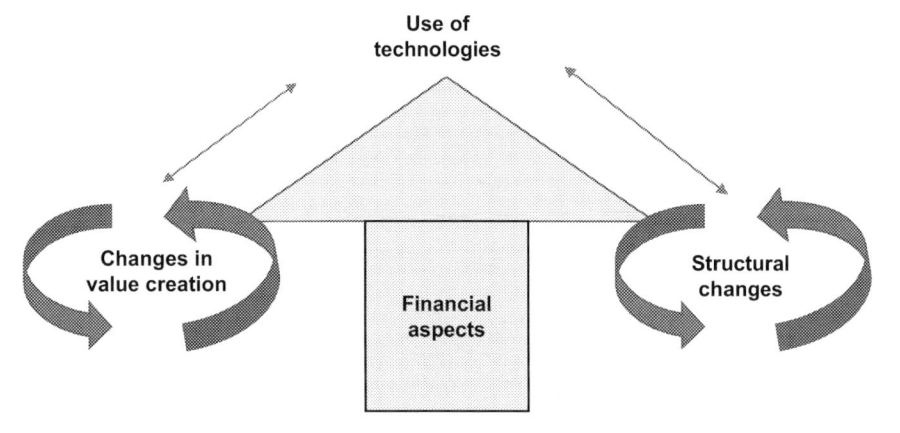

Figure 3.3 Consequences of digital strategies.

The role of technology in a company is important for future changes. If the IT department is just a service department for other departments and companies' functions, it is only supporting and optimizing the present business. The IT strategy is, however, decisive about the role the company wants to play in the marketplace. If a company has the aim to be the cheapest or become a market leader in a certain market, the role of IT will be different. In a stable market a company and the IT strategy will be focused on efficiency, in a dynamic market agility is important to defend customer loyalty and protect against competition (new market entrants, start-ups). In a dynamic market a strong focus on customers and customer needs is needed to protect existing relations. Therefore, dynamic markets are the first reason to change the strategy from supply-driven (product-focused) to demand-driven (relation-focused). It is no longer supporting business processes but is in the core of the processes and company structure. It is obvious that in this case also the values of a company will change. It will be a change from product-related competences to customer-related competences. Machine learning will be essential to give the right value to the network and to the customers. Examples are predictive sales, behavioral based communication, personal services.

To fulfill these changes in creation and to optimize the use of different technologies it is unavoidable to make also changes to the organization and structures of the organization. These are not only processes and skills that will change, but also functions and structures of departments. A purchase department will be affected by predictive sales, lower stock levels and changing customer demands. The financial department will see the influence of new business models, as we will discuss later, like after-sales service, subscription models or network-based cooperation. The marketing department no longer is focused on media and communication to target groups but is focused on customers and communication with individual companies and customers. All these changes are based on the new possibilities and opportunities of machine learning as we will see in the next chapter. All these four dimensions and changes should be part of the digital framework, the blueprint, for overall control and guidance.

Who Is in Control of the Digital Framework and the Transformation?

As we have seen, digitalization has an effect on the total organization and most of the functions and processes. As long as it is only a transformation of a digitalization of existing processes the operational changes are limited. A control from a small team, most of the time business related, is needed. IT will be a leading source because all process and functions will be unchanged, only more efficient (optimized). But if new applications are used like cloud computing, products as a service (PaaS) or platforms as a service, the consequences for the total organization will be significant. Therefore, it is essential that the control is embedded in the total strategy of an organization. The end responsibility lays with the board of directors and finally the CEO. Of course, this is a new focal point with demand, inside knowledge of the impact of changes. Therefore, a transformation manager should lead the total process, not only implementing the IT systems, but also monitoring the transformation process, training and governance. He/she will have assistance from change leaders on every function or level in the organization. The whole transformation process is incremental, small steps with feedback about the results and the progress. The transformation team will use the blueprint of change. In this case it should be completely clear what the purpose is of the transformation and what the aim is. It is not the trip that is important, but the destiny is important for the trip.

Digital transformation strategies have a cross-functional character and need to be aligned with other functional and operational strategies. This alignment can be conducted in practice—not only related to IT strategies, but also from an organizational perspective as we will see later on. The interaction of digital transformation strategies with business development and business models are digital transformation strategies and cut across various other strategies at the same time.

Model of Digital Leadership

According to Gupta's model of digital leadership (Gupta, 2018, pp. 6–7), the first step in transforming your business into one that is demand-driven is to reimagine your business, making a blueprint as described in the last paragraph. This is done through rethinking your scope, business model and organization. This book will focus on how to reimagine your business model to succeed in the new demand-drive economy. By rethinking your business model, you are ultimately changing the way in which you create, capture and deliver value. Digital technology can be leveraged in this process to understand consumer behavior, forecast sales, personalize product offering and predict future trends. Additionally, machine learning can be incorporated to continuously update your insights in this fast-paced environment and give you the guidance you need to change your value chain.

In the past it was always a safe assumption that the expanding marketplace would consume everything that was produced. As a consequence, the primary goal of a company was to produce in the most efficient way and distribute products to the market. However, the old view that a business makes products and then sells them within the supply chain is no longer so relevant or valid, as businesses have come to realize that they can lead a horse to water, but they cannot make it drink. In the future, companies cannot sell products anymore: people will buy from you. This means that the old concept of being supply-driven (company *pushes* products to the market) is being replaced by a pull-concept (the market *pulls* goods from you) where a company understands what their customers need and works backward, deciding how it can satisfy that demand by developing new capabilities. Thinking about business from the outside-in perspective (in other words being demand-driven) is mainly a customer-centric view, where organizations no longer have a sales focus but a buying (customer) focus. And this buying focus requires a different type of strategy (customer-oriented), a different type of organization (agile, flexible) and a different supply proposition and value exchange (based on customer needs). In response to this problem more and more organizations in the past years are shifting from the conventional supply chain management (supply-driven economics) to a more demand-driven supply chain. As the digital economy grows and new digital marketplaces arise, more and more data become available to firms. Thanks to this availability of data, firms can now focus more on demand, trying to shape it so that they can entirely capture profits and have a much better management of their inventory and of their contracts with suppliers. Thanks to these improvements in technology today, a firm can react much faster to a change in the demand, as the information flows almost instantly through the supply chain and as a result the supply chain as a whole (direct material suppliers, manufacturer and retailer) can adapt in a much shorter span of time than before, this is called supply chain visibility.

Marketing plays a crucial role as demand defines the supply chain target, while supply-side capabilities support and sustain demand. The focus of supply chain is on supply of goods and materials, while the focus of demand chain is on market demand.

Marketing tools are used in the process of demand shaping, which is one of the keys in achieving an efficient demand chain, as through demand shaping the accuracy of sales forecasts improves, which translates into an easier management of inventory and of the entire supply chain.

However, the rise of technology and software didn't only change the approach of businesses to supply chains but had them reconsider their entire core business models. Platform business models are becoming more and more popular because of their characteristic of creating value by enabling interactions inside an ecosystem (Choudary, 2015). Giants such as Uber, Facebook and Amazon managed to scale very successfully; thanks to their platform approach they succeeded in creating ecosystems where users can interact and create value while they take care of making available the infrastructure, cultivate the community and leverage the data obtained (Choudary, 2015). This scale is based on customer data. The more products these companies offer to individual customers, the higher the "basket value" and more loyal the customers will be.

In an ever more demand-driven economy, platforms and demand-based organizations enable businesses to better understand customers and to improve matching demand and supply by leveraging data. Data also plays a crucial role in the long-term development of the company; most data keep their value and in time can be used to improve or expand the structure and the community layer of the organization. Because of this today many firms are focusing more on creating ecosystems where value can be created, than in improving the effectiveness of their supply chain. Businesses today do not need to own resources, transform them and channel the products to consumers to be successful. Using a platform strategy companies create value through enabling interactions between potential consumers and producers; in this way competitive advantage comes not from owning the resources but from coordinating and managing the value exchanges in the ecosystem.

These shifts towards new business models (platforms) and agile demand-driven supply chains have been constantly happening in the last 20 to 30 years with an obvious acceleration in recent years due to availability of new technology.

However, the epidemic of Covid-19 at the start of 2020 created a shock that is forcing many firms to rethink their business model; businesses will have to redefine the way in which they create, capture and monetize value to acquire, convert and retain consumers.

Often, this transformation cannot come from "reengineering" and adopting demand-driven tools in your current operational model but requires a "rethinking" of your value chain (Kash & Calhoun, 2010, p. 10). One has to "reshape their manufacturers, retailers, and the media into a collaborative network that will work to the benefit of all who participate" (Kash & Calhoun, 2010, p. 10).

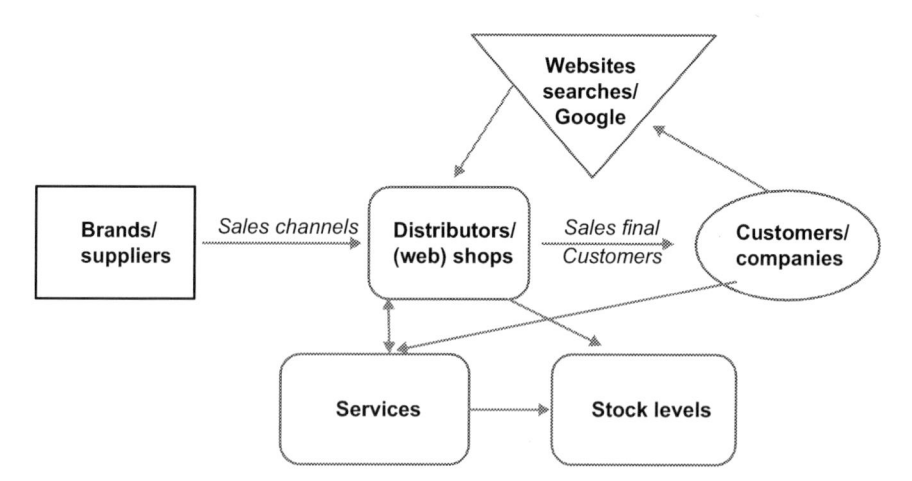

Figure 3.4 Platforms will change the structure of business. The control function of distributors or shops will change.

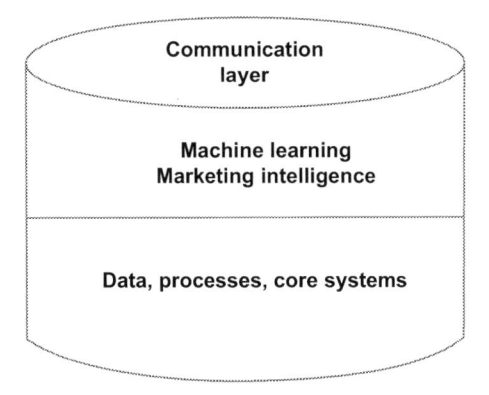

Figure 3.5 Platform concept for demand-driven business model.

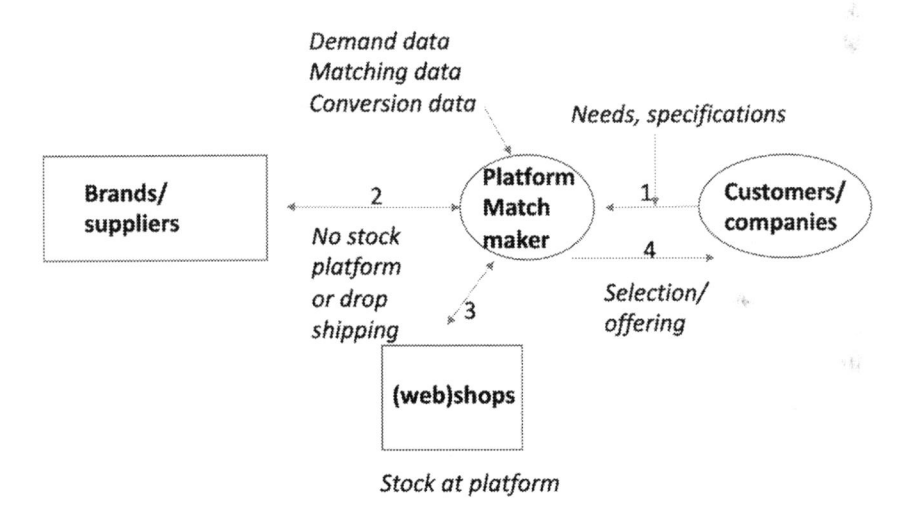

Figure 3.6 The platform (matching) will direct the sales.

The Historical Development: From a Supply- to a Demand-Driven Economy

The shift from a supply- to a demand-driven economy has been fast approaching since the beginning of the 21st century. We have learned from the economic crash in 2007/08 that significant changes were taking place and as such major implications on how companies succeed in this new economic environment (Kash & Calhoun, 2010, p. 28).

According to Kash and Calhoun (2010, p. 30), the economy has shifted from supply- to demand-driven through four stages in transition from the 1940s until presently:

- From the 1940s to the 1990s there was a phase of market equilibrium where there was a continuous managed growth in demand.
- In 1991, supply overtook demand due to many factors such as an aging population in developed nations, industrialization of the developing world and an increase in the productivity of labor due to increased access to digital technology (Kash & Calhoun, 2010, p. 30). Despite oversupply, this consumer spending continues to increase, allowing companies to set up the basic technology infrastructure. In 2000, this bubble burst as companies realized there was simply not enough demand to support the magnitude of supply, leading ultimately to the crash in 2007. Due to this, demand contracted. Globally, many governments were forced to enact stimulus programs to boost consumer spending.
- In 2010, the business cycle eventually restored some level of balance by increasing demand while companies were reducing their supply by lowering production costs and decreasing output (Kash & Calhoun, 2010, pp. 28–31).
- Despite the business cycle restoring some degree of equilibrium, there is still an underlying problem of an economy that leans towards supply. This will likely be made worse by emerging economies characterized by large populations with low incomes. This untapped demand pool perpetuates the cycle of oversupply as most individuals in these emerging economies cannot afford to purchase the goods they produce. Demand is slowly picking up again but there is no evidence that it will be stable and continuous and will always be outpaced by increases in supply leading to downward pressure on prices, lower profits and slower growth (Kash & Calhoun, 2010, pp. 28–31). On top of this the impact and adoption of internet will lead to more transparency, more network effects and data. The focus will shift from supply efficiency to added value and customer contacts.

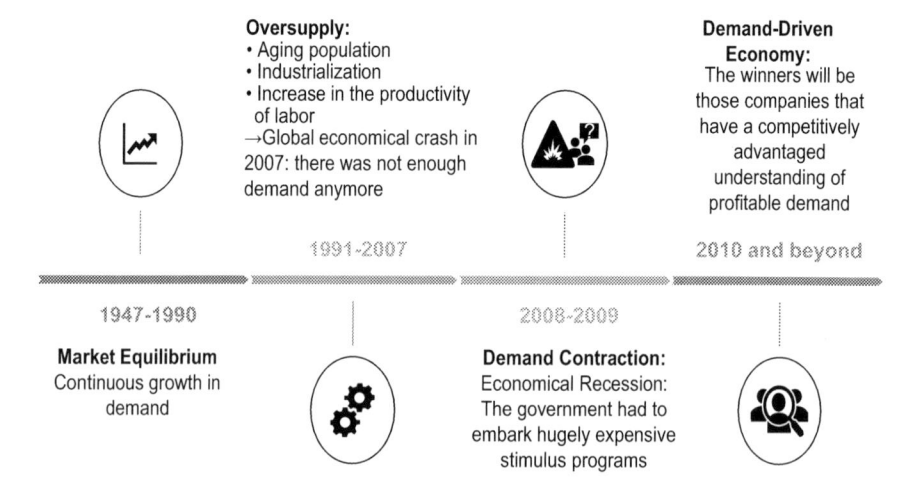

Figure 3.7 The shift from a supply- to a demand-driven economy.

Digital transformation has become imperative to businesses in order to not only adapt to, but also thrive and succeed in this new and innovative market. The concept of digitization is the underlying phenomenon that is shaping this revolution (from innovating the existing supply model to disrupting to a demand-based model). The advent of emerging technologies and disruptive business models is constantly shaping the structure of markets and organizations, leading to a digitalization of business models. This leads to consider digitalization as the use of digital technologies to change a business model and provide new revenue and value-producing opportunities. Digitization is an important driver of "platformization" which represents the inevitable shift from retrieving value from physical products and services to leveraging demand-driven organizations to create value (Nambisan, Zahra & Luo, 2018) and support the buying process of customers.

It is clear that data combined with the latest innovations in artificial intelligence, machine learning and visualization will lead to smarter decisions and automatic actions. This will clearly drive out inefficiencies in processes and in supply chains (like overstock, understock or other losses). It will also lead to a better understanding of customers. A nice example is Zara, the apparel retailer. Zara supports its fast fashion business model through unique buyer-driven supply-chain capabilities. Designers and others at company headquarters monitor real-time information on customer purchases to create new designs and price points. Through standardized product information, Zara can quickly prepare computer-aided designs with clear manufacturing instructions. Complete control over its value chain helps the company to design, produce and deliver new apparel to stores in around fourteen days, where other industry players typically spend about nine months. Zara's smaller batch sizes lead to higher short-term forecast accuracy and lower inventory cost and rate of obsolescence. This reduces markdowns and increases profit margins. Unsold items at Zara account for 10% of stock, compared with an industry average of 17–20%. Just to give an overview of changes as described in this chapter about digitalization, the table of David Rogers is very helpful (Figure 3.8).

Data is the key for change. Without data the old strategies will still be in place. This means as well that without data and the effective use of data there will be a competitive disadvantage. To overcome this, companies start specialized units or branches to get information about the market and focus even more on sales and direct personal communication. In this age, where it is essential to optimize the business model, to limit overstock and to adapt quickly to changes in the market or demand it is imperative that data should be a strategic asset and the fundamentals of strategy.

Data will give more insight into the market, to customers' preferences and opinions and recommendations (unstructured data from social media are an important source). Based on these data profiles of customers, communication can be more targeted, more precise and personalized.

	FROM	TO
Customers	Mass-market Mass communication (media) Product based, transaction focus. One-way value flow Economics of scale	Customer's part of a dynamic network/collaboration. Community-based Customers are key influencers Demand-driven sales Reciprocal value flows Economics of customer value
Competition	Defined competitors Clear distinction between partners and rivals Key assets are held within the company Product-based competition A few dominant competitors per category	Blurred distinction between partners and rivals Competitors cooperate in key areas (like networks, platforms, legislation) Platforms with partners who exchange value Winner takes all due to network effects
Data	Challenge of data storing and the use of data. Controlled by IT department. Only structured data Data is transaction- and production based Data is tool for optimizing processes	Data generation is a continuous process Data turn in valuable information. Unstructured data is valuable through machine learning techniques Data is a key intangible asset for value creation
Technology	Process support Internally focused ERP based (supporting internal functions and departments. Investments based on ROI	Agile and dynamics based on object and dimensions. Linking internal and external systems through API interfaces Low coding for agility challenges Information of data essential
Value	Value based on product features Value based on marketing, 4Ps Value based on business model/ distribution channel	Value proposition is based on meeting customer demands (dynamics) Predictive modelling for personal communication and processes
Organization	Hierarchical Complete control over all assets Top-down decision making	Outside-in processes. Machine learning controlled Functional optimization External links and network integration KPIs are customer based
Business model	Transaction-based Sales through supply channels Standard pricing, market defined	Model based like RFM or profit pools. Subscription modelling Strong customer relationships/ loyalty and interaction. Cluster-like structures

Figure 3.8 Model based on Model strategic assumptions from analogue to digital transformation:
David L. Rogers, *The Digital transformation playbook*, 2016.

Analyzing the data patterns, we will find new patterns based on contextual analyses. But there is more as we will see in the next chapter. These contextual patterns can be used to redefine the "customer journey" and communicate based on the individual orientation process. Later on, we will see these contextual patterns by "browsing" platforms were searching before the sale is analyzed.

However, these results will change in time. Customer behavior is changing due to external circumstances like finance, personal reasons, social media or experiences. A company has to learn how to adapt the strategy and communication based on these changes. For a start all data is relevant, not only data of past contacts and sales but also unstructured data from different sources. Based on the analyses, predictive modelling and contextual clusters are relevant to predict further contact and sales. The result of all action is a feedback of future action. The value driver for customers is based on the exact prediction of needs. This is exactly the transformation that takes place from supply-driven with a focus on products and transaction to demand-driven with a focus on customer needs and behavior.

In the next chapter we will give a few examples of this kind of agility on a personal level.

Conclusion

The shift from supply-driven to demand-driven is facilitated by data and technology. Data of products and sales are typical data sources from a supply-driven approach. For a demand-driven approach data is needed of customers and preferences. By using cluster techniques of machine learning, behavioral patterns can be analyses and are the bases for collaboration. The demand approach is based on individual behavior, collaborations and response.

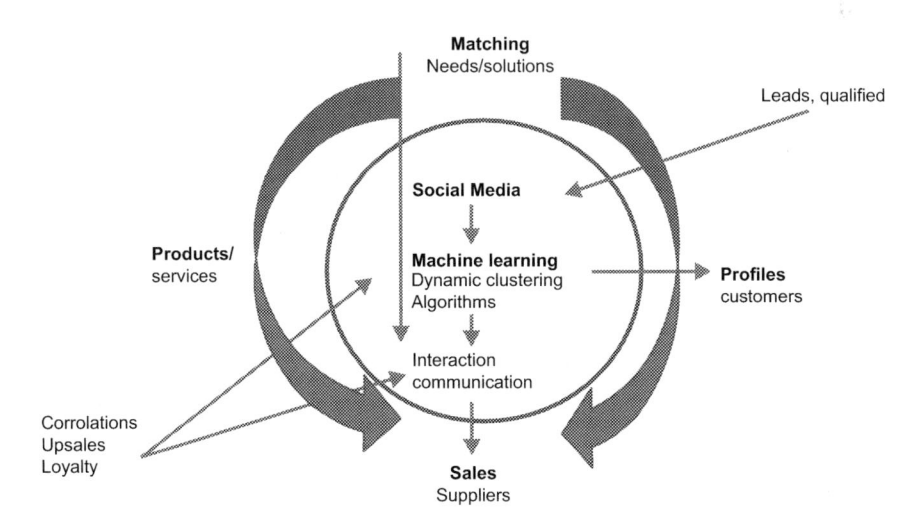

Figure 3.9 A contextual framework of machine learning.

Student's Mind

1   A major change is the impact of data. What is the difference of this approach compared with the historical approach of ERP?
2   Marketing always used data. What is the difference now?
3   What is the core of the business in supply-driven and what in demand-driven?
4   Customers are changing. What is the impact of demand-driven on the behavior and expectations of customers?
5   Is this change only possible for internet-based business models, or also for B2B and physical stores or suppliers?

Discussion Point

Will Google be essential in this transformation or the opposite?

References

Choudary, S. P. (2015). *Platform Scale: How a New Breed of Startups Is Building Large Empires with Minimum Investment*. London: Platform Thinking Labs.
Downes, L. & Nunes, P. (2013). *Big Bang Disruption: Strategy in the Age of Devastating Innovation*. New York: Penguin.
Drnevich, P. L. & Croson, D. C. (2013). Information Technology and Business-Level Strategy: Toward an Integrated Theoretical Perspective. *Mis Quarterly*.
Gupta, S. (2018). *Driving Digital Strategy: A Guide to Reimagining Your Business*. Boston, MA: Harvard Business Review Press.
Kash, R. & Calhoun, D. (2010). *How Companies Win: Profiting from Demand-Driven Business Models No Matter What Business You're in*. London: HarperCollins.
Matt, C. et al. (2015). Digital Transformation Strategies. *Business International Systems*, August 4.
Nambisan, S., Zahra, S. A. & Luo, Y. (2018). Global Platforms and Ecosystems: Implications for International Business Theories. *Journal of International Business Studies*, 50: 1464–1486.
Rogers, D. L. (2016). *The Digital Transformation Playbook*. New York: Columbia University Press.

4 Community-Based Digital Business Models

Platforms

As we have seen in the last chapter, data is crucial for a successful business model. Demand-driven strategies are based on information and data from users, customers and competitors. Based on data, analyses are used to look for similarities, collaborations and causalities. Using these statistical insight, clusters can be formed based on the objectives or based on similarities in the behavior (see next chapter). This way a cluster can be seen as a community with similar characteristics and therefore the same triggers and behavior. The interaction can be based on communication, reviews and the increased attention on openness as a strategic dimension in business model development.

Patricia Wolf and Peter Troxler specified this development in two streams:

- First, there is a stream that uses community-based strategies and business models of firms that emerge from the community by making a company more agile by a mean and lean strategy based on networking, use of shared community resources, work with members of the community as peers and contribute back to the shared resource. This strategy is based on a network of collaborating companies, similar to a supply chain, but now based on the customer demand or on resource sharing as part of the network collaboration (outsource and sharing strategies).
- Second there is a large, comprehensive and substantial stream that investigates community-oriented strategies and business models of which the focus is to extend a central firm's business model with the firm's interaction with a community of user-client-stakeholders (platform based) (Wolf & Troxler, 2016).

Value creation in the context of community-oriented business models implies that focal firms strive "to find an appropriate revenue model that would be both acceptable to their clients and allow them to maximize their profits." Particularly value creation with communities of customers and end-users has attracted high interest as a strategy for business model innovation. Technology facilitates the platform models and are disruptive as a business model. It will also change the role of existing focal companies and will lead to new focal companies with a strong link to the end user. Focal companies are

DOI: 10.4324/9781003226161-4

those companies "that usually (1) rule or govern the supply chain, (2) provide the direct contact to the customer, and (3) design the product or service offered." Especially in a demand-driven economy these focal companies have a strong position because of the contacts with customers and also because of the knowledge they have of customer behavior and customer needs. A focal company can control a network or is leading in a platform. If existing focal companies in a supply chain are not leaders in a community-based network, they will lose their market position. Quite often new start-ups with a fast growth rate will claim this position, as we have seen with Amazon, Uber, Airbnb and Facebook.

The use of data and new technologies like networking changed the traditional balance between customer and supplier and thereby incumbent ways of doing business (Wolf & Troxler, 2016).

The Transition towards Community-Oriented Business

Anderico Adrodegari et al. (2018) conducted research under capital goods manufactures about the possibilities and state of this transformation. Although his conclusion was that most companies where still at the beginning of this community-oriented business model some interesting observations are relevant.

Capital goods manufacturers are moving from product-centric offerings to services and solutions in order to increase and provide steady/balanced revenues during time, and to build sustainable competitive advantage. In particular, services represent one of the main elements to design such new strategies where firms' value propositions move from selling products to provide product-service-systems. Such a phenomenon goes under the name of servitization, encompassing "transformational processes whereby a company shifts from a product-centric to a service-centric business model and logic."

This transformation implies not only a redesign of the value proposition but also companies need to reshape their business models. However, manufacturers undertaking such a shift face numerous challenges that may lead to the so-called service paradox. Also, for this reason, even though several manufacturers are considering service-based paths a limited application of service-oriented business models (SOBMs) has been observed, especially in manufacturing companies.

Manufacturers have to understand deeply their customers' needs and problems first, then develop new value propositions, more customer-oriented, and finally, build new business models that allow generating and delivering expected value.

Customer Data Essential for Community-Based Propositions

As stated above, companies should develop customer-specific value propositions that are linked to specific customer needs. In fact, segmenting customers with specific criteria can enable the development of new, more community-oriented value propositions. Therefore, customers should be segmented using multiple and advanced criteria. Machine learning should be part of this strategy, as we will see in the following chapter.

Computer systems facilitate sharing information and knowledge extracted from data collected among different functions and also towards customers and partners (internal and external networks). Thus, traditional software systems, such as enterprise resource planning (ERP), customer relationship management (CRM), product life cycle management (PLM) and product data management, should be fully integrated, and applications that support supply chain management and collaboration activities should be implemented.

Building and Implementing Network Propositions

In the strategic network perspective, the focal firm directs strategically the activities of the business system. The changing role of actors in the network can be seen as a source of opportunities and risks for individual actors and for the stability of the existing business network. The role of a focal firm is essential for the stability. A dominant player with direct contact with customers can control the network when they really take the lead. To do this, a business model based on direct communication with end users, a network based on connections with suppliers (direct links through APIs), data and machine learning techniques is essential to fulfill this role. The dynamics of buyer–supplier interactions can lead to a change in the role of each actor in the business network. A company which only moved manufacturing processes to the suppliers risks in the long run to lose their central role in the business network (Guercini & Runfola, 2015). The change of a focal company to a focal role in a community-based network is also a change from a supplier's perspective in a supply chain to a role in a demand chain. Knowledge of customers and direct contacts with customers will create the competitive advantage in the market and dependency control of suppliers. Also, in this case a dynamic contact with customers is necessary as well as the use of machine learning techniques to strengthen the focal role. A focal company can choose their own suppliers in the network. The total strength of all suppliers (the network) is decisive for the competitive strength of the total network. Finally, networks will compete with networks, focal company should take the role of competition leaders.

Thus, interaction can be a way for the suppliers to co-create the physical as well as the economic context. For a maximum gain, the manufacturer needed to integrate the key business processes from original suppliers through to the end user, fulfilling customer demands through the most efficient use of resources, including distribution capacity, inventory and labor. Therefore, a manufacturer, whose IT system could be matched with that of the brand it served, ensured a synchronized information flow across the demand chain, including the areas of design, production, forecasting, ordering, manufacturing, transportation, sales and distribution (Guercini & Runfola, 2015).

Under this condition, every member of the network specializes and participates in the overall value creation process, but the focal firm maintains some important competences that justify its position (including data).

The second development in the change to community-based business models is a different collaboration. In the first development we saw the creation of networks where companies are part of the total network and create value to the network. Each company will lose part of its independency and therefore will focus on the core activities. Non-core activities will be outsourced or shared. In the second development that is not the case. Some functions are shared but a company can still stay independent and therefore operate also as an independent supplier. The present development of platforms is a kind of collaboration between companies to share activities or resources.

What is a Platform Exactly?

A platform can be seen as a business model that leverages technology to connect people, brands and organizations in an interactive ecosystem.

Therefore, it is a value creator that orchestrates the cooperation between the different market players. As Gupta (2018) explains, the explosion of platforms stems from the fact that "people act in their own self-interest." Nowadays platforms allow reducing "the transaction cost of finding and selling goods and services" allowing customers to specify their needs and desires in a much more efficient way. Google was the first example of a need-based platform and claimed a role as focal company.

Although it is a service engine linking suppliers to buyers, it is only a middleman to help customers finding the right products or the right suppliers. Suppliers have the opportunity to expose their offerings in a kind of subscription model, media exposure. Customers can link direct to the website of the relevant supplier based on their searches. Hence, the platforms' increasing popularity are the basis of a demand-driven economy. The origin of platforms stems from creating benefits for their users. However, various other advantages have been uncovered by the implementation of digital platforms in brands' business models. Indeed, not only do platforms and demand-driven organizations provide better value to consumers by aggregating a large variety of products and services all together in one place, but they provide greater access to the sellers as well (reversed supply chain equals demand chain). After all, by aggregating brands and their products, platforms and demand-driven organizations facilitate the discovery of certain brands that otherwise would not reach much visibility. It is a win–win situation: suppliers get to have more visibility and consumers get to obtain a larger variety of products from which to choose based on their needs and preferences. These fundamental benefits have substantial consequences. Some of the most visible ones are market growth enabled by lower transaction costs, scalability due to network effect and, inevitably, innovation.

Although platforms seem to be pretty straightforward concepts, they are characterized by innumerable aspects and require substantial knowledge both in the business and in the computer science domain. Indeed, two underlying concepts that are crucial to creating successful demand-driven organizations are understanding and implementing machine learning and application programming interfaces (APIs). Business models and organizational structures have to adapt to demand-driven processes and cooperate in a platform:

- For marketing and customer contacts or for sharing resources.
- In the second purpose platforms can be part of a network where the platform provides a possibility of sharing resources. This can be seen in the IT industry where application can be used as a "service" where before a license agreement was needed. Also, in the entertainment industry this resource sharing can lead to new opportunities like in gaming or entertainment (Netflix a.o.). The "cloud" is important for these kind of business models.

Transforming the Business

By transforming your business to one that is demand-driven, you will be able to survive in this new economic landscape and optimize your value chain. To begin with, if companies are customer-oriented and start with their specific needs, the customer's satisfaction is due to customized products being bigger and customers will become more engaged and loyal. In addition, the new business model:

- On the one hand allows a company to build an asset-light business across the network (Gupta, 2018, pp. 49–50). These savings can be reinvested into market expansion and new product innovations.
- On the other hand, it has been proven that a demand-driven organization leads to an improvement in forecast accuracy (Bursa, 2015, p. 4).

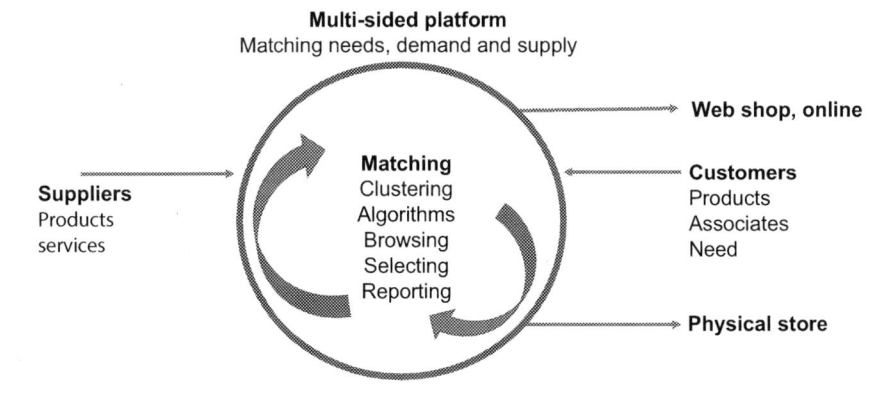

Figure 4.1 Multi-sided platform as part of a network.

With a more focused approach to evaluating demand and the products required to satisfy that demand, accuracy increases. This has a waterfall effect across the supply chain—the bullwhip effect as mentioned before. With a better predictor of demand (some companies like Amazon claims a prediction rate of sales of 80% based on personal data and cluster strategy), you can better align inventory and supply, position inventory accurately, and utilize your production and distribution assets more effectively (Bursa, 2015, p. 4). In this customer-centric view a firm is required to monitor shifts in customer needs precisely and this leads to a better customer service.

Changes to the Traditional Models

Through a platform, suppliers can benefit from the appeal of the network, the customer loyalty and the joint approach to the market. This not only saves costs; it also immediately increases the competitive strength (the network effect).

Collaboration is the basis for the future.

Shift 1: Competitive Strengths Are Used in the Platform Business Model

Platform businesses facilitate the interactions between consumers/buyers and producers/suppliers, whereby the greatest part of the value is created through this network of external users of the platform. The focus in terms of strategy thereby shifts from internal optimization to a maximization of external interaction through collaboration.

Shift 2: From Ownership to a Coordination of Resources

A resource-based view focuses the attention of the management on the company's internal resources in order to identify those assets, capacities and competences that have the potential to gain competitive advantages (Barney, 1991). These are resources that the company owns and/or controls. In linear companies these resources would be tangible assets such as factories, equipment and raw materials, and intangible resources such as brands and intellectual property. In contrast to traditional businesses, platform companies do not produce products and/or provide services themselves; production processes are not organized by the organization, and as a result there is no control of the creation of value within the production process. This value is brought in by external producers and coordinated by the platform company. The network of external producers and consumers is the most important capital of the platform company.

Shift 3: From a Focus on Customer Value to One on the Value of Ecosystems

Linear companies with traditional strategic models aim to maximize the *lifetime value* of individual customers of products and/or services. These customers are located at the end of the linear process; B2C. Platforms, on the other hand, want to maximize the total value of a growing network, whereby that network consists of users who supply a product or service on the one hand, and users who consume that product or service on the other. The users can exchange roles or carry out various roles simultaneously. Eisenmann et al. (2006) suggest that because platforms have a different group of users on either side, the value creation shifts from left to right and from right to left. Users of Uber, for example, may take a taxi ride one day and be a taxi driver the next; travelers may stay the night at an Airbnb on one occasion but then host an Airbnb on another. This change in the value chain is an important feature of a two-sided market (Walton, 2017).

A platform is a collaboration between parties:

- *demand-driven platforms*, the mediator between demand and supply (like Uber, Google and Airbnb);
- *aggregators* (the bundling of supply) whose aim it is to sell on behalf of various parties, like Amazon.com;
- *information platforms* whose aim is to provide specific objective answers to questions (for example regarding science, health or tourist information), like Wikipedia.com; and
- *communication platforms* that mediate the communication between visitors, for example Facebook, as well as video platforms such as YouTube.

Value Creation with Platforms

In a platform business model, value is created by the owner of the platform as an independent intermediary, by matching two (or more) mutually dependent parties, as well as connecting them and facilitating the direct interaction between these parties. Platforms in this context have their own business model because they generate needs and wishes of customers and will match this with supply information. They are the middleman between customers and suppliers, matching needs of customers with offerings of suppliers. This way they generate data from the buying process. Sometimes the sale is facilitated in the platform, mostly the sale is outside the competence of the platform (like Uber or Airbnb). The role of these *demand-based platforms* is an intermediation, which can replace the traditional supply chains. The platform can take the role of a focal company, leading in customer interaction and controlling the offerings and supply chain.

Other platforms are just an *information platform* without a specific business model. Their role is to generate leads for participants. This kind of platforms are still part of the traditional supply chain and will take the role as an advertising medium without special added value for a customer. *Community-based platforms* are not disruptive nor part of the demand-based economy. A digital brochure of products or suppliers with a direct link to their website.

The owner of the platform creates value as an independent intermediary, by matching and connecting two (or more) mutually dependent parties with one another and facilitating the direct interaction between these parties.

The aim of marketing of a platform is no longer focusing on a transaction for a company's product and/or service, but to fulfill a value exchange between supply and demand.

The most important capital of a platform company for providing this value proposition consists of:

- an infrastructure for direct interaction (the platform);
- the presence of network effects that arise when two (or more) sides of the market have an interdependence, supply and demand, resulting in the growth of the network; and
- the availability of data arising from the interaction via the platform, thereby creating matching functionalities and the relevance of the platform.

The most important value activities are the platform management, platform promotion and service provision to the network. The producers can only gain a competitive advantage if they have many frequent customers. It is becoming more difficult for producers to win the loyalty of customers who are no longer loyal to one particular brand, but to a platform that offers practically every brand (are you loyal to a product or to JD.com or Alibaba?). Platforms have made it difficult for producers to win customer loyalty, so producers feel compelled to take advantage of the benefits of these platforms, but the aim is to sell more to existing customers, the so-called loyalty loop, as we will see later. Customers use filters to find the products that best suit their wishes. It is now essential that the producers on these platforms can match as many of these filters as possible. This is done by analyzing popular searches and filters that are used by customers, and on that basis modify the products or the product description where necessary.

Platforms are Service-Driven

For the resource-based view of strategy, management's focus on the company's internal resources is essential in order to identify those assets, capacities and competences that have the potential to achieve competitive advantages. These are resources that the company owns and/or controls. In linear companies these resources would involve both material assets such as factories, equipment and raw materials, as well as immaterial resources such as brands and intellectual property. In a platform business model, however, products and/or services are not produced by the platform itself. Production processes are not organized by the organization either. As a result, there is no control over the creation of value within the production process. This value is created by external producers and is coordinated by the platform company. The owner of the platform creates value as an independent intermediary by matching and connecting these producers (supply) and facilitating direct interaction between consumers (demand). The network of external produccers and consumers is a platform company's most important capital.

Building Knowledge in a Platform

The challenge for platforms is not only in recognizing these different kinds of behavior, but also in identifying the components that lead to this behavior; just as it is important for physicists to be able to break down the individual molecules into atoms. This is not an easy process, as it requires different specializations and different tools. The new technologies offer these tools in the form of big data analyses. By analyzing every aspect of data, as well as examining the links and the connections of the data elements, one can gain knowledge about the buying behavior, and ascribe predictive values. This knowledge is an important source for the competition strategy. If this knowledge is insufficient, or even lacking, any competitors who do possess this knowledge will have a major advantage. Just consider, for example, the lack of this knowledge among shops, while the large internet providers have the information of customers. The adoption of technology by companies in the consumer market has led to an adaptation of the strategy and development of new distribution channels and methods. Knowledge of the customers' buying motives gave rise to a disruption in markets. Therefore, the new opportunities of analyses and machine learning are the core of a platform, as we will see in the next chapter.

B2B, from Efficiency to Disruption

A similar transition is taking place in the B2B market. Here, the focus on the distribution channel is of particular importance. As long as the business connections are based on a complex of buying motives, the traditional values remain important. These include the regular contacts, the delivery times, the collaboration between the various links in the supply chain and the dependency upon one another. There is a strong costs and price focus alongside clear agreements regarding delivery, production and quality. Personal contacts not only ensure bonding, but are also required for necessary information, upstream and downstream. Trade fairs, personal visits and other touchpoints are important too. Due to the limited market size, there is transparency in the market.

The parties look closely at one another from the perspective of the supply. The application of the technology has also changed this market. At first, the cost/price factor was important. Efficiency was important not only for a different price level, but also for better connections. EDI (electronic data interchange), led to efficiency, as well as to a closer connection between parties (on product basis). Most B2B markets are conservative, with a hierarchical organization for efficiency and control. And this is why these organizations respond slowly to changes in the market. The culture is also conservative, resulting in people who work in the organization also being conservative (after all, companies tend to look for people that fit both the job requirements and the company culture). As a result, old methods were, and still are, employed. There are only a few reasons to change if:

- the market changes;
- customers have other wishes and requirements; or
- the competitors have become so successful that the operating results come under pressure.

As long as this does not happen, there is no need to change. But when the market changes, most companies are not able to respond quickly enough, and then suffer the consequences. It is for good reason that Darwin's theory is often referred to, which is all about adapting to changes, for which a company does not necessarily need to be the biggest or the strongest. The many start-ups and successful small and medium-sized businesses are good examples of this.

How Platforms Will Disrupt Traditional Industries

Software is eating existing business, based on knowledge, insight and focused strategies:

- Efficient pipelines ate inefficient pipelines: media, retail at first. But this is only the first stage of disruption.
- Platforms eat pipelines: taxis, hotels, real estate brokers, restaurant services at first, but also Nokia and Blackberry lose from platforms as Google and Apple.
- Internet is no longer a distribution channel but an ecosystem, an infrastructure, and will create new business models.
- A convergence between physical and digital, a platform company leverages external ecosystems to create value in a new way.
- Significant economic advantages are superior marginal economics of production and distribution. Compare Airbnb with a holiday park or hotel.
- Positive network advantages by connecting thousands or millions of remote participants. They have access to more resources than a traditional pipeline company can command. Therefore, firms that continue to compete on the basis of resources that are owned internally are increasingly finding it difficult to compete with platforms.

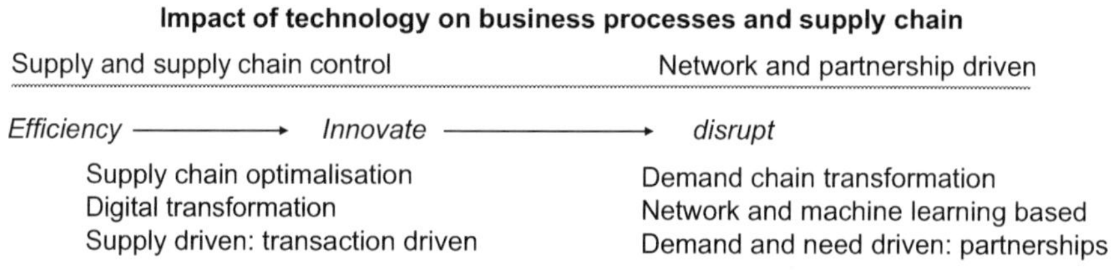

Impact of technology on business processes and supply chain

Supply and supply chain control	Network and partnership driven
Efficiency ———→ Innovate ————→	disrupt
Supply chain optimalisation	Demand chain transformation
Digital transformation	Network and machine learning based
Supply driven: transaction driven	Demand and need driven: partnerships

Figure 4.2 Impact of technology.

The platforms will transform the structure of business by:

- De-linking assets from value: de-link ownership of the physical asset from the value it creates.
- Re-intermediation. In the first stage of internet the expectation and changes were in disintermediation, elimination of middlemen. The fact is now that platforms re-intermediate introducing new kinds of middlemen. Replacing non-scalable and inefficient agent intermediaries with online, often automated tools and systems that offer valuable new goods and services to participants on both sides of the platform. Networked platforms serve as middlemen, the platform offers services to the end consumer or other businesses.
- Market aggregation. Providing information and power to platform users, access to products and services which were before not controlled or shattered.

How Do Platforms Compete?

Platforms seek exclusive access to essential assets. They do this by developing rules, practices and protocols to discourage multi-homing. Multi-homing facilitates switching, when a user abandons one platform in favor of another. Limiting multi-homing is a cardinal competitive tactic for platforms (an Apple strategy, but also adopted by Alibaba). Over the long haul it is in the interest of platform managers to take control of the major sources of value creation and for users in their ecosystem. A platform business will not own all the inimitable resources in its ecosystem, but it will seek to own the resources whose value is greatest. This is the reason why Alibaba and Facebook own search information on their platform, rather than Google, why Microsoft owns Word, PowerPoint and Excel on its platform. Platform businesses can use data to improve their competitive performance tactically and strategically. Like A/B testing. This kind of tactical data usage is quite effective and largely used by Amazon.

Strategic data analysis is broader in its scope. It searches who else is creating, controlling and siphoning value both on and off the platform. Some notable platform strategy battles have been won by companies that took advantage of data supremacy to outpace their rivals.

- Searches are important to help clients find the right solution, better matches facilitated by enhanced data, make both sides happier.
- But also, by identifying unsuccessful user searches reflecting the existence of potential clients in need of business (or product) solutions.
- Finally, to look for new business opportunities and service capabilities.

This way the platform will generate value for users. If competitors don't have the data, they can not create the value, which means they cannot create the interactions which further limits their access to the data. Acquisitions should add value to the users of a platform by means of services, interactions or profitability. Platform businesses don't need to own all the critical assets as long as they have access to them in their ecosystems; platform companies can pursue fewer M&A deals than many traditional firms feel compelled to do. They enjoy several significant benefits:

- Claiming a portion of the value creating is far less than buying a partner.
- Keeping a partner at arm's length reduces the platform's technological complexity.
- A platform that builds on a lean architecture that conducts all its business activity through clean interfaces will offer a much better customer experience.

By comparison with traditional pipeline businesses platform companies can move very rapidly to respond to competitive moves and to mount competitive assaults of their own. In traditional businesses companies compete by attempting to create higher-quality products and services. Platforms compete by trying to improve the quality of the tools they provide to pull in users, facilitate interactions and match producers with consumers. Airbnb allows a person to search through options organized not only according to their own characteristics, but also by quality, number of rooms, price and mapping geolocations. A user can strike deals immediately through Airbnb without going off platform. This makes Airbnb far easier to use and enabled the platform to rapidly outgrow others.

When Advantage is Sustainable: Winner-Takes-All Market

The four forces that most often characterize winner-take-all markets are:

- supply economies of scale;
- strong network effects;
- high multi-homing or switching costs; and
- lack of niche specialization.

Conclusion

When more users join the ecosystem, the value created and the profit margins both increases. Because positive network effects attract more users too when a platform is larger, they are a second force that is likely to strengthen a market's winner-take-all tendency. Another factor is the high multi-homing and switching costs. This might be monetary by paying a fine or non-monetary by inconvenience to move like in Facebook or Twitter. Both higher multi-homing costs and higher switching costs tend to push a market toward higher concentration, dominated by fewer larger companies. See the dominance of Apple in the device market and Android as a mobile infrastructure. A market with little or no niche specialization is susceptible to the winner-takes-all effect. This explains the fierce competition between Uber and Lyft.

Student's Mind

Debenhams has announced it will shut its remaining stores by 15 May 2021, closing the door on more than 200 years of trade on UK high streets.

The move means 49 more shops will go on top of the 52 due to close on 8 May. The Debenhams brand will continue online after being bought by retailer Boohoo for £55m in January. The company traces its roots back to 1778 when William Clark opened a shop in London's West End, selling fabrics, bonnets and parasols.

In 1950 Debenhams had the distinction of being the biggest department store in the UK with 110 stores. Over the years, Debenhams expanded at a rapid rate. In 2006 it announced plans to double its number of stores to 240 and was opening new shops as recently as 2017. However, the chain had struggled for years with falling profits and rising debts, as more shopping moved online. It called in administrators twice in two years, most recently in April 2020.

But the coronavirus pandemic—which saw the enforced closure of non-essential retail outlets—proved to be the final blow for Debenhams and other rival retailers including Top Shop-owner Arcadia. Then in January 2021 Boohoo stepped in to buy the brand but not the shops, signaling the end of Debenhams on the High Street.

Announcing the final closures, Debenhams said: "Over the next 10 days, Debenhams will close its doors on the High Street for the final time in its 242 year history. We hope to see you all one last time in stores before we say a final goodbye to the UK High Street."

(BBC, 2021)

1   Why has Debenhams lost the High Street?
2   What will be the values online?
3   Can Debenhams survive as a platform?
4   What should you do to prepare Debenhams for the online future?

Discussion Point

The business world will be dominated by large-scale platforms. How can companies compete with these platforms, or will it lead to a destruction of the independent companies?

References

Adrodegari, F., Bacchetti, A., Saccani, N., Arnaiz, A. & Meiren, T. (2018). The Transition towards Service-Oriented Business Models: A European Survey on Capital Goods Manufacturers. *International Journal of Engineering Business Management*, 10. (doi:10.1177/1847979018754469)

Barney, J. (1991). *Firm Resources and Sustained Competitive Advantage*. Thousand Oaks, CA: Sage Publications.

BBC. (2021). End of an Era for Debenhams as Final Shops Set to Close. Retrieved from www.bbc.com/news/business-56993816

Bursa, K. (2015). The Impact of Becoming Demand-Driven. *The European Business Review*. Retrieved September 25, 2020 from www.europeanbusinessreview.com/the-impact-of-becoming-demand-driven-2/#

Eisenmann, T. et al. (2006). Strategies for Two-Sided Markets. *HBR*, October.

Guercini, S. & Runfola, A. (2015). Actors' Roles in Interaction and Innovation in Local Systems: A Conceptual Taxonomy. *Journal of Business & Industrial Marketing*, 30(3/4): 269–278.

Gupta, S. (2018). *Driving Digital Strategy: A Guide to Reimagining Your Business*. Boston, MA: Harvard Business Review Press.

Walton, N. (2017). *The Internet as a Technology-Based Ecosystem*. London: Palgrave Macmillan.

Wolf, P. & Troxler, P. (2016). Community-Based Business Models: Insights from an Emerging Maker Economy. *Interaction Design and Architecture(s) Journal*, 30: 75–94.

5 Machine Learning

The Role of Artificial Intelligence in a Demand-Driven Business Model

Machine learning will be the fundament of business. Customers and customer behavior are analyzed and used for more effective marketing strategies. Knowledge of this behavior will be used to predict future sales on an individual level, but also to improve the relationship. Algorithms are tools to automate processes and to react to changes. This will change the competitive strategies of companies but will also have impact on products.

The killing approach for a demand-driven organization is the knowledge of customers and customer behavior. Not so long ago the focus was on target groups and past behavior of customers. But to react to demand it is necessary to know what customers want, maybe even before they know it. New tools like machine learning make predictions more accurate, as we have mentioned in Chapter 4. The approach to do this is called data science and more specifically machine learning. The tools involved will be specified in this chapter.

Data science is an inter-disciplinary field that uses scientific methods, processes, algorithms and systems to extract knowledge and insights from many structural and unstructured data. Data science is related to data mining, machine learning and big data. All these components are relevant for marketing as we will see below.

For Marketing intelligence in this context is the everyday information relevant to a company about customers' behavior and preferences, gathered and analyzed specifically for the purpose of accurate and confident decision making in determining customer needs and behavior processes. Machine learning as part of marketing intelligence can be seen as a process for communication and decision making. First, data have to be collected about customers. Partly this data can be based on traditional data from existing systems, but partly from external sources, as we have seen. All this data (big data) has to be standardized. Making uniform analysis possible. The steps are shown in Figure 5.1.

Check the quality of data and data files. Are all fields consistent? Skip empty field or double field or data (purging). This process is called "merge and purge" to make a so-called clean file which is the basis for analyses. This can at first be done by supervised or non-supervised learning before the clusters are constructed and eventually the algorithms are designed.

DOI: 10.4324/9781003226161-5

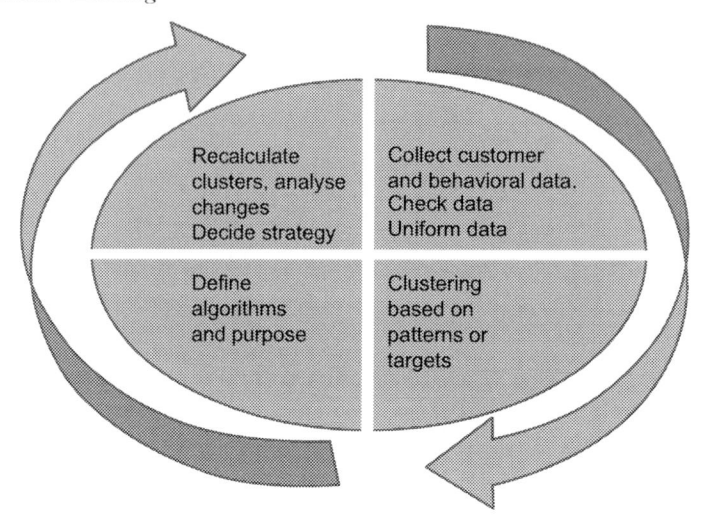

Figure 5.1 Steps for machine learning.

Machine learning involves computers, discovering how they can perform tasks without being explicitly programmed to do so. It involves computer learning from data so that they carry out certain tasks. For simple tasks assigned to computers, it is possible to program algorithms telling the machine how to execute all steps required to solve the problem at hand; on the computer's part, no learning is needed. For more advanced tasks, it can be challenging for a human to manually create the needed algorithms. In practice, it can turn out to be more effective to help the machine develop its own algorithm, rather than having human programmers specify every needed step. This way, algorithms are programmed to decide about new processes or actions and will be part of artificial intelligence. Dynamic customer behavior can be the fundament for constant changes on individual basis of communication but also for defining new clusters.

Machine Learning and Algorithms

Machine learning implies the use of algorithms to find and draw patterns within extensive amounts of data (Hao et al., 2019). More concretely, it is useful to consider all the recommendations received when browsing platforms such as Netflix, Amazon, YouTube and Spotify: they are all part of the so-called big data. It can be text, images, videos or data records. By analyzing this big data, powered by machine learning, pattern can be found in customer behavior. Therefore, it comprises the majority of artificial intelligence applications, created clusters based on behavior and common denominators, and elaborates algorithms in order to predict and anticipate users' preferences and tastes. The outer layer of Figure 5.2 is represented by artificial intelligence which represents the development of intelligent systems enabled to make independent decisions (Shetty, 2019). What

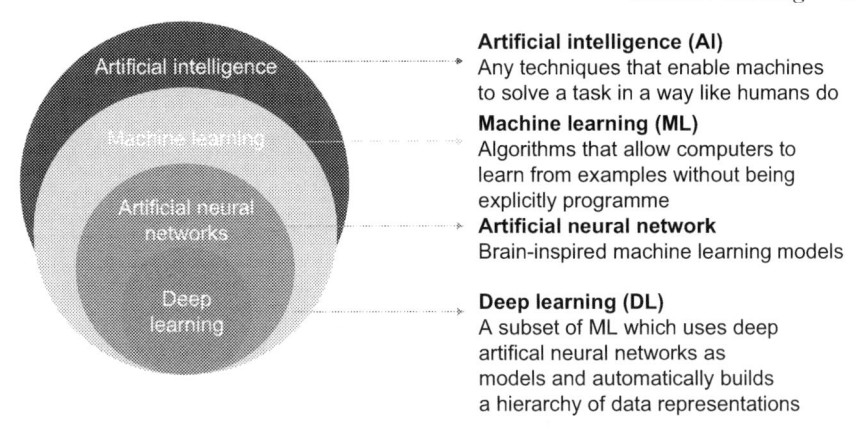

Artificial intelligence (AI)
Any techniques that enable machines
to solve a task in a way like humans do

Machine learning (ML)
Algorithms that allow computers to
learn from examples without being
explicitly programme

Artificial neural network
Brain-inspired machine learning models

Deep learning (DL)
A subset of ML which uses deep
artifical neural networks as
models and automatically builds
a hierarchy of data representations

Figure 5.2 Standard model of relationship between artificial intelligence and deep learning.

contributed to the mainstream adoption of artificial intelligence in various domains is the incredibly extensive amount of data generated each minute which reduces the dependency on humans to accomplish certain tasks (Shetty, 2019). In order to elaborate on people's behavior and online actions, machine learning relies on deep learning which, in turn, leverages neural networks. *Deep learning* is an artificial intelligence (AI) function that imitates the workings of the human brain in processing data and creating patterns for use in decision making.

Therefore, deep learning clusters are some of the applications of machine learning. In 1986, Geoffrey Hinton, the founding father of deep learning, was inspired by human brains' neurons and how they intrinsically work. He developed the so-called deep neural network that entails "layers of simple computational nodes that work together to munch through data and deliver a final result in the form of the prediction" (Hao et al., 2019). At the end of the day, algorithms are the keyword when it comes to touch upon the concept of machine learning. Based on algorithms a company can react to behavior, response and non-response of customers. Algorithms are processes based on behavioral triggers. In the change to a demand-driven organization the knowledge of customer behavior and forecasting individual behavior is a key factor of success. Therefore, knowledge of deep learning and algorithms are essential for marketing decisions.

Algorithms are a set of rules that are essential to be followed to solve a problem. We could think of an algorithm as a set of rules we follow when we get dressed in the morning. Each piece of clothing has a fixed order, otherwise, we would not be able to properly fit in them. Therefore, we first wear underwear and then move on to the outer layers such as t-shirts, trousers, and eventually a jacket. The same goes for algorithms: the right order helps to create codes useful to tell a computer what to do. As Choudary (2015) manages to explain, thanks to their constant reliability and impeccable order, algorithms "are the arbiters of both resource allocation and reputation assignment" and function as gatekeepers:

Algorithms are automated instructions and can be simple or complex, depending on how many layers deep the initial algorithm goes. Machine learning and artificial intelligence are both sets of algorithms, but differ depending on whether the data they receive is structured or unstructured.

The applications of these sciences are various and innumerable. However, a field which has exponentially undergone the advent of machine and deep learning is marketing. Within this domain, AI allows for automation, optimization of processes, and augmentation of workers to alleviate the workload of marketers. These three actions enable some important marketing processes: data collection, insights gathering, and customer engagement which contribute to the "virtuous cycle of personalization" (see Figure 5.2). The latter is achieved by the creation of unique brand experiences through the conversion of any relevant user data into action. Hence, the creation of customized marketing campaigns, where every interaction between the brand and the user represents a new set of data. Cookies are an example. Therefore, there is this continuous loop that a user can hardly escape. Moreover, what makes this loop so hard to escape is the real-time generation of customized content enabled by algorithms (Choudary, 2015). At the end of the day, why would we leave a platform that provides us with everything we want, and even with what we do not know we desire yet, without having to browse countless websites or wander around entire shopping malls?

Analyzing Data: Correlation or Causation

Analyzing the data and looking for patterns may lead to a wrong interpretation of causes. We have to be specifically alerted on the difference between correlation and causation. Correlation shows similar patterns between two data sets (the number of storks and the number of newborn babies, for instance; this is a false correlation). It also happens that there are similar patterns because the reason is the

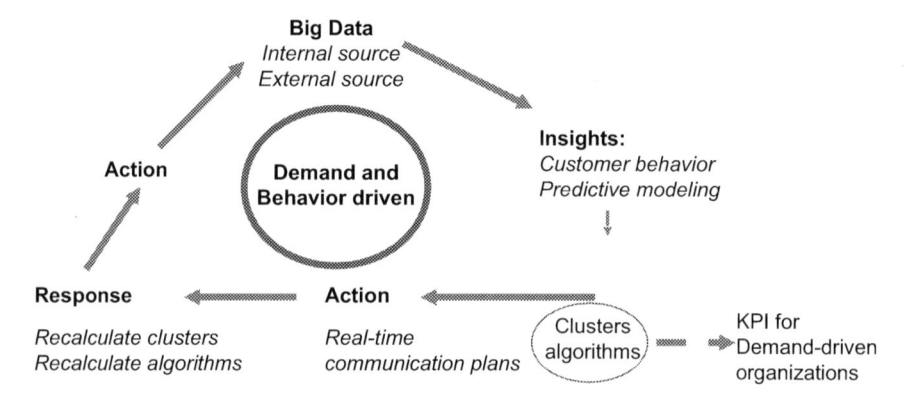

Figure 5.3 Using big data for machine learning.

same. In correlated data, a pair of variables are related in that one thing is likely to change when the other does. This relationship might lead us to assume that a change to one thing causes the change in the other. That kind of faulty thinking will be exposed by explaining correlation, causation, and the bias that often lumps the two together. Here are two examples:

- During 2020 and the Covid-19 crisis more people of over 70 died than any other age group. The conclusion was that people aged over 70 were in danger. But this was a correlation, not causality. The reason some people where more infected than others had to do with the physical health. People with an existing illness or disease, suffering health problems (known and unknown), have less resistance against viruses, especially an aggressive virus such as Covid-19. The older the people are, the less resistance and less physical health. So, the correlation was (too) easily made between age and infection. Therefore, some specialists were advocates of healthy living: healthy food (no fries), no alcohol, no smoking, exercise, and the right vitamins (vitamin D). Quite often it was a case of dying *with* Covid, not *of* Covid.
- The sale of ice creams and the sale of sunburn lotion. The correlation is clear, but it does not mean that we have to increase the sale of ice cream to boost the sale of sunburn. It is just that the cause of the sale of sunburn and ice cream are the same: hot weather. As you can understand we have to know the cause for predicting sales or to stimulate sales. Price elasticity may be the cause for extra sales when the price is lowered. Action of competitors might be the cause for losing sales (maybe not the price level), correlation is simply a relationship.

Correlation and causation are often confused because the human mind likes to find patterns even when they do not exist. We often fabricate these patterns when two variables appear to be so closely associated that one is dependent on the other. That would imply a cause-and-effect relationship where the dependent event is the result of an independent event.

However, we cannot simply assume causation even if we see two events happening, seemingly together, before our eyes. In correlated data, when a pair of variables are related can mean that one thing is likely to change when the other does. This relationship might lead us to assume that a change to one thing causes the change in the other. The human brain simplifies incoming information, so we can make sense of it. Our brains often do that by making assumptions about things based on slight relationships, or bias. But that thinking process isn't foolproof. An example is when we mistake correlation for causation. Bias can make us conclude that one thing must cause another if both change in the same way at the same time.

Despite the immense marketing and business developments that have been enabled by machine learning, it is important to point out some limitations as well. Limitations are present both at a technical level and at an ethical one. The most acknowledged limitation concerns the fact that AI is not human, therefore still has

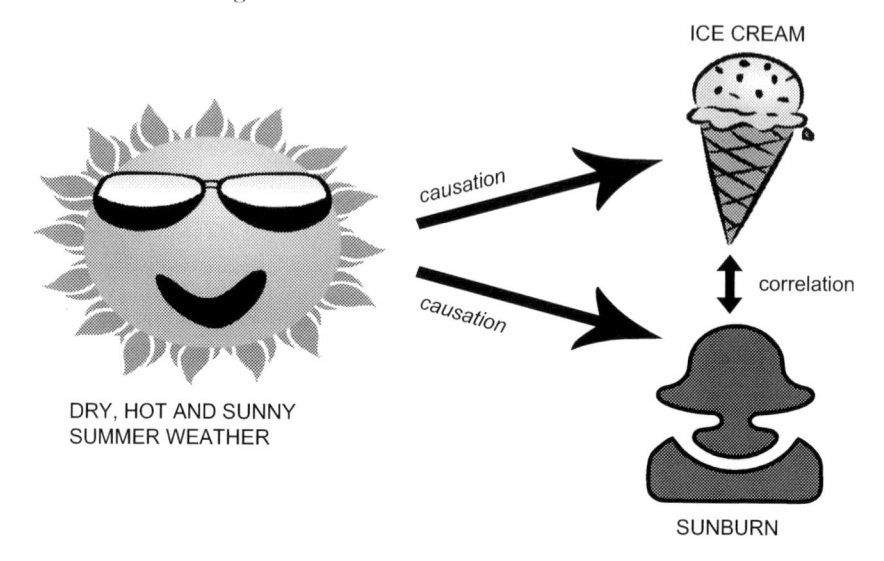

Figure 5.4 Correlation and causation.

limited capabilities and cannot replace jobs involving feelings and ethical thinking. Therefore, scientists came to the conclusion that oftentimes AI is more efficient to empower humans rather than to replace them. Another use of AI is process based.

The application of AI can be divided in algorithms, which are quantitative, a target is defined, and rules of response and reactions will lead to a change of the algorithms. An example is the target, turnover level, response level or loyalties. Artificial application can also be applicable as a support for decision-making. In that case qualitative analytics are more important. For qualitative analytics routines and data are supportive to a decision. This data will be linked to intuition and knowledge of the subject (like market knowledge or personal observations). In the case of objective categories analyses can check continuously external trigger and adjust the algorithms or the category. These analytics should be matched and will make independent decisions and therefore can react to unforeseen circumstances. An example is pricing. When a main competitor is changing the price of certain articles, through AI your company can react immediately by changing the price as well. This is not general for all price changes in the market, but for instance only for price changes of main competitors or certain products (predefined). Artificial intelligence will make use of traditional data, quite often available within the company, other forms of data mostly from external sources and of course data from algorithms (result data and processing data).

Another limitation concerns reliability issues given AI's necessity of disposing of "rich sets of data" in order to draw patterns. Surely, the richer the sets, the more reliable the outcome. However, AI mostly is still a bunch of algorithms and clusters that very few people can totally understand. On top of these, other suggestions mention the inefficiency when marketing stacks are too complicated, and the fact that we hold unrealistic expectations towards AI, rendering it a limitation in certain situations. Regarding the ethical limitations and issues of AI in marketing, the topic is highly discussed. Since traditional marketing is mainly conveying a product's features and value to potential consumers, the ethical issue arises at the moment in which the privacy boundaries of users are crossed by the brands. This will even be a greater issue in demand-driven organization where customer profiles and behavior are leading for product offerings and production. Not only a product is the focus (transaction based) but the needs and preferences of individual customers. Strict data laws are in place to protect the privacy of customers, but also limit the use of data. Sharing data with external parties or competitors within the platform or outside the platform is restricted by legislation. For a business-to-business approach the privacy is not an issue.

According to the Netflix documentary *The Social Dilemma*, nowadays social media and the concept of marketing powered by artificial intelligence have crossed these boundaries to such a great extent that it feels like each and every single one of us is living in our own Truman shows. Such life distortion has been allowed since data have become one of the most, if not the most, valuable asset on the planet. Users' data, including every single small online action and non-action, has become immensely valuable for companies as they provide the basis for the creation of marketing campaigns and customized products and services. Considering that marketing is treated as "the most valuable player of business development," it makes sense for companies to leverage any source available to excel in this field.

In the shift from supply-driven to demand-driven, individual data is the source of product offerings. However, this individual data is used for algorithms but also for aggregation to a cluster level. In that case it is not so much the individual as a person, but the behavior of a person that is relevant.

Regardless of the limitations, it is imperative to acknowledge the high efficiency and uncover the potential of machine learning nowadays. Now that marketers have so much power thanks to algorithms and automated data collection methods, it is entirely up to them to decide how to engage with them. Nevertheless, since fixed boundaries between what is acceptable and what is excessive have not been established yet, government regulations could be a significant step forward to help delineate them.

Defining Clusters

Clusters in a supply-driven economy are predefined clusters based on personal indicators (denominators). Examples are clusters based on income, age, education, gender. The prediction that these denominators represented a certain behavior was sometimes right but was based on averages. A response above average was related to these denominators. Market surveys were trying to underline these assumptions but were never accurate. In the 1980s data analysis was used to analyze the behavior based on lifestyle, socio-demographic or subscriptions. Direct Marketing was part of marketing communication using

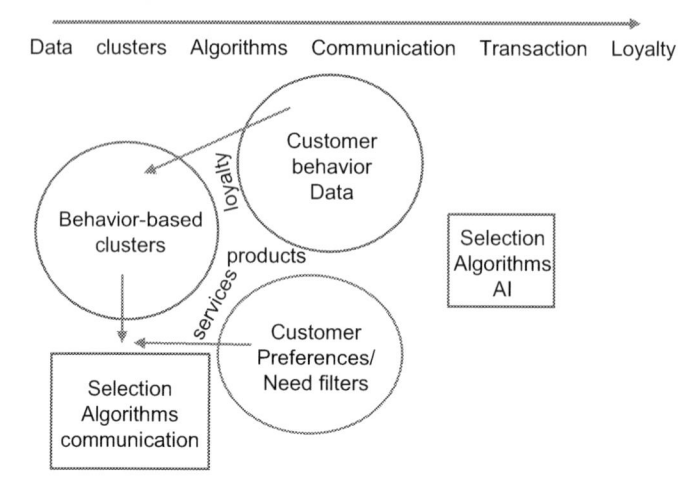

Figure 5.5 Marketing data for machine learning.

databases with addresses and some behavioral issues like subscriptions to certain magazines. The addresses were the basis of selected and directed marketing campaigns. Profiling of prospects was based on the selected list, for instance of a certain magazine and matched with the addresses in a customer database. This procedure was popular with direct writers, insurance companies selling insurance products direct to customers, mail order companies and publishers. Basically, companies with a database of customers and selling their products direct to the market.

Clustering was based on matching external files with the customer database. Direct marketing was based on direct communication with known customers and prospects. Marketing communication in general was based on target media like magazines, papers, television or trade shows. In those cases, communication was based on a target group, whereas direct marketing was based on individuals.

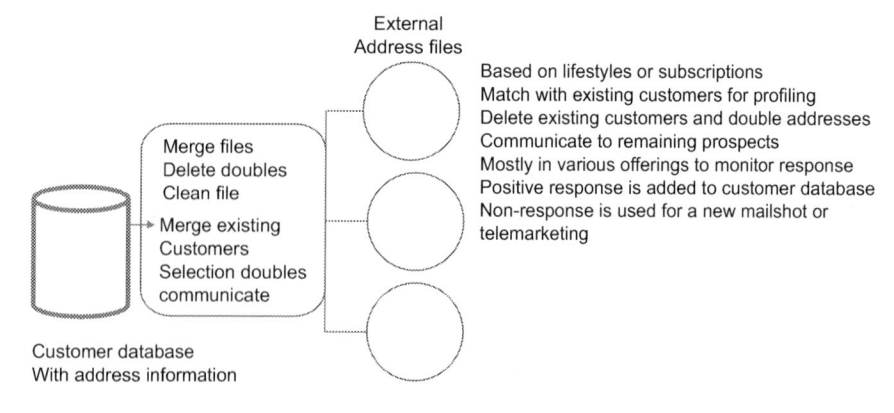

Figure 5.6 Merging data to create a clean file.

A next step came in the 1990s, when the database became a part of the communication with customers. In the case of direct marketing the address files were used to generate transactions/sales. In the nineties the customer files were used to get a better contact with the customers and to register historical communication and contact. The focus of the organization, although still supply-driven, changed from transactions to relationships. The historical data was used to communicate direct, phone and (e)mail. The database and customer files became part of a customer focus of organization. Customer relationship management was based on the customer data, contact and transactions. The sales of products and services was more based on the relationship with customers. Repeat sales, loyalty and customer ranking (gold, silver and bronze) became part of the marketing and marketing communication strategy. Analyses and clustering were based on the level of communication with customers and the level of sales transactions.

As said, clusters in marketing were used in direct marketing to get new customers. Direct marketing was also used to improve the relationship with the customers and to predict the sales better. Also repeat sales and loyalty, as key focus points, could be improved by using clusters, especially behavioral based clusters.

As an example, I will specify three possible clusters for marketing based on a different focus or source data:

- a RFM clustering strategy for forecasting;
- a pool-based clustering; and
- a loyalty-based clustering.

RFM and Other Clusters

A method which was used by companies with direct sales and identified customers was a RFM-based clustering. In the RFM-based clusters customers where ranked based on the last visiting date, the frequency of sales and the money spent. The loyalty of a customer and therefore the success rate of further sales was ranked as:

- Recency: last visiting date.
- Frequency: how often does a customer buy something.
- Monetary value: what is the amount spent per sale or in a certain timeframe?

RFM stands for *recency, frequency* and *monetary value*, each corresponding to some key customer trait. These RFM metrics are important indicators of a customer's behavior because frequency and monetary value affect a customer lifetime value, and recency affects retention, a measure of engagement.

Businesses that lack the monetary aspect, like viewership, readership, or surfing-oriented products, could use engagement parameters instead of monetary factors. This results in using RFE, a variation of RFM. Furthermore, this engagement parameter could be defined as a composite value based on metrics such as bounce rate, visit duration, number of pages visited, time spent per page, etc. These parameters can be ranked based on importance or number of hits. This is especially important in ranking prospects based on website analyses and forming the clusters in a demand-driven business model.

RFM factors illustrate these facts:

- the more recent the purchase, the more responsive the customer is to promotions;
- the more frequently the customer buys, the more engaged and satisfied they are; and
- monetary value differentiates heavy spenders from low-value purchasers.

Based on these criteria a behavioral definition can be made like:

- Recency: last 6 months, between 6 months and 24 months older than 24 months.
- Frequency: more than 6 times in 2 years, between 3 and 6 times, 0, 1 or 2 times.
- Monetary value: more than €500, between €200 and €500, less than €200.

RFM-recency	RFM-frequency	RFM-monetary	Percentage
3	1	1	12%
3	1	3	8%
3	3	2	8%
2	1	1	7%
3	1	2	7%
1	1	1	6%
3	3	3	5%

	Classification	Factor
Recency:	last 6 months	3
	between 6 months and 124 months	2
	olderthan 24 months	1
Frequency:	more than 6 times 2 in years	3
	between 6 times and 3 times	2
	2,1 or 0 times	1
	More than €500	3
Monetary value	Between €500 and €200	2
	less than € 200	1

Figure 5.7 Clusters based on RFM analyses.

Those 27 clusters (3 × 3 × 3) group the customer based on behavior and indicate the loyalty level. Campaigns can be based on each cluster. Response and non-response will give a more insight in a cluster but will split the cluster in two segments. This information can be used to qualify the segment but can also be an indication of a shift of individuals to a different cluster: response can lead to an upgrade, higher cluster; non-response can lead to churn, a lower cluster. On itself when a change of cluster is likely, a special algorithm can be used to stop the change or to motivate the change.

Matching the customers within a cluster is relevant too. Because within the cluster they share identical behavior or have the same common denominator as profit (profit pool, like age, education or social commitments like being married). Variables are indications for behavior. Matching difference within the cluster can indicate opportunities. For instance, if 70% of the customers in a certain cluster bought a certain product, the remaining 30% are likely to buy this product too. A special algorithm will help to stimulate sales.

Further analyses of behavior in various clusters can predict future sales, on product level and on customer level. A demand-driven strategy based on this RFM analysis will lead to more insight in possible sales, customer needs and behavior and loyalty. This is an example based on collaborative filtering.

Collaborative filtering is a method of making automatic predictions (filtering) about the interests of a user by collecting preferences or taste information from many users (collaborating).

Collaborative filtering based on behavioral clusters is a method of making automatic predictions (filtering) about the interests of a user by collecting preferences or taste information from many users (collaborating). The underlying

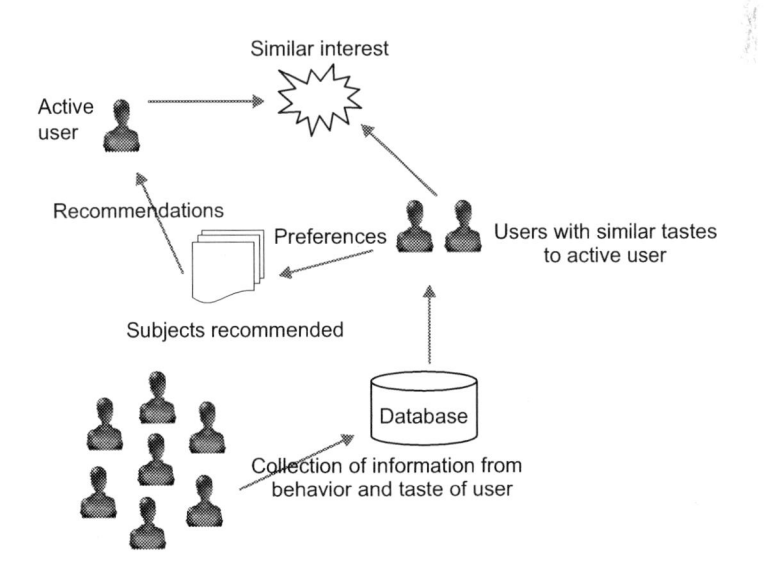

Figure 5.8 Collaborative filtering for creating clusters and predictions.

assumption of the collaborative filtering approach is that if a person *A* has the same opinion as a person *B* on an issue, A is more likely to have B's opinion on a different issue than that of a randomly chosen person.

RFM is a method that can be used if the indicators RFM are known on an individual basis.

If we analyze the table of Figure 5.7, we can use this high-level representation as a forecasting tool. Looking at the classification, where 3 is the best and 1 the lowest in ranking as we have defined earlier, we can see that in the biggest cluster frequency and monetary value are low, but recency is high. That means that there was recent contact with the people in this group, but the frequency is low and so is the expenditure This is a dangerous position because the regularity of contact is an indicator for loyalty. Churning is very likely. This will lead to less turnover. A special strategy (algorithms) is needed to get in contact again with these customers.

On the other hand, we see on the second line a similar group of customers where the contact is also low, but they spend more. In the first example the strategy is aimed at creating returns and communication, but in the second example we should only focus on a higher frequency. Based on this kind of analyses we can predict future sales, based on behavior: frequency, recency and value. It is also possible to replace the indicators recency, frequency or monetary value with other indicators. As mentioned before, RFE is a possibility where a certain engagement parameter is used like cross-sales, repeat sales or response rate. The advantage is that a strict analysis on preset parameters make it possible to compare customers and create clusters based on similar behavior and link this to algorithms. On the other hand, when the indicators are not so strict, other cluster techniques can be used:

- Skipping an indicator, so cluster based on one or two sets indicators.
- Add a special indicator in place of the standard 3 or add a number 4.
- Create flexible data pools.

The term *data pool* refers to a related set of values obtained from a centralized database. The data can be anything from supply chain information to employee records. The data can be generated automatically or manually for analysis using the entire data set or a subset of values.

For creating data pools based on indicators, clusters are created based on behavioral indicators, postal codes, other selection criteria. The pools can be temporary like for a campaign, or permanent based on collaborative filtering (what do users have in common) or after analyses the database for correlations between behavior of buyers or visitors (to a website).

With Figure 5.2 the principles of machine learning were explained based on three layers:

- deep learning;
- artificial neural networks; and
- machine learning.

In Figure 5.9 the process of similarity analyses is explained based on two principles: supervised and unsupervised. In unsupervised analyses the system is looking for elements that data have in common (common denominators) to form clusters. This can be based upon a number of clusters that had to be formed and the data is grouped around a common denominator. The number can be small, so large clusters are created but with a high variety, or the number of clusters are more where the variety is less (this can be an indicator), but the data elements (customer behavior has a high correlation factor). In all cases data pools are formed as an aggregation for algorithms, communication or further analyses.

On the other hand, also a supervised analysis of the database is possible. In that case the factors of analyses are predefined. Look for people who bought something the last month, or who bought also for more than €100 per sale, or whatever. This way targeted clusters are formed for action.

All clusters, the data pools, are flexible and can change based on reactions or specified analyses.

The Role of APIs in Platforms' Design

Together with AI, another underlying concept, vital to the creation of successful platforms as a basis for demand-based business models, is APIs. An API is a special interface program to link external sources to the platform. This can be a link to activate external software application or web shops. Also, a link to external source and the platform is possible to generate data or special information (e.g. about products, stock levels or delivery). Thanks to the high

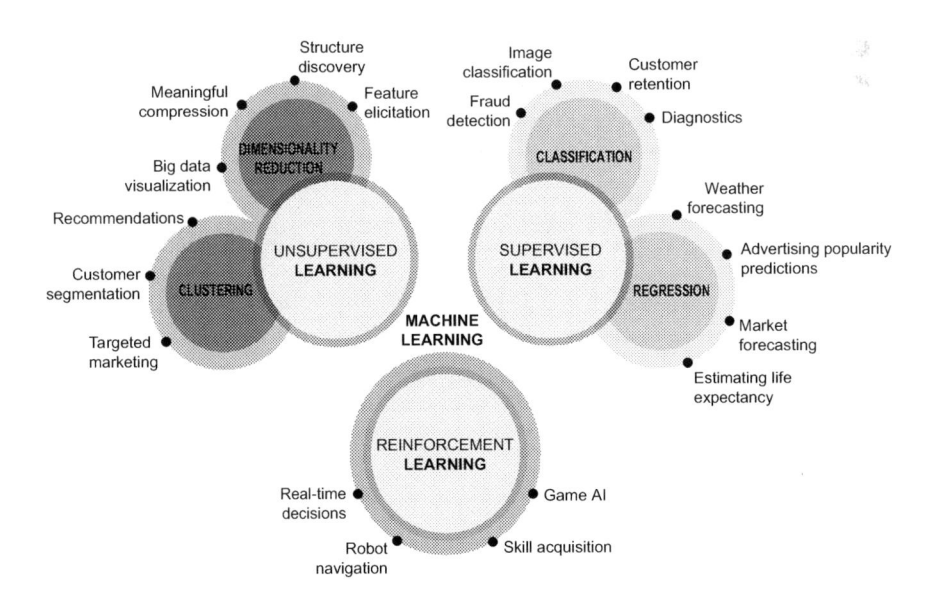

Figure 5.9 A model generally used to explain the various steps of machine learning.

business scalability that platforms allow, an increasing number of companies are joining platforms or creating new ones so that they do not fall behind in the race to gain competitive advantage. The most significant competitive advantage created by platforms is the network effect: the more people join a platform, the higher the possibility of word-of-mouth, the higher the chance of thriving.

However, the basis of this loop is understanding consumers' behavior and triggering customers' willingness to repeatedly visit your platform. Surely there are infinite components that contribute to achieving this, nonetheless, a platform's interface and ease of browsing can substantially make the difference. After all, platforms in the first place were built to indulge people's necessity to obtain what they desired in a quicker and more efficient way. This is where application programming interfaces (APIs) come into play. They are interfaces that represent a point of interaction between a number of systems. APIs represent a way for businesses to innovate and gain significant competitive advantage: they enable a new form of business development and innovation by "coalescing an external ecosystem of developer-partners" (Choudary, 2015, p.45). On top of this, APIs have the power to create value on platforms. Together with algorithms, they encourage user participation of platforms and match the supply with the respective demand (Choudary, 2015).

Technically speaking, APIs represent the messenger that takes requests and tells a system what you want to do. They then bring back the response to you exactly like waiters in restaurants. Therefore, an API is responsible for all the interactivity that occurs in relationship with a platform. Whenever we select filters, insert keywords and scroll up and down a page, APIs are there to make sure that the user gets what they want. Consequently, correct and well-functioning interfaces are vital to the success of a platform. That is the competitive advantage of a demand-driven business model. In sales-driven platforms like Amazon, searches are based on products they offer. Communication and registration are based on sales data. In a demand-based model the needs and preferences of a visitor are dominant for searches. Machine learning is supporting the match between the need and preferences and the service or products. This is why machine learning and other types of analyses are based on general behavior and objective criteria, not on sales. In supply-driven platforms (like web shops), a match is made based on a product request. The platform gives customers exactly what they want with no delay and no imperfection whatsoever. In this day and age there is an oversupply of products and an unlimited number of (web)shops. Buying is not a problem anymore but selling is. Therefore, an advanced strategy on demand detecting, direct communication and loyalty based on interaction and support are needed. This outlines the need for a demand-driven business model to be successful in the future.

Conclusion

Technically speaking, APIs represent the messenger that takes requests and tells a system what you want to do. They then bring back the response to you exactly like waiters in restaurants. Therefore, an API is responsible for all the interactivity that occurs in a platform and between the platform and other connections like suppliers, news or other sources. Whenever we select filters, insert keywords and scroll up and down a page, APIs are there to make sure that the user gets what they want. Consequently, correct and well-functioning interfaces are vital to the success of a platform. That is also why it is so difficult for platforms to compete with Amazon. The platform gives customers exactly what they want with no time delay and no imperfection whatsoever. Since we are now used to such a high degree of perfection, it is almost impossible to choose another platform over a general platform like Amazon. Indeed, APIs contribute as well to the creation of the virtuous cycle of personalization. After all, APIs are powered by machine learning too.

Student's Mind

1   How can machine learning support focal companies?
2   How can network effects support focal companies?[1]
3   What is the relationship (or constraints) between privacy and machine learning?
4   What are the consequences when a company bases strategy on RFM analyses?
5   Can you mention other successful analyses based on machine learning?
6   What are the financial consequences of the impact of machine learning?
7   How is loyalty built with machine learning?

Discussion Point

Why do people prefer to buy from a platform? And what are the negative aspects for customers?

Note

1   Companies governing over the supply chains, providing direct contact to end customers, and having bargain power over other actors in the supply chain. Because of the impact of focal companies on competition, new legislation is drafted by the European Union to restrict their power.

References

Choudary, P. S. (2015). *Platform Scale: How an Emerging Business Model Helps Startups Build Large Empires with Minimum Investment*. London: Platform Thinking Labs.

Hao, T., Elith, J., Guillera-Arroita, G. & Lahoz-Monfort, J. J. (2019). A Review of Evidence about Use and Performance of Species Distribution Modelling Ensembles like BIOMOD. *Diversity and Distribution*, 25(5): 839–852.

Shetty, S. (2019). Analysis of Machine Learning Classifiers for LULC Classification on Google Earth Engine. Thesis, University of Twente, Enschede, The Netherlands. Retrieved from https://library.itc.utwente.nl/papers_2019/msc/gfm/shetty.pdfWhat is a Focal Company?

6 Transforming Existing Business to Succeed in a Demand-Driven Economy

The transformation from a focus on supply to a focus on value creation is a major change in the strategy and structure of an organization. A supply chain was a process approach linking companies to process goods from producer to consumer. A process approach strongly focusing on efficiency and optimalization. The flow of buying data and buying preference on an individual level was not relevant. In a demand-driven approach it is relevant, it is the fundament of every organization in a value chain approach, putting customers in the focus point. Customer data is the driving force in a value chain, customer contacts are essential. The power of focal companies is almost unlimited.

Role of Technology in the Shift from a Supply- to a Demand-Driven Economy

The world is in the midst of the Fourth Industrial Revolution and the main catalyst of this shift to a demand-driven economy is continuous technological development.

On the supply side, technological development, optimalization and innovation, has led to an unparalleled increase in productivity and output. The benefits of using technology on the supply side of business to reduce costs, improve efficiency and output are evident. However, due to the changed economic landscape of oversupply where there is simply not enough demand to fill supply, technology needs to be leveraged to capture and enhance the demand side of your business. In addition, in the last few years people are realizing the power of utilizing (the adaption) of technology on the demand side of businesses. Increased access to technology has fundamentally changed the way in which consumers engage with businesses, since they are better informed and consequently more assertive. The impact of internet on the buying behavior of companies and consumers is evident but the real impact is just beginning. Consumers now expect more. If a company does not have exactly what we are looking for or offer the experience we seek, we have the power to switch to a different supplier at the click of a mouse (Kash & Calhoun, 2010, pp. 28–31). Consequently, to survive, businesses have to have a deeper understanding of their consumers. Technology can be leveraged to analyze, predict and develop this competitively advantaged

DOI: 10.4324/9781003226161-6

understanding of demand and use this information to change the way in which their business functions across all areas of their value chain while still remaining agile in this fast-paced new landscape (Kash & Calhoun, 2010, pp. 28–31). However, for companies the distribution is no longer a supply chain focusing on products, but also a choice of selling opportunities: physical through shops, agents, or salesman, but also an opportunity to sell through internet. New companies on internet will use the possibilities of internet, technology and data to create knowledge of customers. The producing companies are now in a kind of channel conflict:

- Selling through the original distributors based on a relationship of years, probably longer.
- Or maybe, selling also direct through internet or web shops and create a channel.

In addition, for companies to survive in a world where buyers (customers) determine who will succeed and who will fail "it is imperative that you construct a framework in your company that encompasses and aligns everyone toward meeting not just the current but the latent and emerging demand of your highest-profit customers and consumers" (Gupta, 2018, pp. 6–7). It is important to keep in mind that in comparison to a supply-driven economy, "the demand-driven company not only thinks about today and tomorrow, but next year and the next five years" (Kash & Calhoun, 2010, p. 28). Often this shift from a supply- to a demand-driven company requires an entire shift in the business model to acquire, convert and retain consumers (Gupta, 2018, p. 31).

Introduction to Business Models and Business Model Canvas

Platforms have been exploited right from the beginning by companies to transform established industries and trigger a digital transformation (Gupta, 2018). However, joining a platform and crossing fingers that everything goes according to plan was never the right approach to adopt. That is the reason why companies that successfully managed to shift to a platform-based business had to change some components of their business model. Gupta (2018) sees a business model as a model (tools and processes) "that defines the way a firm creates, delivers, and captures value" (p. 42). The implementation of platforms in a business model would require a business model innovation: enforcing the model with a new business logic that would potentially have visible changes in the logic of the model itself (Gatautis, 2017). A company can have different business models depending on its main focus and objective. In the book *The Discipline of Market Leaders*, Treacy and Wiersema (1995) explained three possible value disciplines that characterize every business, showing how different purposes require different business models. According to the authors, a business could focus on:

- the operational excellence, where the objective is to guarantee low prices and smooth services; or
- the product leadership, with the aim of providing the best products of the market; or
- the customer intimacy, which aims at creating a close relationship with customers by offering tailored products and services.

These objectives can be interpreted as the businesses' value propositions for a supply-driven economy. Therefore, a business model can be portrayed as the architecture that firms leverage to design the way to deliver value to consumers and its mechanisms (Rachinger et al., 2019).

The value proposition is only one of the components of the business model canvas and usually aims at solving customers' problems. A business model canvas is a graphic way to describe in a detailed way every element that a business must implement in order to be successful on the market. Each component of the canvas has a very specific role. For instance, the customer segment indicates who the value proposition is for, meaning the initial target audience. The key partners include the stakeholders, the key resources who and what is necessary to implement the strategy, the key activities delineate each indispensable step, the revenue streams focus on how to make profit, the channels on the ways in which the proposition will be communicated and sold, the customer relationship entails nurturing clients, and the cost structure refers to the money needed for the proposition to become reality. The business model canvas gained relevance on the moment in which companies realized that having a nice and functioning product was not enough to thrive. Companies need to provide value to customers, listen to them, understand their pain points, and provide them with tailored and quick solutions. As a consequence, lucrative businesses locate the customer at the center and build the other components around it (Gupta, 2018).

Value Analyses as Starting Point for Demand Transformation

Placing the consumers at the beginning of the strategy can be seen as the backbone of every platform-business. Platforms' value is centered on the network effect and not on the products. In order to achieve so, it is important to blur the linear process of the value chain where the supply represents the initial point and the consumers the end one. Consumers will contribute to value creation and are vital to the establishment of a network effect. Network effects arise when users create value for other users. The larger the network, the greater the quantity of disposable data, the easier it is to enter the virtuous cycle of personalization and keep users on the platforms. That is why consumers cannot be ignored. They are the key to success.

As a consequence, business models experienced a significant shift with the increased importance of platforms, as value propositions need to focus on delivering value to customers, indulge them and make sure that they will not choose another platform or network in case of new purchases. After all, data is what makes a platform and a network thrive in the first place. As it is noticeable in Figure 6.1,

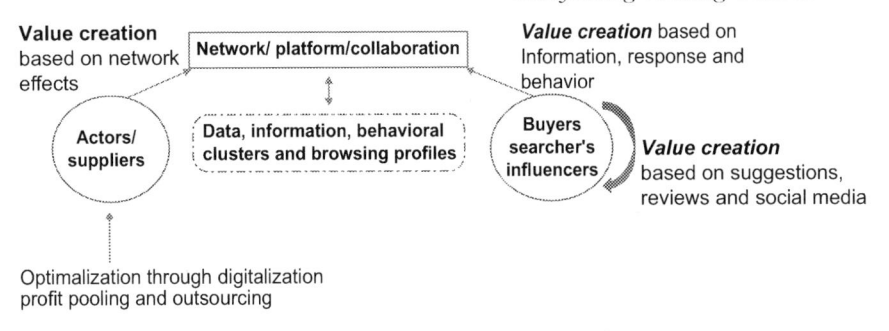

Figure 6.1 The two markets: suppliers and buyers.

the customer relationship segment is occupied by "network effect" and one of the possible value propositions is establishing and controlling trust between the different players of the platform. This indicates the relevance of prioritizing close supervision of customers. Process analyses are looking for opportunities to improve production and to lower the costs. Process analyses are based on producing products and deliver the best product to the market. This, however, is not so relevant in a demand-driven company. It is no longer the process that should be optimized but the value for customers leading to profit for companies. In the next chapter we analyze the possibilities of profit pooling to optimize profitability, but for transforming an organization from supply-driven to demand-driven a value analysis is the fundament of change.

Value Streaming

Value-stream mapping, also known as *material- and information-flow mapping*, is a lean-management method for analyzing the current state and designing a future state for the series of events that take a product or service from the beginning of the specific process until it reaches the customer. A value stream is not the same as a process analysis. The purpose of process mapping is for organizations and businesses to improve efficiency. Process maps provide insight into a process, help teams brainstorm ideas for process improvement, increase communication and provide process documentation. Process mapping will identify bottlenecks, repetition and delays.

In a supply chain approach processes are dominant, and the focus is to optimize the flow of goods from producer to seller. The added value is limited (for the customers). In a value chain the focus is on creating value for the customer, therefore a direct contact with the customer is essential. Most new business concepts, including platforms, are based on value creating and direct contact with customers. These new concepts and platforms are focal companies. Therefore they are a real thread to existing businesses (supply chain), disruptive in markets (creating value for the customers) and relevant for producers (information sharing).

Value delivery spans all stages from ideation to deployment in production and buying objectives of customers. The objective of value delivery is to enable customer success, so value delivery management is broader than value stream management and actually means a transformation of the whole enterprise into an organization centered around value and enabling the success of its external and internal customers.

The first step in value stream mapping is to create a current state map. This map can help identify waste such as delays, restrictions, inefficiencies and excess inventories. These are then eliminated in the ideal state map, which gives the organization a working plan to achieve lean efficiency.

Value stream maps are most suited for improving services, production and distribution. Internally it links the business model and the network, externally it is the basis of networking. It highlights the product cycle-time and wait-time between major production functions and the demand of customers. On the other hand, *process maps* improve decision making by better evaluating information flow between departments and the next link in a process (supply chain). Value mapping improves decision making based on behavioral clusters and customer classification, creating communities.

Easily combine sections of your value stream into a value chain. The value stream analysis considers the dependencies of these subsections of your value stream based on the data stored in the system. In addition, you can group sub-processes to obtain a better overview without losing the level of detail. This way, you can identify correlations in a targeted manner, work out the right starting point for changes, or provide concrete feedback on optimization proposals for critical production steps.

This model is based on multi-sided platforms and networks as described above. The change from a supply-driven strategy to matching demand and finally to a demand-driven strategy is shown in this model in the two lines. Also, the supply for segments is an obvious link. Some corrections are needed to fulfill the changeover. Finance can still be based on transaction fees; the value is in the right offer for the right needs. We have seen, however, that changes can be based on permanent relations like media (Netflix) or services (software). In that case a subscription model will guarantee a continuous link with customers, some may call it loyalty, but in that case, it is a form of structural loyalty. For a supplier it is a predictable, continuous earning. Customer segments and clusters are linked to the value proposition and can be different for each cluster, segment or organizations.

Multi-sided platforms and networks create value for their participants by:

- Facilitating the exchange of goods and services. New companies and sellers can start to sell their products with low investment, saving especially on advertising. And the buyers have the convenience to purchase goods from home, in a safer, and often cheaper way. The transaction platform creates value by benefiting both sellers and buyers. And, as for the platform itself, it doesn't have to produce or store the products.

Key partners
- Suppliers
- Distributors
	Key activities
	- Collecting & using
	  browsing data.
	- Matching needs
	  with solutions.
	- Giving
	  transparent
	  advice.
		Value proposition
		Browsing data
		and advice.
		
		- Perfect
		  matching
			Customer
			relationships
			Advice on
			data, higher
			customer
			satisfaction
			due to perfect
			matching
			more impact
			in the market
			Independent
			information &
			solutions,
			perfect match
			for needs
				Customer
				segments 2 types
				
				S/d side:
				- Suppliers
				- Distributors
				
				C side:
				- Cluster
				profiles

Cost structure - Licenses - Development platform - Marketing - Organization				

	Key resources
	- offering products,
	  providing
	  information
	  traffic on
	  platform and
	  browsing data,
	  buying products
		Transparent,
		demand-driven
		
		Revenue streams
		- Subscription
		  fees
		- Commission
				Channels
				- Platform
				- Social media:
				  Facebook,
				  LinkedIn
				- App

Figure 6.2 Business canvas model for platforms.

- That's not only true for retail, like eBay or Alibaba. It works the same way for sharing platforms, such as Airbnb or Uber. The owners and the drivers can enjoy the marketing and knowhow of the app to reach their customers, who, in their turn, can have a car or a place within reach of a smartphone. And the platform, again, doesn't have to invest in the assets, like homes or cars.

Providing a Network

Social media and content platforms offer a digital environment to the users, who became the content generators, feeding the environment while providing data for the demand side. The demand side, therefore, can run highly targeted campaigns.

The changeover from supply-driven to demand-driven will be an incremental process, step by step. It is a total restructuring of a company, the organization, technology/data management, and the distribution. On top of it, the strategy of the company should be based on sharing and collaboration. Therefore, it is necessary to know what the purpose is, what the steps for change are and what the expected end result should be. In other words, rethink the business for the network economy.

The first step is the roadmap: where are we and where do we want to go? In this chapter we outlined this approach by making a current state map and an ideal state map (a destiny map).

This mapping process can be seen as a roadmap for change (Figure 6.4).

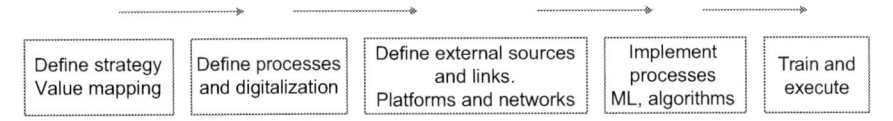

Define strategy Value mapping	Define processes and digitalization	Define external sources and links. Platforms and networks	Implement processes ML, algorithms	Train and execute

Figure 6.3 Steps in the changing process.

Focus point.	Current state map.	Ideal state map
Organizational structure	hierarchical	Value added clusters
processes	Production based	Network based
departments	Specify and prioritize	Specify and prioritize
distribution	Channel, agents, shops	Multi-point collaboration
products	Standard based on customer segments	Demand driven, integration services, product and customize
services	After sales for distribution points (shops)	Linked to demand and use of products
Data management	Production, stock and product sales	Based on behavioral clusters, predictive modeling and cooperation
Data sources	Internal and market data	Network, machine learning, browsing and transactions
Decision making	Based on KPI	Algorithms and strategy
reporting	Monthly based on budget	Weekly on basis of algorithms, responses and predictions
Analyses	What has happened	What is going on, based on predictions, changes and dynamics
Profit sources	Profit on products	Profit pool analyses, customer behavioral clusters
Cost sources	Production, distribution, communication, organization	Internal costs, external costs, network costs
Drivers of change	Competition, turnover, profits	Customer demand, market changes

Figure 6.4 Elements of a road map.

The step after this roadmap is to make a digital structure for a company, a change from doing digital to being digital. New entrants to the market are based on the possibilities of digitalization (being digital); existing companies, however, have a history. Digital became a more recent possibility to adjust functions based on internet technology and application. Every function is analyzed on the possible digital advantages. Normally it is a three-step approach: optimalization, innovation and disruption. This approach starts with an existing structure of the company and step by step it will change according to market developments and changes in customer behavior.

A company's ability to deliver the value as described above, relies on four distinct but interconnected capabilities:

- *Technology* streamlines journey steps and connects functions internally and externally. While automation of processes is highly technical, the focus is on enabling simple, useful and increasingly engaging experiences.
- *Proactive personalization* uses information about a customer—either based on past interactions or collected from external sources—to instantaneously customize the experience. The integration with machine learning is essential to personalize and predict. Remembering customer preferences is

a basic example of this capability, but it extends to personalizing and optimizing the next steps in a customer's journey, such as immediately responding based on algorithms and on regular basis reclustering.

- *Contextual interaction* uses knowledge about where a customer is in a journey to deliver them to the next set of interactions, such as a retail site showing a customer the status of a recent order on the home page. For every step special information is available based on the needs of the customer.
- *Journey innovation* extends the interaction to new sources of value, such as new services, for both the customer and the brand. Companies analyze their data and insights about a customer to figure out what adjacent service he or she might appreciate, a matching within the cluster is good indication.

It starts with the existing processes and structures. What can be digitized, which optimalization is possible and what can be changed. Obviously, based on the existing focus from supply, there is a strong aim of cost reduction which will lead to higher profitability. This kind of decisions are mostly based on ROI, return of investment. However, that is a financial focus based on present market circumstances. The focus should shift to demand-driven, customer behavior and value drivers. The strategy of profit pooling can help to re-evaluate the existing processes and strategy.

The next step is to decide what should be done by the company and what can be outsourced, and which role is important in the network or platform. Based on the value drivers and profit pools the processes are defined and implemented. This way the company is restructured, and the process is defined based on demand and the collaboration in a network. The uncertainty of the demand and demand-drivers are analyzed based on browsing analyses, cluster analyses and correlations. Therefore, data will be the essence of the new "supply" chains. As we have seen before, the contact with buyers and data about the buying and search process is of vital importance.

Knowledge of the browsing process is important to communicate directly with customers, but also to analyze later on the total buying process from transaction to initial contact. This approach requires marketers to find new ways to get their products and services included in the initial consideration set that consumers develop as they begin their decision journey. The process is a two-way conversation, marketers need a more systematic way to satisfy customer demands and manage word-of-mouth. This is the beginning of a value chain, adding value to customers. Therefore, the steps to define the buying process are:

- Knowing the demand of customers based on their browsing patterns or the browsing patterns of another member of the defined cluster.
- This so-called browsing process is the search process of customers for information or for the right product.
- Based on the browsing process (need detecting) suggestions can be made for the right products or services and suggestions can be made where to buy this product.

- This demand-driven approach prevents a possible channel conflict. A customer will decide about their point of sale out of the options offered based on their preferences and the value proposal.

For a company it is important to align all elements of marketing, strategy, profit pooling, channel management and communication with the journey that consumers undertake when they make a purchase decision, but also to integrate those elements across the organization and within the network. When companies understand this journey and direct their spending and messaging to the contact moments, they can help the customer in the buying process and create value.

Nike+

An example is Nike. Traditionally they build their business through a combination of innovative products, intensive brand building through multimedia platforms and efficient operations. As the possibilities of the new digital technology emerged, Nike quickly capitalized on all three areas. Nike transformed its customer experience by introducing new selling processes and connecting athletes worldwide and its operations with new design and manufacturing methods. Nike did not start by strategizing on its business model, but rather looked at ways it could provide even more value to its connected customers. Nike decided to weave its technology and information together into a new business model: Nike+.

Nike+ includes multiple connected components: a shoe, sensor, an internet platform, and a device like iPod, iPhone, Xbox, a GPS watch or a band. The band uses geo-tracking, following a person throughout the day giving users real-time updates on how many calories they have burned, the number of steps and providing real motivation for athletes. Runners can also share their performance and routes with their friends (just like Strava) on Twitter and Facebook. Nike of course get valuable data about users, their products, and the community. Nike has changed its business model from providing only apparel to providing new hardware, technology, rich data and useful add-on service for its customers. Nike is now attracting external partners to continually enhance the service on the Nike+ platform. Nike has increased its market share and developed new revenue streams (profit pools) with a range of add-on products and services. It understood the nature of its customers' needs for engagement and asked, "How do we provide more value?" In this way Nike engineered a coherent digital platform that interconnects its products and services to the benefit of the athletes.

More companies are in this kind of changing processes, not only doing digital but being digital. Later, the Volvo case will show the integration between Volvo, the dealers, social media and users of the product, connecting, collaboration and profit pooling as underlaying principle. All demand-driven strategies with involvement of buyers and customers. Many companies will stay too close to existing models and are too afraid to change (channel conflicts, data conflicts), but other companies are using new opportunities of technology and data to enhance their value proposition, others have used the data they already possess to create new value propositions based on the data itself. In that case machine learning, clustering and algorithms are inevitable tools.

In all cases the strategy, design experiment and implementation of new business models is a task for business leaders. Functional managers will not have sufficient authority to drive new business model experimentation across business silos, data silos and separate activities. In the next chapter the transformation of an organization from supply-driven to demand-driven is explained. The orientation model can be used to visualize this change. Later, a further description will indicate organizational changes. In this chapter the role of information technology is important. Existing organizations have an infrastructure which fits the existing orientation of a company.

Conclusion

The change from supply chain to a value chain is a fundamental change in the strategy of a company. Adding value to the customer is not only product driven but based on the needs and preferences of a customer. Using new technologies in the supply chain will lead to efficiency and optimalization. But in a value chain it should improve the customer relation and preferences. Therefore, not only the focus of a company will change, but also the organization and partnerships. New business concepts like multi-sided platforms and selling platforms will control the customer relations and will act as a focal company.

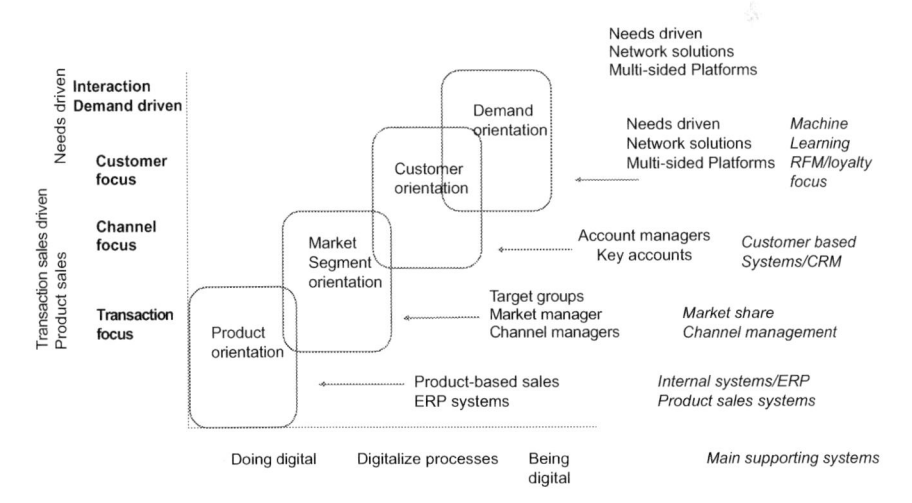

Figure 6.5 Orientation model as guide for internal change of the organization and systems.

Student's Mind

1   What are the most important drivers for a change of the business model?
2   What is the difference between a classical canvas model and a value model?
3   Why is a value model relevant for change in this time?
4   What are the drivers of the value chain?
5   How can the Nike+ approach also be implemented in different markets?
6   What are the marketing needs, constraints for this approach?

Discussion Point

The main drawback of change is the organization itself. How can you it increase the sense of urgency to change?

References

Gatautis, R. (2017). The Rise of the Platforms: Business Model Innovation Perspectives. *Engineering Economics*, 28(5).

Gupta, S. (2018). *Driving Digital Strategy: A Guide to Reimagining Your Business*. Boston, MA: Harvard Business Review Press.

Kash, R. & Calhoun, D. (2010). *How Companies Win: Profiting from Demand-Driven Business Models No Matter What Business You're in*. London: HarperCollins.

Rachinger, M., Rauter, R., Muller, C., Vorrader, W. & Schirgi, E. (2019). Digitalization and its Influence on Business Model Innovation. *Journal of Manufacturing Technology Management*, 30(8): 1143–1160.

Treacy, M. & Wiersema, F. (1995). *The Discipline of Market Leaders*. Reading, MA: Addison-Wesley.

7 Building a Demand-Driven Business Model

Business models define "the way a firm creates, delivers, and captures value" (Gupta, 2018, p. 31). The journey of becoming a demand-driven organization requires a shift in mindset and a new way of thinking and approaching strategy in all its dimensions (the supply chain; business models; redefining your scope, core competencies, segmentation and targeting, etc.). In addition, business model innovation goes hand in hand with technological development, changes in consumer behavior and the emergence of new competitors (Gupta, 2018, p. 31). As such, in the new demand-driven economy it is important to re-evaluate how your firm functions, evaluate new demand-driven operational models and alternative revenue streams. It is also important to analyze the value chain to decide what the focus of a company is and which role the company should play in a supply/demand chain.

A demand-driven business model represents a shift in perspective from a traditional product-centric model to one that is consumer-centric. It involves looking at demand that already exists or is emerging and developing strategies to fill it. This chapter discusses some tools that can be used to develop a

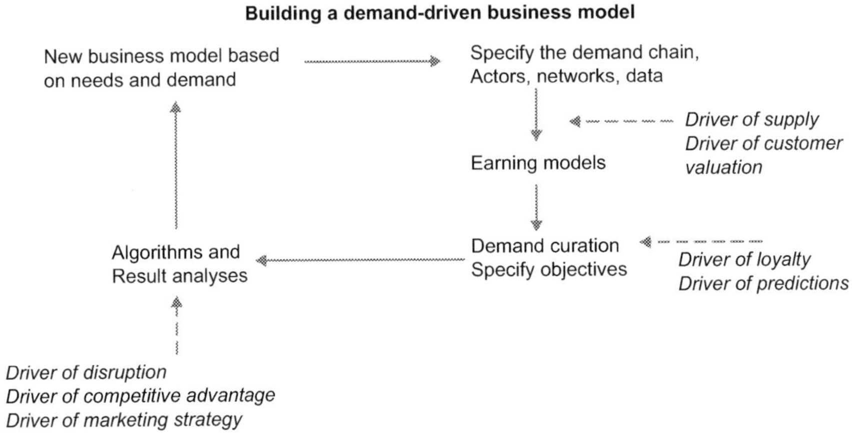

Building a demand-driven business model

New business model based on needs and demand → Specify the demand chain, Actors, networks, data

↓ Driver of supply / Driver of customer valuation

Earning models

↓

Algorithms and Result analyses ← Demand curation / Specify objectives ← Driver of loyalty / Driver of predictions

Driver of disruption
Driver of competitive advantage
Driver of marketing strategy

Figure 7.1 Building a demand-driven business model.

DOI: 10.4324/9781003226161-7

competitively advantaged understanding of demand and create a demand-driven business model, and furthermore, analyzes the specific demand-driven business models that focus on flexible consumption.

Tools to Create a Demand–Driven Business Model

A demand-driven business model will need a new toolset based on customer data, companies' objectives and value drivers:

- demand profit pooling;
- digitalization and data;
- machine learning;
- algorithms; and
- supply chain management/ process optimalization.

In the digital age, the previous marketing axioms that competitive advantage revolves around either being the lowest cost provider or product differentiation are no longer relevant as companies rethink their core competencies and strive to find new ways to create value (Gupta, 2018, p. 21). Data is at the core of this struggle to find new ways to create value.

The traditional value approach of Treacy and Wiersema (1995), focusing on customer intimacy, operational excellence or product leadership is being replace by a value chain, a network approach. We have seen that outsourcing and collaboration are part of a value chain. A company will focus on their core competence as part of this network, but this means that a thorough analysis of profitability is needed. Before the profitability was a complex of values and costs, which will lead to transactional profits. However, if the demand of their customer is the focal point, the network will be redefined. A company should decide which role they want to play. In this decision-making process profits are more important than revenue and customer data and contacts are leading for decision making. The company should focus on profit pools based on the needs of the network, the demand of customers and their own core competence.

As such, businesses should transform their traditional segmenting and targeting techniques to create "demand profit pools," which group activities together based on the common needs of customers and the role in the value chain they want satisfied and the degree of profitability they represent (Kash & Calhoun, 2010, pp. 56–70). By changing the segmentation strategy to demand clusters, profit pooling businesses can understand how their business creates value to individuals who have similar motivations for buying a product.

A *profit pool analysis* is a savvy way of looking at the financial portfolio of any given business, prioritized by its largest operational margins. It's a real and honest way of looking at what makes the most money for a business and how much volume that margin represents of a firm's gross revenue. It is also a way to optimize value drivers for customers.

- It is a strategy model that can help managers or companies focus on profits rather than revenue growth.
- By definition, a profit pool is the total profit earned in a company at all points in a company's value chain. A value chain is a business model that describes the full range of activities that are needed to create a product or service. For customers, profit pool is a type of framework that uses an industry's financial history for strategic decisions for the future. Whereas profit margins are generally considered for a specific period. Profit pools are usually industry/company-specific in a supply approach but based on customer clusters in a demand approach. Nowadays a network of collaborating companies and linked activities is formed to generate and share data and data analyses.

Profit Pool Mapping

Profit pool mapping is done by using value chain analysis for a particular industry.

- This framework analyzes how profits are distributed among the various activities that form a value chain of an industry.
- Profit pools prove that the highest revenue does not always necessarily convert to the highest profits.
- Start-ups looking forward to disrupting various industries use customer data to control customer contacts and will act as a focal company and will use the value chain of existing companies to be different.
- It will also give them a competitive advantage over others in terms of hitting profitability early.

In order to create demand profit pools, you will need to construct a demand landscape from which you can assess which groups are the most profitable as well as potential untapped demand pools. Therefore, you need tools such as machine learning to create insight knowledge of the customers and cluster the customers based on profit per transaction and profit in time (RFM would also be possible). By grouping individuals in such a way, you have the ability to assess and monitor who and why some demand pools/clusters are more profitable as well as augment your pricing strategy and identify potential untapped profit pools. Using this information about purchasing motivations, you will be able to allocate resources in your business effectively and capture a larger share of the profitable market than your competitors, use this to differentiate and manage your brand/product portfolio as well as redesigning your branding, marketing packaging and channels to effectively meet the expectations of the different demand pools (Kash & Calhoun, 2010, pp. 56–70). The need of machine learning is inevitable, algorithms can be used to act on customer behavior.

Essentially, using data and technology to create a demand landscape is the first step in developing a demand-driven business model as this gives the opportunity to assess how the business delivers value above and beyond their competitors to acquire and retain customers. The forward-looking demand scale is something that is continuously changing and as such implementing machine learning to continuously gather information about why people are buying your product and developments in the market and rapidly implementing these into strategy (Kash & Calhoun, 2010, pp. 56–70).

Once the demand profit pools have been established and this strategy is part of the business strategy, it can be matched with the needs of the clusters defined by machine learning. Using real-time data to construct predictive models and microtargeting different profit-based clusters is a way to spread the specific message that needs to be communicated to each group (cluster). Additionally, individual level data can also be used to predict which behavioral cluster each consumer is likely to belong to and as such provide them with the correct personalized marketing messages, distribution channel and price point that creates the most value for everyone (Kash & Calhoun, 2010, pp. 56–70).

By using data to understand the motivations of individuals in different clusters, manufacturers, retailers and media companies can work together to share real-time information which can determine what is sold, how it is distributed, how it is packaged and/or which promotions to run. This network of information can be referred to as the demand chain and allows firms to deliver the "right product more precisely." The demand chain can be viewed as an integrated business model with information flowing in the opposite direction than it would in a traditional supply chain model. Information about demand and results drives and defines capabilities and business scope and through the collaboration of different points along the demand chain greater growth and profits can be achieved (Kash & Calhoun, 2010, pp. 56–70).

The demand chain model is different from a regular model as there is real-time communication between the manufacturer, the distribution channels, and the media. Traditionally the manufacturer would develop the understanding of demand and translate that information into strategy and communications alone. Now this intellectual capital is created and shared with all consumer touchpoints and the media to prompt alignment and integrated strategy (Kash & Calhoun, 2010, p. 183). Understanding that different distribution channels serve distinctly different demand profit pools is essential for the successful implementation of this model. If real-time information is shared between manufacturers and the distribution channels together, they can personalize their product offering and communications to align with the demand pool who uses each channel. This creates the ability to offer a more personalized customer experience as well as build pricing power and loyalty among consumers (Kash & Calhoun, 2010, p. 184). As an added advantage the channel conflict which appeared with internet will be solved. It is a close cooperation between the supplier, the value chain, and the distributors/shops. In addition to optimizing the customer experience through each channel the media can be used in this process as well. With the growth of big data, identifying the correct media platforms to advertise on for each demand pool/cluster is becoming more and more accessible. Data can be used to identify which demand profit pool each person may belong to and as such provide them with the most compelling message that demonstrates why a product or service has value to each individual (Kash & Calhoun, 2010, p. 185).

Overall, the demand chain model is a concept that can be used to create a holistic approach to customer acquisition, retention, and conversion. This technique can exist alongside the traditional supply-chain if used to guide the business operations. This mutually beneficial network aims to create a more intimate and effective connection between the manufacturers, distribution channels, media and consumers. Manufacturers will be able to optimize their product offering and point of sales information while simultaneously each distribution channel will benefit by having the correct product for their most valuable profit pools. The media will also benefit in the sense that their profits depend on their precision of matching the correct product with the highest value targets (Kash & Calhoun, 2010, p. 186).

Flexible Consumption Models: Earning Models

Product as a Service, from Ownership to Access

The shift from a supply- to a demand-driven economy is an essential trend that leads to the rise of several different business models. In the flexible consumption model, the integration of a network is essential (using cloud options).

A flexible consumption model offers customers product delivery and payment options that allow them to purchase access to products as a service. Specifically, *product as a service* (PaaS) is a business model that allows customers to use a product rather than buying it. The rise of PaaS as a service model is an attempt for firms to capture value in a growing "sharing" and "on-demand" economy which has been facilitated by the creation of platforms that connect demand with spare capacity in a form of *collaborative consumption*. Additionally, the shift of mentality to focus not on ownership but usage makes this business

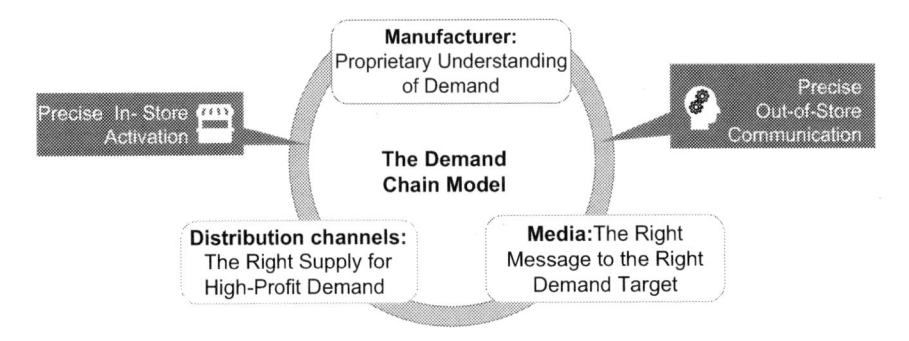

Figure 7.2 The demand chain model.

model one that is fit to survive the new sustainable circular economy model. PaaS models are a way in which the production and consumption patterns are changing to decouple value creation from resource consumption. Fundamentally, when the firm retains ownership, they are more likely to create a product that is of higher quality and has a longer life cycle ultimately promoting the principles of the circular economy. This strategy fits in a profit pooling strategy, as we have seen above.

Viewing a business as selling solutions, not only products, is fundamentally demand-driven as it is customer-centric as opposed to the product-centric traditional models. Transitioning to a PaaS model requires a shift in operational model that has capabilities to support the unique characteristics of a PaaS model such as recurring billing, revenue recognition and strong customer support systems. Additionally, transitioning may be complex as the products generally have different value propositions to different demand pools, so it may be a strong likelihood that one needs to create multiple PaaS models to cater to the most profitable demand pools.

From Transaction–Based to Subscription–Based Models

Over the last few decades, there has been a constant move away from the natural opinion of ownership or transaction-based to the subscription-based model. In fact, several industries have begun to adopt subscription-based models. This subscription-based model is a form of using PaaS and is defined by a continuous delivery of its value proposition for a periodic recurring fee (Gassmann et al., 2013, pp. 22–23). With the subscription model users are charged a periodic daily, monthly, or annual fee to subscribe to a service, regardless of the actual user rate.

If we look at the historical application of subscription models (Figure 7.3), we can see that they have already been used in the early 16th century by European map publishers to update conquered empires (Rudolph et al., 2017). A century later, subscription models have been used to get access to newspapers and books. In the early 1960s the aircraft turbine manufacturer Rolls-Royce established an innovative business model called "power-by-the-hour," which was introduced as a usage-based

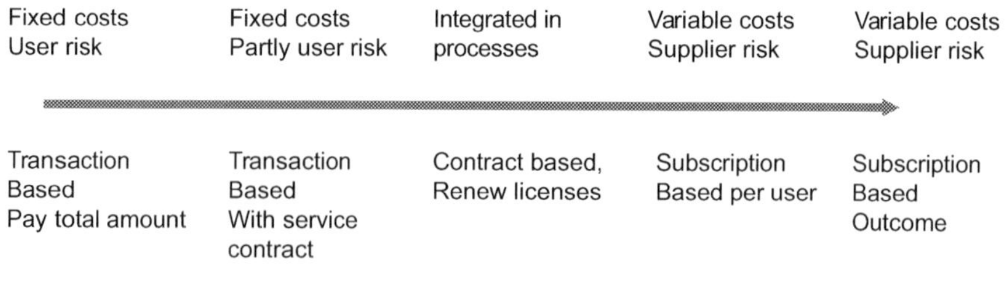

Fixed costs	Fixed costs	Integrated in	Variable costs	Variable costs
User risk	Partly user risk	processes	Supplier risk	Supplier risk

→

Transaction	Transaction	Contract based,	Subscription	Subscription
Based	Based	Renew licenses	Based per user	Based
Pay total amount	With service contract			Outcome

Figure 7.3 Earning models.

subscription model and focused on the usage instead of the turbine itself. Then, with the ongoing process of digitization and dynamic changes in customer behavior and needs, various subscription models were established within the IT sector (like Netflix or Spotify). For instance, Netflix, a retailer that provides initially movie DVDs for rental, also uses subscription pricing. You pay a monthly fee and have access to an unlimited number of rentals. Due to the subscription-based model Netflix received a much better understanding of their customers' needs and could transform itself from a DVD distributor to one of the most successful series and movie producers. Later on, subscription models were introduced to other industries, for example to the automotive industry. For instance, automotive OEMs offers customers access to a pool of vehicles for a recurring payment. Or the German printing machine manufacturer Heidelberger Druckmaschinen offers its customers that they pay for a defined monthly print volume instead of the whole printing machine.

There is an ongoing process away from the actual ownership of a product or service to an outcome-based model, or PaaS model. This shows that, as we move forward toward a demand-driven economy, access, not ownership of products, will drive the success of business (Gupta, 2018, pp. 54–58). However, it must be taken into account that the introduction of new business models is associated with a variety of strategic and operational activities for companies, which confronts companies with a lot of challenges.

Benefits, Limitations and Challenges of Subscription-Based Models

Despite the many challenges that may arise, PaaS models have numerous benefits for both consumers and firms.

To begin with the benefits for companies, in contrast to a one-time product-oriented transaction, the subscription-based model enables a company to focus on offering integrated bundles of products and services. Simultaneously, the retention-oriented model facilitates ongoing communication with customers which allows for greater data collection and ultimately a deeper understanding of what they want, which can be translated into more customer-centric product offerings, as well as different schemes to cater better to the needs of each demand profit pool. Insights into how customers interact with products are the basis for a wide range of business choices, like product alterations or new products and marketing decisions. Due to this ongoing communication, a long-term relationship between supplier and customer is being created. Companies can use the subscription model to focus on a continuous fulfillment of their customers' needs, as well as customer retention, and less on making new sales (Riesener et al., 2020, pp. 730–731; Gassmann et al., 2013, p. 305).

There are several benefits for consumers and suppliers:

- First, the initial payment is lower, making services seem more affordable. For instance, when a product is priced as monthly payment, it is a psychological effect of appearing affordable.

- Also, the convenience of using subscriptions is very high.
- Next, if people make monthly subscriptions, it can encourage them to consume more, to get their money's worth.
- Because of this, by increasing consumption, it encourages brand loyalty and consumers are more likely to reorder a product or service.

Sometimes, a free monthly trial is offered, consumers are more likely to give the product a try. Also, once we have a subscription to a service paid by direct debit it is easier to keep the customer paying because of consumer inertia and not wanting to try to change.

However, there are also some downsides and challenges resulting from the usage of a subscription-based model.

- To begin with, although it is good for business, consumers may become burnt out from having to sign up to more subscriptions in the future.
- Also, a company needs to add more services over time. For instance, Netflix needs to produce its own content to keep its subscribers engaged, and due to high costs, this procedure is not possible for every company.
- A company needs to manage the churn rates, since repetitive purchasing is one of the key benefits of adopting a subscription business model. Consumers are quick to cancel services that don't deliver a superior experience—for example, because of poor product quality, dissatisfaction with the assortment or a lack or perceived value.
- To end with, the competition is extremely high, since the volume of subscription options in the market is huge and increasing.

As we can see, apart from the challenges and disadvantages, there are numerous reasons for a company to adopt the new business model.

Business Models and Demand-Driven Organizations

To realize a demand-driven organization it is important to stay in contact with your customers. Feedback on all activities will generate data to analyze the customer behavior and to predict further behavior.

The use of algorithms in AI and machine learning will greatly affect traditional companies. Facial recognition, as mentioned earlier, is being used in retail to transform the way we shop. From the moment you walk into a shop, facial recognition (identification) algorithms will be able to identify your average spend, buying preferences, and notify the shopkeeper of your emotions of purchase. Algorithms are the basis for most technological advancements happening in industries such as retail, which consequently will change the face of retail dramatically in just a few years. Take machine learning algorithms one step further by going "beyond pattern recognition and learn about cause and effect" and predictions a completely new business model and strategy is needed.

If an algorithm can explain the "why" side of approaching questions, then AI will be able to act and think even more like humans do.

Next Wave of Disruption through Algorithms

As mentioned before, algorithms already have changed businesses, especially in the retail and marketing sector on a large scale. However, this path is a continuously changing process which is only at its beginning and will transform the markets relentlessly.

The next wave of disruption in the retail market though is the use of independent curation engines based on algorithms. These curation search engines will be able to tailor refined recommendations for their user and then search the internet for the best available product, like market mappers such as a Skyscanner for the retail branch. This will make the buying process even more transparent through a seemingly unlimited number of choices, which will be rated on factors like price, delivery options and service quality of the shop. The system will automatically weigh up hundreds of factors of thousands of shops to find the perfect product, which suits your needs the most.

This could become a huge industry, where the customers are increasing the quality of it by approving or ignoring offers of the search engine. These service platforms will support their users as digital personal shopper assistants by algorithms learning from their previous purchase behavior, (brand-) preferences and returns. This method can also be used for physical retail with geo-fencing. A customer can specify the needs and the engine will look for the best offer, or availability in a certain area. This will lead to a virtual integration between online offerings and offline availability. Virtual means in the mind of a customer. These curation engines will restructure retail and are only possible with support of retailers and suppliers. For this disruption to happen:

- Search engines must have access to all the different APIs of small and also huge retail-platforms like Amazon or Alibaba.
- The data from retailers (based on delivery information from suppliers) should be available and updated.
- In addition, the algorithms must be able to deal with the vast scale and diversity of data which comes along with this border-crossing.
- Moreover, the prices of the products in the retail sector are much less than for example in the airline (travel) industry where it is worth it to get help from travel platforms.
- In the retail sector, the success of this system will depend on higher volumes of supervised sales due to the lower prices and therefore smaller margins.
- And of a new earning models based on agreements with suppliers/brands.

Companies should observe and understand the rating and decision criteria of the analyses, since it will be crucial and a huge competitive advantage to be able to influence the algorithms. It will be key to obtain and evolve your company's technical skills to ensure always being up to date when it comes to understanding algorithms and data.

Another important point in the process is the change of brand-recognition and identity, since it will play a minor role compared to the dynamic algorithms which decide what a customer will buy. In addition, the enhanced curation engines will offer thousands of alternatives, so the brand is under pressure to constantly justify their products and cannot only rely on customer loyalty anymore. So again, the question rises of how you can ensure that the curation or search engines will choose your product and not one from a competitor who has maybe a higher rating for one criterion (like better ratings on overall fabric quality). It will be a key capability to continually develop products and generate new content so that your offerings are able to align with the consumer's needs. "This will require brands to sharpen their differentiation; increase their ability to compete on speed, quality, and cost; and recognize and respond to rapid or subtle shifts in consumer tastes."

User Acceptance of Algorithms

One critical aspect for the success of the future systems of algorithms is user acceptance. Consumers must face the choice between relying on humans or algorithms. Until now, most of the research shows that users rely more on humans even if this leads to worse outcomes. Research shows that people prefer humans over artificial intelligence when it comes to medical treatment since they believe that algorithms would ignore their personal circumstances and feelings. Unlike humans, algorithms do not have the ability to explain or communicate their behavior and draw the conclusion that user acceptance depends on the type of task and the trust in the algorithm. The trust in the algorithm is split between two dimensions:

- The *cognitive dimension* can be found in the performance-beliefs of the algorithm.
- The *affective dimension* can be independent from this, and deals with the feelings toward using the system. Since you cannot sufficiently influence the affective side through a good working system, you have to find other ways to increase the overall trust of the users.

It is always helpful to shape your system at some points to be more human-like and give it personal attributes such as a voice. This makes it easier for the customers to relate emotionally. The perceived users' control over the output of the algorithm-based system is also very important to be more tolerant with errors and in general more content with its ability to forecast. Investing in building consumer-trust towards the product will have a huge impact on the users' personal life and most of the future systems will know them better than some of their closest friends. This requires a lot of trust. Even if this may be more problematic in the older generations, it should be well understood by companies which factors of algorithms influence the user's (acceptance) to prevent a potential algorithm aversion. This is not only important for the marketing or development sector, but it is also a key factor when it comes to increasingly algorithm-based HR systems which can have high user-resistance.

Downsides of Algorithms

Although many are excited about the rise of algorithms and all the benefits and opportunities they bring, possible drawbacks of using them should also be considered. Only by considering all aspects of algorithms can one unleash their full potential. One very unique characteristic of algorithms is their apparent objectivity when predicting and profiling people's behavior, but is this always true? There could be a great danger if algorithms are biased, since they combine data to close gaps of knowledge or create a new meaning about subjects, which could have a great impact on the subjects' lives. Not algorithms themselves create biases, but their people-component does.

The teams of algorithm developers, who shape the algorithm with their values and assumptions, are often not diverse enough, which can lead to biases. They have to make the decision on which criteria are relevant for the algorithm and how this is weighted and, therefore, isolate certain characteristics. The most dangerous part about this is that this can happen unconsciously without being aware of your own biases. But not only the producers of algorithms shape the bias, also the users can boost it through their confirmation-bias. If the outcomes of the algorithm confirm our beliefs, we tend to give good feedback, which is then sent to the feedback loop which further develops the algorithms. Biased behavior in algorithms is rarely intentional and rather caused by "poorly selected data; incomplete, incorrect, or outdated data; selection bias; poorly designed matching systems; personalization and recommendation services that narrow instead of expand user options." Another people-related factor which results in biases is that algorithms only give; what we will do with them, how we present them and how we interpret them is completely up to humans. Since the occurrence and development of algorithms came at a very fast pace, maybe we are not trained well enough yet to do this job sufficiently.

Conclusion

Building a demand-driven business model is based on the needs of the buyer and a focus on demand. In the old business models the focus was on supply, the distribution channel and distribution points. The strategy was based on a special market position based on competitive advantages (between other suppliers). Treacy and Wiersema (1995) specified the possible strategies as a focus point: product leadership, operational excellence and customer intimacy.

A demand-driven business needs the feedback and contact with buyers. The data of buying behavior, needs and demands are the core of the system. A close contact with companies who have these contacts is of vital importance. There-fore, a demand-driven business model is based upon:

- having a network of collaboration companies adding value to a value chain;
- sharing data of customer behavior and needs;
- applying the possibilities of machine learning and predictive modelling; and
- working on an integrated business model from production to distribution.

Because of the value chain collaboration, the focus on profit pools and restricted roles, the choice of the last contact is a choice of the buyer, not anymore of the supplier. A channel conflict is a souvenir from the traditional supply-based models.

Student's Mind

1   Algorithms are important for further marketing; how can we prevent the ratio mechanism in communication?
2   What is the link between community-based marketing and algorithms?
3   What is the link between loyalty, clusters and algorithms?
4   Demand-based marketing has a challenge to know the demand. What can be done?
5   What is the difference between fast movers and shopping goods for a demand-based approach?

Discussion Point

Will algorithms and data take the emotional factor out of marketing?

References

Gassmann, O., Frankenberger, K. & Csik, M. (2013). *Geschäftsmodelle entwickeln: 55 Innovative Konzepte mit dem St. Galler Business Model Navigator*. Munich: Hanser.

Gupta, S. (2018). *Driving Digital Strategy: A Guide to Reimagining Your Business*. Boston, MA: Harvard Business Review Press.

Kash, R. & Calhoun, D. (2010). *How Companies Win: Profiting from Demand-Driven Business Models No Matter What Business You're in*. London: HarperCollins.

Riesener, M., Doelle, C., Ebi, M. & Perau, S. (2020). *Methodology for the Implementation of Subscription Models in Machinery and Plant Engineering*. Aachen: Aachen University.

Rudolph, T., Bischof, S. F., Böttger, T. M. & Weiler, N. (2017). Disruption at the Door: A Taxonomy on Subscription Models in Retailing. *Marketing Review St Gallen*, 5: 18–25.

Treacy, M. & Wiersema, F. (1995). *The Discipline of Market Leaders*. Reading, MA: Addison-Wesley.

8 Marketing in a Demand-Driven Economy

Data as Competitive Advantage

On the one hand, digital technologies have enabled the emergence of new and exciting business models. On the other hand, business models that are based on technologies have had disruptive impacts on many industries and other business models. They threatened the businesses and organizations of many conventional and old-fashioned businesses, who aren't adapting fast enough to keep up with the time. It's important for business to know how to use and influence consumer behavior to improve business performance, reputation and profit. As we have seen, the shift from supply-driven to demand-driven can be done by adding value for the consumer. With the rapidly changing world, there are various aspects they have to deal with. Looking at the customer journey and the associated data that can be collected from customers today, we have to use this data to investigate what is the best approach for companies and how they can create value for customers. We have to know what the best way is to create value for the consumer by companies through using social media, communication and machine learning.

Have the Marketing Strategies Changed Over Time? What Works Now?

In the past twenty years a lot has changed in marketing strategies. This is due to liberalization, globalization and privatization. Although marketing has been around for as long as business itself, a definition has only recently emerged. The development of marketing has not only started with digitization. It began as early as the First Industrial Revolution from 1900 to 1950. In this period production was a central focus. This changed rapidly after the Second World War. People become more and more aware of the use of products and attach more and more value to the quality of products. As a result, from 1950 to 1960, the product took center stage. From 1960 to 1970, with the rise of mass media like television, the sale of the product came to the fore. This changed the focus from financial to non-financial within marketing. Initially the focus for marketing was on profit, sales and cash flow, but now it shifted to customer satisfaction, customer loyalty and brand equity. This was due to the arrival of mass media and later the internet. People got more and more opportunities to use advertising on a larger scale.

DOI: 10.4324/9781003226161-8

Also, with the use of mass media and the internet came the opportunity to communicate people's opinions widely. This gave rise to a new form of "word of mouth" that is still one of the most important marketing strategies today (Clark, 1999). Nowadays, marketing is no longer a separate part of the company's strategy, but is part of the overall business strategy. The marketing strategy also faces more and more challenges in this rapidly changing new world. Multi-channeling, individualistic customers, data, internet just to mention a few. People are increasingly unpredictable in their behavior and more and more difficult to reach. Customers are in contact with each other day and night via social media and internet. This has also changed the buying process of customers compared to a few years ago. Companies need to respond faster and more effectively to the rapidly changing needs and expectations of customers.

Customer Experience

Changing customer demand has led to an increasing focus on customer experience, customer service, customer satisfaction and customer loyalty. The customer experience across all contact channels, customer processes and touchpoints are crucial to win and retain customers. This is because global competition means that customers have more and more choice in products and can compare better. So, the customer is now the determining factor, and this means taking a customer's focus. Marketers use sophisticated analytics and machine learning to process vast amounts of data on consumer behavior. This behavior is analyzed using clustering techniques and algorithms. Companies like Amazon, Uber, Alibaba and booking.com use all contractual data to analyze and predict behavior. The communication to individual contacts is based on these algorithms.

In the traditional supply-driven economy, the knowledge of products is dominant, the knowledge of customer behavior and interest is a guess based on market research. Mostly target groups are formed based on some generic criteria or objects. There is, however, a gap in the customer expectation of the product to be delivered

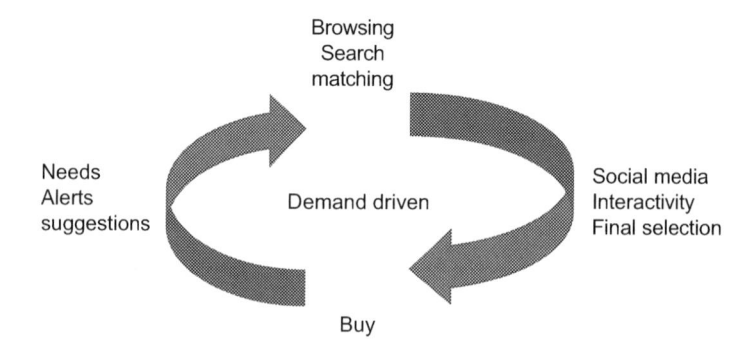

Figure 8.1 A demand-driven customer journey.

and the perception of the actual service or products delivered. The four gaps in the Customer Adaptation Process (CAP) model (Figure 8.2) are called provider gaps, and each gap is a potential cause for a company's failure to meet customer needs and expectations. Those provider gaps are a result of a supply-driven strategy. The focus on the products does not always lead to the right matching with needs. At the top of the model, bridging the customer gap and providing the right match is "need detection," a demand-driven approach. Through a series of questions and answers the needs of a customer have to be related to a specific product or service. It is essential that not the product qualifications are matched but the user's experience or product application. So, the need is: "why do you need a certain product or what do you want to do with the product." We can call this a need gap, the matching between the specific need and the product possibility, which is quite often a standard or standardized product offering. Demand-based multi-sided platforms like Airbnb or Uber have a strong matching module to match the specific needs and wishes of customer with the possible solutions/offerings.

The customer focus is divided in four specific groups:

1   the need/offering focus;
2   the expectation focus;
3   the experience focus; and
4   the algorithm focus.

At its most basic level, the logic of the model suggests that the customer focus is a function of any one or all of the four provider focuses, but can be bridges by the demand approach. First listen and detect the needs before products or services are offered.

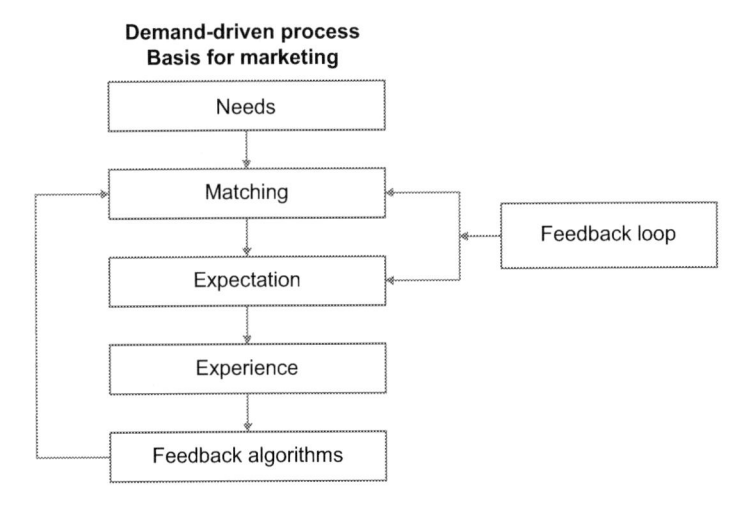

Figure 8.2 Expectation versus delivery.

Focus 1: The Need/Offering Focus

The problem for many companies is that they don't listen to customers. So, it is important that companies stay in touch with customers and discuss their needs and problems with them. The companies have to focus on listening to customers in multiple ways through "Q&A" need detection, algorithms and behavior analyses. Second, on building relationships by understanding and meeting customer needs over time, proactive based on clusters and algorithms as explained in Chapter 5. The last key focus point is to know and act on what customers expect and what they experience as a delivery failure. This is not a standard procedure in a supply-driven strategy but is the basic need in a demand-driven strategy.

Focus 2: The Expectation Focus

This focus is concerned with translating customer needs into actual product/service offerings and developing standards to measure matching operations against customer expectations. In the supply approach this focus is based on the expectation of the product description and advertising. The mindset is influenced because of sophisticated advertising methods, and producers (over-selling) their products. You can also call this transaction focused selling. As long as you can make the transaction, who cares? There are important strategies for focus 2, part of the demand focus: Employ well-defined new matching experiences and innovation practices. Understand the total customer needs based on all relevant circumstances like the surroundings of use (the context), sport-, home-, work-related, and comparing with the defined behavioral cluster. Measure service operations via customer-defined rather than products-defined standards, and the last strategy is to incorporate cluster-based behavior and experiences.

Focus 3: The Experience Focus

When the experience of the product of service level does not meet customer expectations, the added value of listening and selling will be a negative. By ensuring that all the resources required to meet the needs and wishes are used to close focus 3, the customer gap can be reduced. The key strategies for closing focus 3 are behavioral data align with needs and collaborate with similar customers (cluster-driven approach) to define customers' needs and integrate technology effectively and appropriately to motivate and incentivize. Reviews, repeat sales supported by customer services are important performance indicators to indicate satisfaction with the product.

Focus 4: The Algorithm Focus

Even if the company has completed all the work suggested in the other three areas to ensure the quality of service, but when the communication about the service does not match the service provided, it may still be unable to meet customer expectations. Therefore, the final supplier focus that must be bridged is the communication focus, or algorithm focus. This focus looks at the difference between needs, preferences and expectations and the information communicated to customers through advertising, pricing and other forms of communication. An automatic process of communication is based on experiences of the similar users in a group or the individual customer (algorithms). Several key strategies for closing focus 4 are: communication strategies based on triggers, predictive modelling based on behavioral clusters, and use algorithms for the right communication. This is an interactive process to manage customer perception and proactively predictions.

These are important focus points to consider. After all, customer behavior is difficult and unpredictable, but can still be used as a guideline for customer loyalty and future forecasting. That is why the focus points of every gap must be looked at over and over again. These gaps are a mismatch based on a supply-driven strategy. What is needed is a demand-driven approach where those gaps are not relevant, because you fulfill the needs of the buyer based on their behavior and preferences. The customer decision journey understands the motives and behavior of customers.

Some established retailers already offer services to help customers find the most suitable products. Amazon collects user reviews and makes customized suggestions based on learning algorithms. In the United Kingdom, womenswear retailer Topshop and department store John Lewis partner with online engine provider Dressipi to create personalized outfit recommendations based on initial profiling followed by machine learning applied to preferences.

Both companies fit in the retail curation model when companies use external specialized service as part of their own business strategy. This way they can focus better on their own target (maybe profit pools), but still collect the data. For customers it is a seamless process.

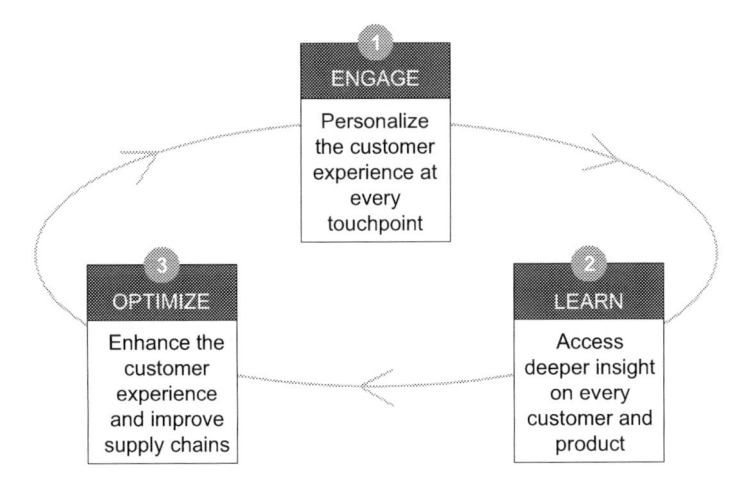

Figure 8.3 Dressipi model for demand-driven services.

Machine Learning to Solve the Supply Gaps

In the demand approach, knowledge and behavior of customers are relevant. As we have seen before with machine learning we use all kinds of data sources, including social media, to understand the customer and the behavior of customers. Based on this knowledge clusters are formed: based on certain objective/ measures like RFM for loyalty, personal features or behavioral criteria. After we have formed clusters, algorithms are linked to these clusters based on a marketing perspective or targets. These algorithms can be based on direct communication leading to a response or a change in behavior. These changes are the basics for knowledge and re-clustering. Focus points are not used in this place, only behavior and response. With a set of algorithms, the reaction is monitored and will lead to more action. This can lead to re-clustering of these customers, forming a new cluster or activate certain algorithms.

Gibbs and Harrison (2019) expect that retail curators will become an industry on their own, changing the structure of the retail sector and capturing a significant share of retail sales. Retail curation will be a major tool for retailers, online and offline. To be sure, technology advances and differences between retail curators make direct comparisons difficult. But digital retailers like Amazon and Alibaba are already blurring traditional retail boundaries and consumers have demonstrated a large and growing appetite for digital retail. It seems fair to assume that retail curation will ultimately decide about the future of retailing.

What Is a Retail Curator?

In Latin, the term "curator" means "to take care of." This is what you do as a retail curator. You take care of your merchandise, brand, story, space and customer. You use external providers for certain specialized functions as part of a total buying process, like in the example of John Lewis and Topshop. Retail curation is linked to the profit pools strategy.

Cluster and Algorithms Strategy

For this cluster strategy machine learning is essential. If we use the same example as before we have formed 27 clusters, on every focus point 3 alternatives. We used three focus points, so $3 \times 3 \times 3$ are 27 clusters. Focus should be *numerical* and *normative*. Normative generally means relating to an evaluative standard. Normativity is the phenomenon in human societies of designating some actions or outcomes as good or desirable or permissible and others as bad or undesirable or impermissible.

The numbers refer to a table: 3 is best and 1 is the lowest. Obviously, a customer who scores less than the number 1 segment is a target. But at the same time, we should be aware for churning, customers moving to a lower segment.

Therefore, a strategy should be in place to improve customer loyalty and sales and at the same time to avoid churning for other customers. This strategy and communication are based on customer behavior, correlations and customer data. Based on the RFM module and the customer profiles in each of the 27 segments the strategy is decided, and the algorithms are defined. Now it is a matter of analyzing the response.

First, behavioral clusters are defined like the RFM clusters. This is a status quo for our marketing actions. Based on the segments a special focus and strategy is defined. After the first round of communication, we see the reactions: response as a guideline and redefine the clusters. Normally a communication cycle has at least a three-step approach: response and non-response and a strategy for changes. This should be a full schedule for a certain season which is specified in a tree diagram. Because all reactions and non-reactions are foreseen, a dynamic (and agile) approach is possible. Normally we have various sources we can use, but also activate:

- internet sources like transactions, payments, visits, or quotes;
- external sources like social media, platforms or other websites including google data.

A response can be linked to all external sources and activate a communication issue. Now we see the impact of a network based on interaction or contact within the network leading to a better customer profile.

Based on the defined strategy a certain target is set for the 27 clusters. Each strategy for each of the 27 segments has targets, like upgrading, reducing churn,

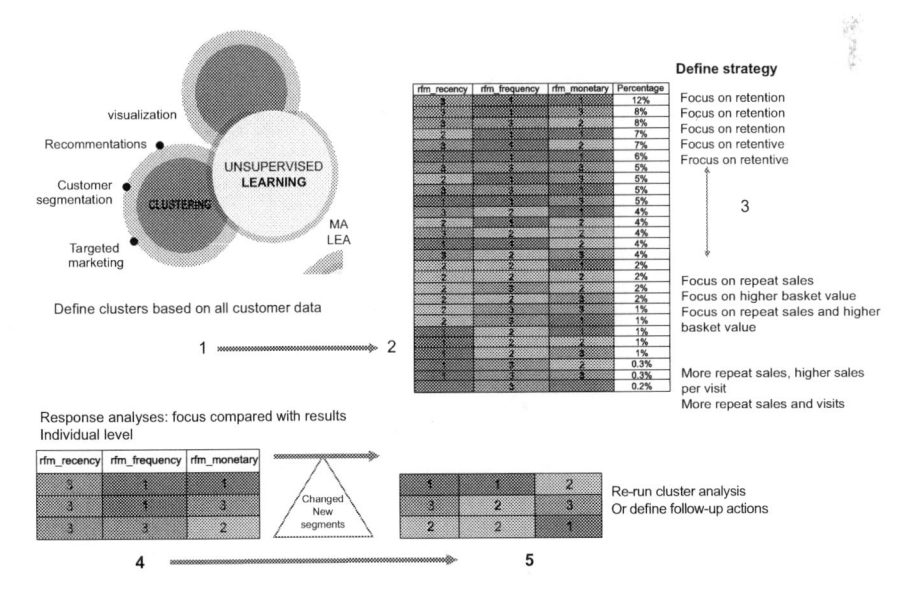

Figure 8.4 RFM process.

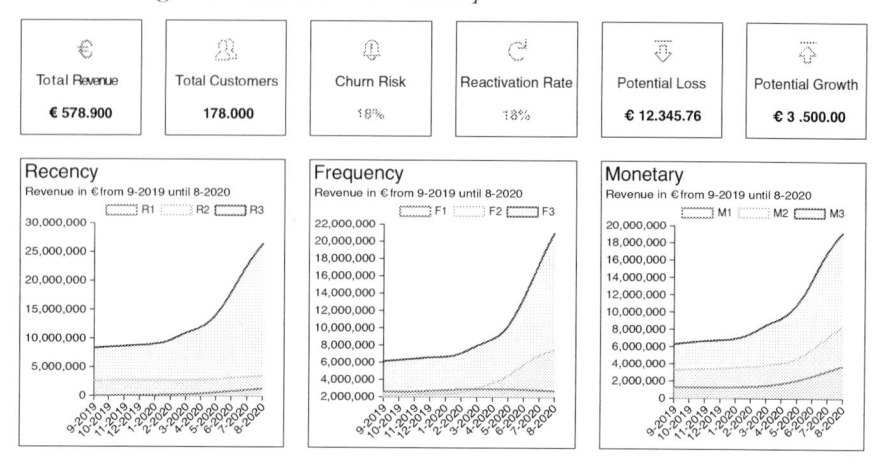

Figure 8.5 RFM analyses.

increasing share of wallet, increasing repeats or trying to get contact again. Response can be seen because of the strategy and can be measured in each of the three focus points (*recency, frequency* and *monetary value*) and after that to the effect on the cluster. Now a decision is made to re-activate the non-response or negative response. Also, a new strategy can be defined for the response (upgrade or churn) and set new targets. After a certain time, or after the strategy cycle it might be advisable to re-cluster the database: new clusters with common denominators, change tracking for special campaigns or define changes in separate clusters. Now we reach a higher level of complexity and artificial intelligence will take over. Now algorithms can be set for communication and product offerings. Now we see that the system takes a leading role. All results, like the analyses per segments and the movement of cluster, will be monitored by marketing. Marketing will no longer define the actions but concentrate on strategic issues based on the results. Strategic insights might be: predictive modelling per segment or product. This prediction can be linked to production, stock levels and investment or cash flow expectations. Now machine learning is no longer a tool for marketing but embedded in systems as part of the monitoring of the performance of a company. Special analyses can be used for more specific information, like "what if" analyses, financial scenarios or competitive strategies.

Customer Decision Journey

The customer journey begins long before they buy a product. It starts when they open the internet to search for a product (browsing). This is the zero moment of truth (ZMOT). This is an important moment, a Google study shows 84% of shoppers claimed that ZMOT shaped their decisions of which brand to buy (Lecinski, 2011). It is important to get data from

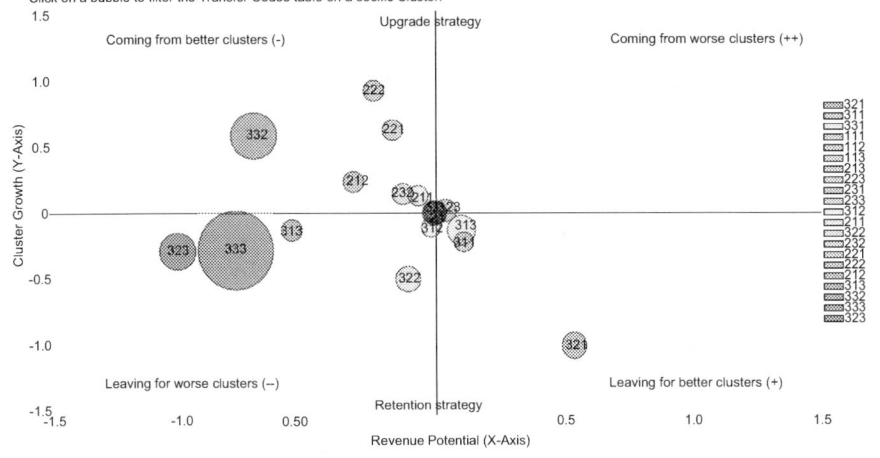

Cluster Growth vs Revenue Potential
This chart shows the change in cluster size and produced revenue calculated over all predicted transfers. The size of a bubble is relative to a cluster's total revenue. Use the legend on the right to show/hide individual clusters. The dark dots, left, 332,323,333,313 have a negative potential. The lighter dots, right, 331, 311,321 have a positive potential. The others round the centre are neutral.
Click on a bubble to filter the Transfer Codes table on a secific Cluster.

Figure 8.6 RFM strategy.

customers to get more information about this phase of customers. This will be more and more a role for a demand-driven platform. Google creates for example heat maps to visualize how and when consumers actively searched for a product. Also, through Google analytics you can see the key words used for the search. The rise of social media and the increasing use of reviews by consumers have made the third moment of truth (TMOT) a critical factor. This is when loyal customers of a product become passionate advocates for it on social media and consumer-review sites. This phase has become more important due to the popularity of social media. Customers have access to information themselves. Customers are no longer interested in what a company says about its own product, but rather in customer experience. No longer will this be based on product criteria or product-based information, but more on matching needs and possibilities. "What is in it for me?" That's why this phase has become so important. Machine learning is essential in knowing the motives of a customer. Data from search engines and social media are important for detecting needs (searches) and behavior (browsing). This data is partly available from external sources and partly available from internal databases. Therefore, the customer journey has changed to a data process, as fundament for algorithms. As mentioned before, business intelligence is explaining what has happened, machine learning is explaining what is going to happen based on behavior of clusters or individuals.

Developing a deep knowledge of how consumers make decisions is the first step. For most marketers, the difficult part is focusing strategies and spend on the most influential touch points. In some cases, the marketing effort's direction must change, from focusing brand advertising on the initial-consideration phase to developing a demand-based communication that help consumers gain a better understanding of the brand when they actively evaluate it. Other marketers may need to retool their loyalty programs by focusing on active rather than passive loyalists or to spend money on in-store activities or word-of-mouth programs. The increasing complexity of the consumer decision journey will force virtually all companies to adopt new ways of measuring consumer attitudes, brand performance, and the effectiveness of marketing expenditures across the whole process. Besides these analyses it is important to predict behavior and to match other functions to this prediction, like finance, investment and cashflows, stocks, channel management and marketing communication.

Social Media: Not Only a Communication Tool, but Also a Tool for Behavioral Data

Social media is a collective name for all online platforms that enable interaction between users. Users on social media can communicate with each other via various channels, publish photos and videos, share information with each other, enter into a discussion (Boora & Singh, 2011). In this book, we take the perspective of social media as a marketing tool for generating data. The largest social media players are Facebook, YouTube, LinkedIn, Twitter, Instagram and Snapchat. Social media is not only used for entertainment, social interaction or obtaining information, but is often also used to develop a personal identity or to influence others. Therefore, this data is relevant for machine learning. Social data is information that's collected from social media platforms. It shows how users view, share and engage with your content. On Facebook, social media data includes numbers of likes, increases in followers, or number of sharing. On Instagram, hashtag usage and engagement rates are included in the raw data. Mainly, this data is used to analyze the effectiveness of campaigns or the website/web shop. Therefore, not all data is relevant.

Once social media data is collected, it's measured or analyzed to see what is and isn't working. Brands are gathering data around the clock, by the way. Every time someone likes a post or engages your brand, that's a data point. Social media data is the raw source you get when you mine or analyze your social networks. The data from external sources are under observation because of the various privacy laws. In the future, personal data from external sources might be limited, because of legislation.

The exact KPIs will vary for each user, but very likely they will be driven by metrics that fall under one of the following areas:

- content optimization;
- customer care analysis;
- competitive benchmarking;
- audience analysis;
- engagement analysis;
- ad analytics; and
- demographics analytics.

On the one hand, digital technologies have enabled the emergence of new and exciting business models. Business models which are based on technologies have disruptive impacts on many industries and business models. They threatened the businesses and organizations of many conventional and old-fashioned businesses, who aren't adapting fast enough to keep up with the times (Gupta, 2018). It's important for business to know how to use and influence consumer social communications to improve business performance, reputation and profit (Fan & Gordon, 2014). This can be done by adding value for the consumer. With the rapidly changing world, there are various aspects they have to deal with. Looking at the customer journey and the associated data that can be collected from customers today, we have to decide what is the best approach for companies and how they can create value for customers. Then we decide how companies can best use the data for their marketing. We will analyze the customer behavior by collecting response data from communication and websites and which social platforms companies can be linked. By examining the above aspects, we want to know what is the best way to create value for the consumer by companies through using social media.

Choice of Social Platform

It's important to determine which specific social platform is the best fit to create the most value for your customers. It starts by recognizing that no single social platform is going to be enough for social media activities. It is unlikely that your potential customers are using only one exclusive form of the social platforms, so-called multi-homing (Petersen, 2011). Research showed that users are most of the time active on two or three social platforms (Belch & Belch, 2012). Another assumption is that consumers will go from one social platform to another as time moves on. Also, marketing on multiple social platforms isn't much more expensive than marketing through one. By choosing a few social platforms, you can reach different audiences in different ways. In this way you can generate much more data to cluster and so on (Peterson, 2011). The best way is putting the right effort into marketing on the few social media platforms that attract the customers you want to reach. You can start by looking at the audiences with which you want to interact and exchange value with. You also have to look where your customers participate the most.

The most important thing is learning about your customers. You have to research and understand where your customers and potential customers are spending most of their time. To do this, you have to research on which platform the most customers can have the highest level of engagement (Peterson, 2011). So, you have to investigate on which social platform the most amount of time is spend, what they specifically do. To get to know the way they interact with each other is very important. It all starts and ends with understanding how the user behaves on social media (Boora & Singh, 2011). For example, if you're a solutions provider from business-to-business, business-related interactions are most likely to be on LinkedIn, despite the fact that they may spend more time on Facebook or Instagram (Peterson, 2011).

Not only do you have to study your customers, but also the social platforms. You have to watch the macro trends of the social platform and decide if it's emerging, has settled or that it is declining (Peterson, 2011). After that, you have to determine if the social platform is a place where your company is going to have the permission to participate and if it's one in which you want to participate. You have to look if it's all convergent with the value of the company and if it will contribute to the creation of value for your customers. In which platform you seem more likely to add value too, is probably the best social platform to create value for your (potential) customers (Peterson, 2011).

Building Blocks of Social Media

From a traditional perspective, consumers used social media simply to communicate. But now, consumers are utilizing platforms, where they share content, blogs and social networking. In this way they create, modify, share and discuss internet content in their own social media domain. This is also known as the social media phenomenon (Kietzmann et al., 2011). It's seen as a communication platform, where social media tracks everything you do. Some may say, social media knows more about you than you do yourself. Location-based services are one of the many services and functions to generate data. But, because of this transparency there may also be an additional drawback, which includes fake news or false information. Because of the high amount of data that is obtained, it can be linked and tracked down, which results in groups and clustering.

It is easy to collect data from online platforms. They can track everything from a customer's process to the actual purchase. However, this is different for physical stores. They can only obtain the data of the customer behavior at the time in the store. Therefore, it is important for companies to look for a good transition. They must use an online platform or a collaboration through which they obtain data. The key to managing this transition is to think of different channels as complements, not as substitutes. Each channel is best suited for certain products, for a specific group of customers, or for a certain part of a consumer's decision journey. The trick is to identify these complementarities and build around them (Frazer & Stiehler, 2014). In a supply-driven economy this might lead to a channel conflict. However, if a customer decides about the buying point and if every channel can add value on a specific way to the buying process, the channels are supplementary.

Operational Use of Data

For example, Disney has installed thousands of sensors throughout the park, which communicate with the MagicBands, a stylish rubber wristband with a built-in RFID chip, and convert the park into a giant computer system. You just tap your MagicBand at the gate, at rides, or at restaurants. If the sensors detect too many visitors approaching a ride, Disney can, in real time, start a parade around the corner to entertain guests without them experiencing the pain of waiting for their ride. The technology and data about customers also allow Disney employees to optimize their time. They can now spend more time with guests and help create magical memories instead of handling tickets and payments. This is an example of blending the digital and physical worlds, and a perfect omnichannel strategy (Gupta, 2018). The personal data and contacts can be used again for other purposes, for communication and for customer profiling (clustering).

Software runs the millions of daily ad auctions at Google and Baidu. Its algorithms decide which cars offer rides on Didi, Grab, Lyft and Uber. It sets the prices of headphones and polo shirts on Amazon and runs the robots that clean floors in some Walmart locations. It enables customer service bots at Fidelity and interprets X-rays at Zebra Medical. In each case the machine learning applications treat decision-making as a science. Analytics systematically convert internal and external data into predictive modelling based on numerous variable and cluster profiles, insights and choices, which in turn guide and automate operational workflows.

Part of the use of social media marketing is the phenomenon of machine learning. The development of machine learning (ML) is realized with the expectation that marketing can be more efficient, personal and humane. Regardless of whether it is embedded in the cognitive system in marketing software, it provides power for every functional area of marketing and every step of the costumer journey[1]. Artificial intelligence-driven marketing uses

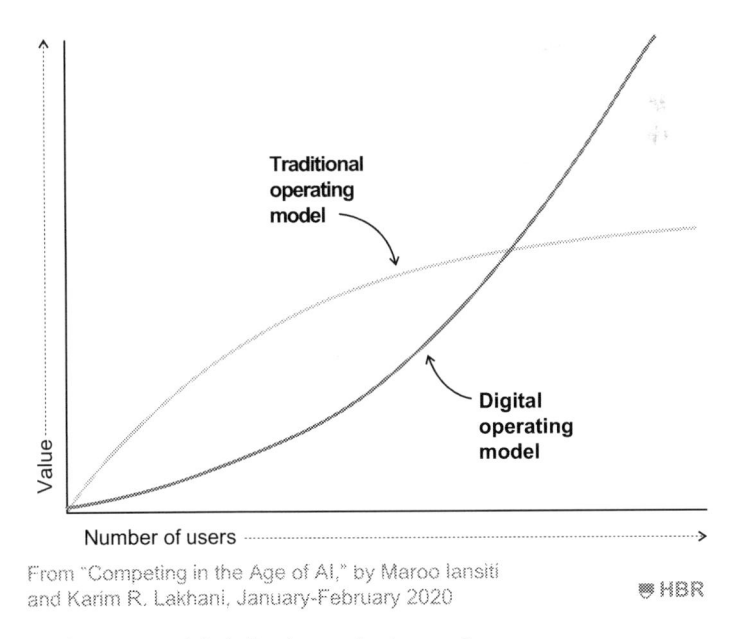

From "Competing in the Age of AI," by Maroo Iansiti and Karim R. Lakhani, January–February 2020 — HBR

Figure 8.7 The impact of digitalization on business value.
Source: *HBR*, January–February 2020

models to automate, optimize and enhance the conversion process that converts data into actions and interactions, and has the scope of predicting behavior, predicting demand, and hyper-personalized messages (Mari, 2019, p. 1).

Machine learning is a part of artificial intelligence and a way of creating problem-solving systems. With the help of machine learning, statistical techniques can help us teach computers to learn without requiring strict rule sets.

Machine learning relies on a bottom-up, data-based approach to recognize patterns. When there is a large amount of (behavioral) data, pattern recognition is most effective. This is where the power of big data is obvious. Today, there are several ways to train machines to perform tasks normally performed by humans.

Customer Knowledge

The first one is "supervised learning." Google is using this for example to recognize spam emails. Supervised learning involves the use of large amounts of "training" data, such as emails, which are first classified or marked as spam or non-spam by humans. These emails are then fed to the computer to see if it can correctly identify spam. No rules are specified for identifying spam. Instead, the machine will automatically learn the phrase or sentence to focus on based on the accuracy of its prediction. As more data became available, this trial-and-error process improved (Gupta, 2018, p. 217). This method can also be used to detect new trends or topics which are relevant. Companies should adapt their marketing to these trends. Bol.com in The Netherlands and companies like Amazon or booking.com are companies that anticipate current trends and convert this in their marketing strategy on social media.

On the other hand, there is unsupervised learning. This method effectively requires the machine to find interesting patterns in the data without telling the machine what to look for. Also, to look for similarities in the data itself, common denominators. This method can be used to find remarkable correlations and causalities in a data set. To expand this knowledge, we can create a context for customers, profiles or behavior. In that case we talk about contextual marketing.

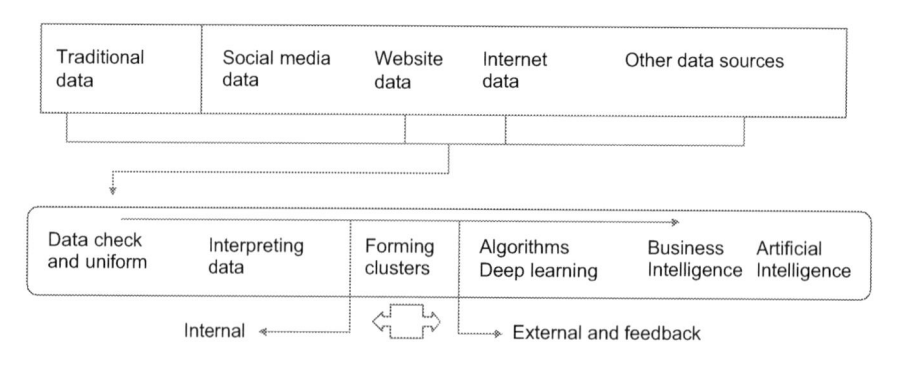

Figure 8.8 Process flow machine learning.

Contextual marketing is a strategy that's guided by the behaviors and conditions surrounding marketing efforts so all content is relevant to the person receiving it.

Customer knowledge and behavior are the basis for the marketing; "contextual" means you are more capable of adding to the customer profile. In order to do this it all starts with the data. Companies need to be able to identify customers, enrich their understanding of them and they need the technological capability to interact with them. A company can respond to this when choosing a marketing strategy. Clustering is a method of unsupervised learning and is a common technique for statistical data analysis used in many fields. Clustering is a machine learning technique that involves grouping data points. Given a set of data points, we can use a clustering algorithm to classify each data point into a specific group.

Theoretically, data points in the same group should have similar attributes and/or characteristics, while data points in different groups should have different attributes and/or characteristics. Clustering can be used for analysis to gain some valuable insights from the collected data by seeing what groups the data points fall into when we apply a clustering algorithm. This is a new way of making segments in the market. Instead of segments we talk about clusters, behavioral clusters (Seif, 2019). Clustering is very useful for online marketing. A company can divide people with the same attributes in clusters, for example they make a cluster based on age, gender or hobbies. If companies have done this, it is much easier for them to choose which people to target with their commercials. Also, if companies want to use hyper-personalized ads, clustering data is very eligible. Hyper-personalized messages mean the delivery of relevant messages at the right time and channel. AI marketing enables the collection and analysis of data, generation of insights, and definition of actions that more effectively reach the individual. Nowadays we understand what the customer is looking for now and what might be of interest to him next. Design-driven relevance of hyper-personalized experiences has become a major priority for most organizations (Mari, 2019, p. 13).

In between these two approaches is reinforcement learning. The machine starts with unsupervised learning. When an interesting pattern is found, the researcher sends a positive reinforcement signal to the machine to guide its search. By recognizing the excess data, the company can then use supervised learning to process the data (Gupta, 2018, p. 218).

Process of Machine Learning

Artificial intelligence (AI) helps to automate, optimize and enhance three basic marketing processes:

- data collection;
- insights collected through data analysis; and
- interaction with customers.

Modern marketing is based on intelligence technology to capture relevant user data from interactions with brands. From a long-term perspective, the benefit to users is that they can better assist immediate expressed needs and unexpressed needs.

The personalization process is a continuous cycle, controlled by algorithms, that provides companies with opportunities to attract consumers one-to-one and build self-reinforcing relationships. The company continues to improve its personalization process through repeated feedback loops, thus forming a "virtuous cycle of personalization." However, managers sometimes have different views on which type of personalization is suitable for each moment, which has sparked heated debate. Generally speaking, personalization constitutes a repeating process that can be defined by the three phases of the "understand-deliver-measure" cycle (Mari, 2019, p. 10).

The "AI first" strategy needs to consider why and how to strategically inject AI into consumer-centric (demand-driven) data collection, promotional activities and customer interactions. Creating a unique brand experience requires marketers to convert any relevant user data into actions or activities. Each customer's response to a predefined activity will generate a series of interactions at different touchpoints. For example, the call-to-action phrase "book a test drive" in the message will interact with users on social media, stores and contact centers. Each interaction between the brand and the user represents a new set of separate data, which is collected explicitly or silently via cookies. The company must capture, organize and analyze this information to enrich the individual's personal data. The central idea of this data-driven marketing combined with machine learning makes the cycle from data to operation to interaction shorter and more intelligent. The three sequential steps of the relationship driven by AI are closely linked and require a good integration of technology and process. Create a model, run tests, and get results from interactions (Mari, 2019, p.10). Machine learning continuously updates its data into a course of action. However, the speed of improvement will stop at some point, and will remain in a steady state until you make changes.

Data

Companies are using cognitive technology to make the utmost use of data and knowledge. Cognitive technologies, or "thinking" technologies, fall within a broad category that includes algorithms, robotic process automation, machine learning, natural language processing and natural language generation, reaching into the realm of artificial intelligence (AI).

Cognitive technology requires the use of customer-specific data to provide a unique brand experience. This data comes from consumer activities such as web browsing, social media posts, and mobile usage—and increasingly from sensors built into machines. AI algorithms themselves are not smart and are not giving elaborated usable data. They only analyze data to generalize learning. Artificial intelligence helps companies automate, optimize or expand the process of data collection, analysis, and storage. Sasha Srdanovic, chief solutions expert for artificial intelligence, said: "Artificial intelligence can help improve data quality by automatically screening and checking data pools and databases. For example, you can avoid duplication or consider different data capture options." So, in the future no company or marketing manager is expected to succeed without using collected data well (Mari, 2019, p. 10), and to use this data for demand-driven processes or to use the data at contact points.

The quality of data is more important than the amount of data, the well-known term big data specifies only the size of a database not the usefulness. Another misunderstanding is that data collection, integration and preparation are far more time-consuming than building a machine learning model itself. The last misconceptions. Companies should consider that a machine learning model is automated; it will not continue to create algorithms over time without manual control. Since the environment outside the model is dynamically changing, key business users need to view the model and provide new data sets regularly. This prevents biased data (Mari, 2019, p. 10).

Data needs to be visualized as a source of action and self-improvement. Algorithms can absorb real-time data, process it, and then perform real-time operations. Among other things, artificial intelligence helps companies automate, optimize or expand the process of scoring, positioning and campaigning. Delivering unique communications on a large scale requires marketers to move from classic segmentation to advanced technologies that use machine learning and intelligent scoring to attract audiences and predict each customer's conversion probability (cluster based) (Mari, 2019, p. 10).

Benefits of Using Machine Learning on Digital Marketing

It can be concluded that machine learning can be based on extensive data processing to provide necessary information for the decision-making process of marketing experts. The application of machine learning-driven tools in digital marketing brings a variety of new challenges and opportunities. The biggest benefits of using these tools in marketing are (Miklosik et al., 2019):

- Optimal performance, machines perform steadily at 100% because they cannot be disturbed or distracted.
- Faster decision making—machine decision-making time is determined by the available data. After a quick calculation, machines can decide (almost) immediately. The decision is not affected by subjective factors such as feelings, personal preferences, opinions.
- Automatization of predictable activities—machine learning can very effectively automate routine activities. For example, in digital marketing, ML can assist with generation of regular reports on advertising campaigns in social media marketing.
- Reducing error rates, eliminating errors normally caused by human factors. Machines perform a task by always following the predefined procedure.

- Digital assistants, machine learning-driven systems can handle complicated tasks and optimize daily routines, as personal human assistants nowadays do.
- Exploring areas unavailable to humans. In many areas a person is unable to perform the required tasks for various reasons, process large amounts of data that are generated every minute on the internet or do tasks in very tiny places. Machines can be adapted to almost any condition, and computing can handle even the most difficult mathematical-statistical operations.

Machine Learning Technique Usable for Social Media

Many marketers prefer to use AI to convert data into valuable customer insights. Information gathering involves identifying the benefits of online marketing to improve information gathering and feedback. Most users use social media platforms to share their views on products of interest and their expected demand (Arasu et al., 2020). Each segment has a different machine learning tool that fits them best. For machine learning in combination with social media marketing, sample data sets are collected and analyzed.

Customer Loyalty

The basic rules in the supply world apply also in the demand world as for creating loyalty. But there are also huge differences, such as knowledge of the individual customers, trust, complementarity, community and above all behavioral data. Communication is direct and makes it easier to collect customer information which can be used to create new interactions. The purpose of a firm has to be to create customers (Boora & Singh, 2011). This ties in with the demand-driven and customer-centric economy, which was discussed before. To create satisfied customers, there has to be customer loyalty. In a world of platforms, loyalty programs result in the wanted customer loyalty by looking at the behavior design (Choudary, 2015). Interactive direct communication based on predictive needs and demand will build loyalty automatically. There will be a feeling: "They know and understand me."

Platforms, like Facebook and Instagram, created a huge customer database with potentially relevant customers for companies. Namely, data itself is the source of value (Belch & Belch, 2012). Companies have to see these opportunities and have to start focusing on retail loyalty platforms. Namely, data itself is the source of value. The retail loyalty platform will attract consumers' interest based on past consumption, so as to provide them with more shopping transactions in the future. On the retail loyalty platform, consumer data is a unit of value. For retailers interested in targeting this consumer, this is a source of core value (Choudary, 2015).

Merchants can use loyalty platforms to offer discounts to the customer base they already have. In this way, these customers maintain more inter-action with the merchant. Companies also see the value of consumer-oriented applications of promoting them to their customer base. As a result, the merchants bring their existing customer base to the loyalty platform. The platform will understand their customers better, because they have insight into purchasing preferences because of the flow of consumer data (Boora & Singh, 2011). This will result in cross-pollination by consumers to other non-competitive businesses. This increases the power of network effects even more (Choudary, 2015). The success of a focus on loyalty depends on the speed at which the data is used in a buying process. So again: companies have to be agile and flexible (Butscher, 2002). A satisfied customer is the result of a business (Boora & Singh, 2011).

Consumer's Perspective on Personal, Demand-Driven, Marketing

It's important to know what customers expect from geting a demand-driven communication. Their thoughts may influence, sometimes unconsciously, the way they behave (Butscher, 2002). Their behavior is what companies are most likely to measure, because behavior leads to (not) buying behavior. Knowing what customers' drive is, is an important aspect to aquire new customers. Acquiring new customers is a major driver of growth, and growth is a key priority for every business (Gupta, 2018). Ultimately, the true goal of the economy is to create value (Cinquini et al., 2012).

There are three ways a firm can provide information and influence consumers:

- The first one is through paid media, where you can think of ads on TV and radio.
- The second one is owned media, which is for example the company's website. Also, the ranking in online searches can be influenced this way.
- The last one is through direct communication based on past behavior and predictions.

As described before, the key for companies is to focus on what the customer wants. This shift, from product orientation to customer focus, has a couple of effects. The product tunes in better with the customer's needs. It also increases satisfaction, creates loyalty and results in a more concentrated strategy for companies. That demand-driven perspective is a prerequisite to create a good customer experience, but also means that a company has to be agile and flex-ible. A company has to be as structured as possible, because this makes them more flexible and allows for quick adaptability when needed. As discussed earlier, it's important to be flexible to be able to respond to opportunities that arise by looking at what the customer wants. It's also meaningful for "being digital" and to implement new technologies.

Creating Exchange Value

Marketers create exchange value when they effectively match their offerings to specific customer needs. That requires recognizing when customers are looking for a particular product or service, understanding what problem they are trying to solve, and figuring out what offerings will suit them best—in real time. It calls for sharp *conversion, personalization* and *prediction* capabilities.

Value creating has four dimensions for customers:

- functional;
- economic;
- emotional; and
- cohesion.

The functional value is linked to the product, the economic value to the price (or ROI), the emotional value is based on personal criteria, and cohesion is linked to attachment or belonging to a certain group. For marketing, it is essential to decide which value is relevant for each target group or cluster. The precise tuning of the value offer to each group will increase the competitive advantage of a supplier. Obviously, this is more so in the demand approach.

Marketers can increase engagement value by encouraging customers to interact with one another, asking questions, sharing knowledge, and collaborating. To this end, Salesforce created the Trailblazer Community, where customers can join dozens of user groups across industries to share their experiences with the company's products. Similarly, Glossier, a direct-to-consumer beauty-products brand, facilitates community groups focused on pertinent topics. User groups help these companies understand customer needs, enhance retention, lower acquisition costs, generate product ideas, and smooth the introduction of innovations. For instance, Glossier is exploring social commerce that involves community members who act as influencers and even sell its products. Marketing leaders can also play a central role in creating or identifying new business models and technologies that spur customer demand. For example, many large companies—Unilever among them—have established units to manage investments in start-ups and new ventures in emerging marketing technology or entertainment services that, among other things, can help shape product, service, or marketing efforts.

Also, they foster an organizational culture that focuses on customer needs and more-fluid interactions between areas of expertise. One tool for that purpose was *key behavioral indicators* (KBIs), such as levels of interpersonal trust and transparency, which were accorded the same status as KPIs in performance evaluations. That's because when performance on KBIs falls, one manager stated once that the time needed for alignment and coordination increases, reducing speed to market.

In its role representing the "voice of the customer," the marketing function can create knowledge value, principally through the astute use of data science. Some established customer-intelligence activities, such as user-needs assessments and sentiment tracking, remain important. But newer technologies open up further opportunities. For example, AI-powered data analytics systems can increasingly tease the causal relationship between marketing investments and business outcomes, creation and management, leveraging market and customer intelligence, and advancing marketing analytics.

In addition, new technologies are enabling ever more innovative ways for companies to capture market signals and use data. For instance, the Freestyle vending machine installed by Coca-Cola across thousands of quick-service restaurants allows customers to select from dozens of flavor mixes, which are individually dispensed. By tracking and reporting these orders, the machines provide granular, real-time, first-party data on consumer preferences: a highly valuable asset for a non-direct-to-consumer firm. The company has used this data to inform its R&D and to launch new products.

As a major producer and user of data, marketing can also create knowledge value by collaborating with IT and data science teams to generate a single source of market intelligence, devise ways to define and measure key marketing metrics, and develop mechanisms for protecting customer information. Adobe executives credit the creation of such a "single source of truth" as a key turning point in accelerating the company's transformation effort. Marketing leaders have recognized and acted on the need to change their organizations. But most have struggled to carry out changes in ways that advance marketing's operating effectiveness. The framework presented here brings clarity to the process and guides the design of a marketing organization for our time—one built as a coalition to create value and drive company growth.

Digitization has changed the buying process of consumers in recent years. The rise of platforms has changed the buying for customers and companies. Consumers can find all the information about the products themselves and they are increasingly listening to reviews from other consumers. So, companies are forced to react differently to customers. Where they first looked at a company's profits, retaining customers has become more important in today's times. As a result, it has become more important to know what is behind customer behavior, the customer decision journey. Nowadays this can be well analyzed by means of data.

Machine learning is an important development that is changing (online) marketing strategies. Machine learning ensures that the data collected by companies, using artificial intelligence, is converted into valuable insights of the customer. Machine learning helps in clustering consumers by recognizing attributes and characteristics and thus placing the customer in a particular cluster. Machine learning software also recognizes where a customer's interests lie. With this information it is much easier for a company to get the right personalized ads to the customer on social media. By targeting the right customers, the chances are much higher that the advertising will result in a purchase from the company.

Companies have to keep their focus on keeping their brand and the customer loop as valuable as can be. This can be done by showing empathy and transparency towards their customers. Regarding operations, it's important to use marketing in more agile ways, which on their way can create more empathy during this pandemic. Internally there has to be adaptation to new ways of working to keep delivering value for customers. Companies can create value on social media for customers if they ensure that the collected data is converted into valuable insights for the customer. The most important thing is that companies look at the customer loop over and over again, because the world is changing very fast and so is customer behavior. Social media is a good platform to collect the necessary data and then quickly anticipate changes because social media is a huge platform. This allows companies to give the customer an optimal personalized experience in the buying process.

Competitive Advantage

Finally, what is the competitive advantage of data, as part of a demand-driven strategy. In an article by Hagiu and Wright (2020) they specified the sustainability in six important questions:

1   How much value is added by customer data relative to the standalone value of offering?
2   How quickly does the marginal value of data-enabled learning lose value?
3   How fast does the relevance of the user data depreciate?
4   Is the data proprietary, meaning it can't be purchased from other sources, easily, or reverse engineered?
5   How hard is it to imitate product improvements that are based on customer data?
6   Does the data from one user help improve the product for the same user or for others?

In all cases the strategic use of data has a competitive advantage in the relationship with customers, but what is the importance for suppliers in the network or for every individual supplier? Especially data is used for the relationship with customers (demand-based) but the data can also be used for product innovation. A good example is Nike, we have explained the customer focus and demand drive of Nike+, but the data is also used for specific product innovations like the carbon layer:

- The Nike ZoomX VaporflyNEXT% is the fast you've never seen—or felt—before. By combining our two most innovative technologies, Nike ZoomX foam and VaporWeave material, it's the fastest shoe we've ever made. Learn more about the future of racing shoes.
- A full-length carbon-fiber plate underfoot provides a propulsive sensation to help you push the pace.

- The VaporWeave material is insanely strong and crazy lightweight. It's also water resistant so go ahead and pour water over your head; these shoes won't soak it all up.
- Added Nike ZoomX foam in the forefoot delivers exceptional energy return.(www.nike.com/nl/en/running/vaporfly)

Conclusion

Data is the new marketing tool to gain competitive advantage. The demand-driven approach is based on customer and behavioral data, but also on machine learning. With machine learning you give knowledge to the data, and you use the data for predictions. In this way the organization can react quickly to changes (agility) but can also communicate directly with customers (and customers in clusters). For profiling the customers, the data should be used to create clusters based on common denominators and changing responses. This is a new marketing approach but will decide about the future success of organizations. The next step will be the adoption by the organization based on this strategy and the new tools.

Student's Mind

1 What is the major change for marketing?
2 What is the difference between data from direct marketing and data from today?
3 Will the use of machine learning be supportive or leading for the marketing strategy?
4 Cluster techniques is a different form of marketing, what will be the consequences?
5 How do you integrate all data sources for marketing?

Discussion Point

Marketing used to focus on the impact on markets. By using machine learning the focus will shift to an impact on buyers' markets. What influence will this have on the skills of marketing people?

Note

1 Cognitive technologies, or 'thinking' technologies, fall within a broad category that includes algorithms, robotic process automation, machine learning, natural language processing and natural language generation, reaching into the realm of artificial intelligence (AI).

References

Arasu, B. S., Seelan, B. J. B. & Thamaraiselvan, N. (2020). A Machine Learning-Based Approach to Enhancing Social Media Marketing. *Computers & Electrical Engineering*, 86.

Belch, G. E. & Belch, M. A. (2012). *Advertising and Promotion: An Integrated Marketing Communications Perspective*, 9th ed. London: McGraw-Hill/Irwin.

Boora, K. & Singh, H. (2011). Customer Loyalty and its Antecedents: A Conceptual Framework. Retrieved from www.researchgate.net/publication/339527575_Custom er_loyalty_and_its_antecedents_a_conceptual_framework

Butscher, S. A. (2002). *Customer Loyalty Programmes and Clubs*, 2nd ed. London: Gower Publications.

Choudary, S. P. (2015). *Platform Scale: How a New Breed of Startups is Building Large Empires with Minimum Investment*. London: Platform Thinking Labs.

Cinquini, L., Di Minin, A. & Varaldo, R. (Eds.). (2012). *New Business Models and Value Creation: A Service Science Perspective*. New York: Springer.

Clark, B. H. (1999). Marketing Performance Measures: History and Interrelationships. *Journal of Marketing Management*, 15(8).

Fan, W. & Gordon, M. D. (2014). The Power of Social Media Analytics. *Commun. ACM57*, 6 (June): 74–81.

Frazer, M. & Stiehler, B. E. (2014). Omnichannel Retailing: The Merging of the Online and Off-line Environment. *Global Conference on Business & Finance Proceedings*, 9(1): 655.

Gibbs, B. & Harrison, N. (2019). How Retail Changes When Algorithms Curate Everything We Buy. Retrieved from https://hbr.org/2019/01/how-retail-changes-when-algorithms-curate-everything-we-buy

Gupta, S. (2018). *Driving Digital Strategy*. London: Reed Business Education.

Hagiu, A. & Wright, J. (2020). When Data Creates Competitive Advantage. *HBR*, January–February.

Kietzmann, J. H. et al. (2011). Social Media? Get Serious! Understanding the Functional Building Blocks of Social Media. *Business Horizons*, 54(3): 241–251.

Lecinski, J. (2011). Winning the Zero Moment of Truth. Google report, June. Retrieved from www.thinkwithgoogle.com/future-of-marketing/emerging-technol ogy/2011-winning-zmot-ebook/

Mari, A. (2019). The Rise of Machine Learning in Marketing. Retrieved from www. zora.uzh.ch/id/eprint/197751/

Miklosik, A., Kuchta, M., Evans, N. & Zak, S. (2019). Towards the Adoption of Machine Learning-Based Analytical Tools in Digital Marketing. Retrieved from https:// ieeexplore.ieee.org/document/8746184

Petersen, M. (2011). *Agile Marketing*. New York: Apress.

Seif, G. (2019). The 5 Clustering Algorithms Data Scientists Need to Know. Retrieved from https://towardsdatascience.com/the-5-clustering-algorithms-data-scientists-need -to-know-a36d136ef68

9 Transforming Organizations
From Digital to Demand-Driven

Digitization is the process of converting information from a physical format into a digital one. When this process is leveraged to improve business processes, it is called digitalization. The results of this process are called digital transformation. Digitalization is the use of digital technologies to change a business model and provide new revenue and value-producing opportunities; it is the process of moving to a digital business. Digitalization is a process of converting information into a digital format.

The result is the uniform representation of an object, image, sound, document or signal. Because of digitalization it is possible to connect data resources even if they have a different format. We can connect traditional data with, for instance, social media data and numeric data with images. This way it is possible to build big data warehouses and analyze processes, behavior and other relevant sources.

Transforming Organizations to Demand-Driven

Transforming an organization from a supply-driven organization with a strong focus on internal processes and optimalization to a demand-driven organization with a strong need for external data and interaction digitalization is a first step in creating uniform data sources. The first step of machine learning is to analyze data on uniformity on field level and transferring this data to a uniform set of data. These first steps are the same as steps taken for digitalization, getting data and standardizing format. For some companies a total change of strategy and operation is a "bridge too far." Therefore the first step is quite often very close to the existing business, only it optimizes processes and functions. The quality improvement and the cost saving are good motivators for change. The second step is harder. Based on the optimalization of existing processes and lower cost (implementing digitalization) the next step will be to make use of the new opportunities of digitalization in the use of software and for strategy. New ways to improve the organization and activity will lead to innovation. Do things differently. An innovation is an idea that has been transformed into practical reality. For a business, this is a product, process or business concept, or combinations that have been activated in the market and produce new profits and growth for the organization. The innovation is still based on the existing

DOI: 10.4324/9781003226161-9

business processes and values. But using this kind of technology will lead to a disruption because of adoption of the market (competitors and consumers), but also to adaption of strategy (competitors) and behavior (consumers).

The Reason for Transformation: Disruption

Transforming Customer Experience

At the heart of digital is customer data. More data is needed of customers to analyze the needs and possible sales to individual customers. Therefore, a direct contact is needed or a link to a database with all the relevant data. Many companies are increasingly aware of this and are looking for opportunities to get in touch with potential customers, like through their own website or web shop, by collaborating within the supply chain, with the last link in a supply chain or selling or communicating direct to the end user. This will lead to restructuring of business processes but also to reconsidering business partners (a restructuring of the supply chain).

More Data-Based Insights

When you go digital, you can track metrics and analyze the data that you capture during your digital marketing efforts. Using data-driven insights can help to understand customers better, and also rethink business strategies, assisting with better decision-making, better forecasting and to optimize existing business drivers like stocks or production.

Greater Collaboration across Departments

Digitalization offers an opportunity to restructure the organization based on linking independent departments in a customer-based approach, to monitor activities better and to collaborate with external parties. When you find everyone aligned to a common purpose (customer-needs driven) the processes based on machine learning and demand-driven strategies will effectively create a network,

Improved Agility and Innovation

Based upon the dynamics in markets and dynamics in customer needs and behavior it is essential to react timely to these changes. Agility is based on triggers, exceptions and forecasts and will activate processes and activities. "Go with the flow" is a key strategy for companies active in these kinds of markets.

It sounds logical and simple but to transfer a business model which was successful over the last 150 years, with a management who are brought up with hierarchy in decision making and control barriers are obvious. Outside pressure from customers, new entrants in the market and diminishing profits will put a strain on decision-making for the traditional managers. Markets and customer behavior are changing rapidly and quite often unpredictable. This is the main reason to act accordingly. In stable markets and stable customer needs, direct interaction and the detection of "needs" was not needed. However, this has changed and since 2000 the tools are available to implement a dynamic strategy to know, analyze, interact and respond to the changes. Since 2000 new start-ups used the new available technology to change businesses. First in a classical business model like Amazon (first competitive advantage was online ordering and home delivery). After Amazon has proved a need for this kind of "mail ordering," new start-ups followed but also new technologies became available. Somewhere round 2007 digital communication became the core of a business model. Social media became very popular, individual communication based on smartphone made a barriers-free use of internet possible and Facebook became the "cliffhanger" for internet use. This was the start of a worldwide adoption of internet, personal communication and communities on internet. This was also the realization for existing companies to change their business. It was not a coincidence that at the same time a worldwide financial crisis was the start of a recession until about 2012.

The Build-up to Digitalization

1998–2004

New start-ups using internet as core business structure. New business models using "scale" as business horizon (geography is not an issue anymore). Traditional companies became aware of changes because of using new techniques. A struggle on business view and business decision was a struggle between new business entrants and existing companies. Especially the focus on profit changed to a focus on company value based on prospective market growth and prospective revenues. Why was a loss-making company as Amazon more valuable than a profit-making car factory or consumer products company? Results from the past were replaced by possible results in the future.

2004–2010

2004–2010 was a time of realization that internet is here to stay and would transform supply chains and companies. A focus on agility to meet demand and customer behavior dynamics, new start-ups in markets, more international connections were a result of a better and faster internet structure. New technologies made it possible to optimize production so more product features could be produced in a shorter time frame. Custom-made production, bespoke products and producing for small groups was possible because of the new scale of the market.

A traditional mail-order company as Landsend used the time between ordering and delivering for adapting standard product. A bespoke shirt was possible when you gave the right measurements. Initials where possible, any-place on a shirt. Also, special logos or other changes to the garment became standard. It was normal that you had to wait for these special features. This became of course a successful weapon against physical retailers, but also data was gathered about the customers that could be used for future offerings.

Amazon was the first to use collaborative filtering for products in communication with customers.

Using the search engine of Amazon for product they gave suggestions for other products: "Other customers also bought ..." This was of course a strategy to increase basket value. Later on this whole process was optimized with advanced cluster technique, but also linking product suggestions to all the clusters and to the product search.

Well-known is also the bespoke jeans of Levi's. If you measure your size and order online you got a bespoke pair of jeans. This was more a marketing gimmick, but went well in this period suggesting that a customer can influence the production process. The jeans were not really bespoke, but all possible sizes (10,000) were stored in a general warehouse where the online orders were produced.

Another development used geography as competitive tool; ordering wine in France direct from the castle, order cheese direct in The Netherlands or ordering direct in Asia for authentic products.

This was the time to use the new possibilities for new business models and to reach out to new customers and markets. It was also the time that traditional companies were trying to change within their own structure, New start-ups within a company were responsible for the web shop and internet sales (although, using standard financial criteria.) Traditional companies bought new start-ups to get inside knowledge of customers but also of the new techniques. New software was used to optimize the business processes.

The financial crisis of 2007 and the following recession was also the time to realize that the business world was on the eve of transformation.

2010–2020

This was an era for connection. Companies evaluated their cost structure. Technology improved vastly. Companies realized to get competitive advantages demands new technologies and updates of their systems were essential, However, the cost would be considerable in software and upgrading hardware. Two strategic developments became evident:

- cloud computing; and
- service computing.

Looking back, these developments were essential for the future applications like machine learning and networking.

Cloud Computing

Cloud computing is the on-demand availability of computer system resources, especially data storage (cloud storage) and computer power, without direct active management by the user. The term is generally used to describe data centers available to many users over the internet. Large clouds are predominant today, and often have functions distributed over multiple locations from central servers. If the connection to the user is relatively close, it may be designated as an edge server. Clouds may be limited to a single organization (enterprise clouds), or be available to multiple organizations (public cloud). Cloud computing relies on sharing of resources to achieve coherence and economies of scale.

Advocates of public and hybrid clouds note that cloud computing allows companies to avoid or minimize up-front IT infrastructure costs. Proponents also claim that cloud computing allows enterprises to get their applications up and running faster, with improved manageability and less maintenance, and that it enables IT teams to more rapidly adjust resources to meet fluctuating and unpredictable demand, providing the burst computing capability: high computing power at certain periods of peak demand. Cloud providers typically use a "pay-as-you-go" model, which can lead to unexpected operating expenses if administrators are not familiarized with cloud-pricing models.

The availability of high-capacity networks, low-cost computers and storage devices as well as the widespread adoption of hardware visualization, service-oriented architecture and autonomic and utility computing has led to growth in cloud computing. By 2019, Linux was the most widely used operating system, including in Microsoft's offerings and is thus described as dominant. The most used clouds are Amazon's webservices and Microsoft's Azure. Also, Google cloud is a prominent alternative. The group of networked elements providing services need not be individually addressed or managed by users; instead, the entire provider-managed suite of hardware and software can be thought of as an amorphous cloud.

By 2020 the focus is no longer anymore on optimalization or innovation, but now the focus is on disruption. How can we competitively use the new software and applications as a strategic tool. It is no longer enough to optimize business processes (an inside strategy) but also to use the new tool for competition on the market. The changes have to lead to transformation of the business concept and business strategy. This transformation has just started, we see the impact of platforms, machine learning and outsourcing of activities (Mean and lean agile operations) as a new development changing organizations and market structures. The supply-driven economy will be a demand-driven economy with a direct interaction between customers and suppliers, a need-based offering, communities and same kind clustering, anytime, anywhere and anyhow contacts between companies and customers. Another major change is the impact of worldwide platforms like Amazon, Alibaba, Uber and Airbnb. Connecting customers, analyzing behavior, creating same kind of clusters and work in networks of suppliers and customers are just some challenges companies are facing.

Service Computing

Service computing is using a pay-as-you-go model, you only pay for the use of the cloud or an application. Major software companies like SAP, Oracle and Salesforces have changed their license model where the user buys a license to use the software in a service contract.

Service computing has become a cross-discipline that covers the science and technology of bridging the gap between business services and IT services. Service computing is a cross-disciplinary field that covers science and technology, and represents a promising direction for distributed computing and software development methodologies. It aims to bridge the gap between business services and IT services by supporting the whole lifecycle of services innovation. A few examples of service computing are:

- software as a service;
- infrastructure as a service;
- platform as a service;
- data storage as a service; and
- analytics as a service.

Software as a Service

Software as a service (SaaS) is probably the most well-known application for cloud computing. Essentially, SaaS products distribute data online, and are accessible from a browser on any device, which allows those companies to continue to host the software. The ease of use, upfront, subscription-based pricing and lowered costs make SaaS one of the most attractive sectors in all of business and tech. Well-known companies using SaaS are Salesforce, Slack and Zoom.

Infrastructure as a Service

Infrastructure as a service (IaaS) provides a virtualized computing infrastructure managed entirely over the internet. IaaS is typically used in a few different ways, including as a testing environment for app development, as a website host and even as a platform for big data analysis. IaaS is becoming a popular option because of its business continuity and its efficiency in delivering apps. IBM is a leading company in this field.

Platform as a Service

Platform as a service (PaaS) is a cloud computing model that provides users with hosted development kits, applications management capabilities and database tools, the virtual resources a company needs to build, deploy and launch their software applications. By outsourcing hosting, database security and data storage, companies avoid long-term investments (saving them lots of money). Amazon webservices and Azure by Microsoft are well-known companies using PaaS.

Data Storage as a Service

File sharing and data storage account for lots of cloud use, with individuals and businesses sharing large files through cloud-based softwares and outsourcing their data storage to off-premises data centers. Pay-as-you-go models help businesses manage and scale data sharing and storage based on current needs. Best of all, there's no limit on either one. Dropbox is a well-known supplier of capacity for big data.

Analytics as a Service

Data storage is only one aspect of cloud computing. As cloud-based security companies attempt to outmaneuver hackers and stay ahead of invasions, it's also an increasingly secure way to protect sensitive data from cyber marauders. Because big data companies require massive amounts of storage and processing power for analysis purposes, lots of them are turning to the cloud for greater amounts of both, plus enhanced security for business records.

Transforming an Organization Based on Data

To transform a traditional organization to a demand-driven organization is a total restructuring of the organization. In *The Digital Transformation Playbook* (Rogers, 2016) five domains of change were detected. Customers (of course), competition, data, innovation and value.

Customers should get more attention in the strategy of a company, there should be a focus on customer value. A two-way communication is essential to get the right data and knowledge of customers.

Customers as target group, sales focus → Individual customer behavior

Competitors will work together in platforms. Because platforms are combining supply and match supply with needs of customers as we have seen it is more a matter of the right match than selling products. Within a platform they will cooperate for the best match; however, outside the platform they can still be competitors.

Competing on sales, product features → Competing on needs matching and direct communication

Data is crucial, it's a continuous process of gathering, restructuring, analyzing and deploying. Data is needed to create value for customers and to optimize processes for companies. The type of data and the use of data is different from the past. Individual behavioral data is important to predict future contacts and sales.

Data of internal processes (ERP based) → Data of customers and preferences

Innovation is the second step in transformation: optimize, innovate, disrupt. All process and structure are analyzed for the possible impact and change of digitalization. First based on existing structures, soon to be followed by innovation. From digitalization of existing processes to processes based on digitalization.

Changes made on ROI basis → Changes made on possible impact on customers

The fifth focus is on *value,* customer value. Knowing the reasons why customers buy, analyze the behavior, cluster similar behavior, detect predictive behavior and analyze (and re-cluster) again. Slowly the organization will change from a product (or service) selling organization to a matching offering based upon customer needs and data analyses.

Selling the right product on customer preference → Matching the customer needs based upon best match

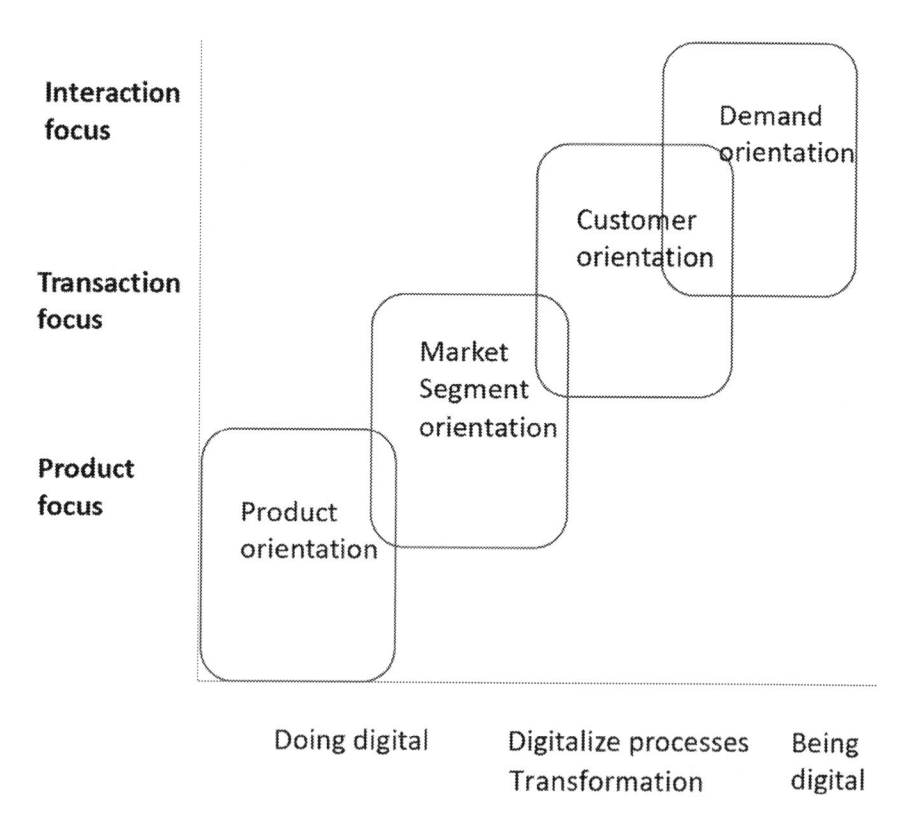

Figure 9.1 A dynamic orientation model, combining focus with digital.

In the dynamic orientation model, the different orientations of an organization are indicated. As we have seen in the traditional supplier's model organizations are organized to produce articles. In this production role, a distribution channel is usually used to bring the articles to the end user. There is a strong focus on the quality of products and the efficiency of the distribution channel. Technology is used to support these functions, including the use of internet. Contacts with customers usually go through the distribution channel. For product support there is a call center or email handling.

With a market orientation, there is still a focus on the production of articles, but the production is partly focused on the market share within a certain market segment. It is supply-driven, although the illusion exists that there is a customer focus, but the focus is on the need of a certain market segment. This market orientation is based on a target group approach. The relationship with the target group will also be part of the marketing strategy. The application of technology will be supported by the wishes of the target group and will be strongly focused on doing digital, supported by production and distribution. There is an orientation break in the customer orientation because this is the change from supply to demand. This is the change which takes place because of the impact of internet and machine learning on customer behavior and business models as we have seen earlier. We no longer deliver to unknown customers, but attempts are made to integrate customer knowledge within the business model. This often refers to customer-oriented or "customer-facing." The terms already indicate that there is an increasing involvement of customers.

The product concept is adapted by adapting the physical product and services are used as an important addition. Through a clear brand strategy for a specific target group, supported by interaction, a relationship is established with individual customers. This phase is the switchover of the model. The customer is becoming increasingly important, there is interaction with the customer and direct communication. The focus is still on the product, but in an interactive process. Share of wallet, how much does the customer buy and how often does the customer come (RFM) is an important measuring instrument as we have seen. Many web stores are customer-oriented due to individual communication, behavior-based analyses and interaction via social media. The greatest involvement of customers is in customer participation and interaction, the platform orientation, demand-driven. The involvement of customers is maximized here. Interaction and communication are the important drivers. In this phase there is no longer a focus on the old marketing tools, the 4Ps, but that the focus is on the customers, connection, communication, and commitment, supplemented with collaboration and interaction.

The change from a product focus to a platform focus cannot be done in one go. This requires a change of the organizational structure, the functions, but also of the market approach. The technology will be much more based on interaction, behavior registration and communication. This integral change process is essential to be successful. A partial adjustment will inevitably lead to frictions such as customer contact centers that close at 6 p.m., slow response to emails, slow delivery times or no insight into stocks or customer behavior.

Orientation	Product orientation	Market orientation	Customer orientation	Customer participation/ Platform orientation demand driven
Focus	Product	Target group/ segments	Relation / loyalty	Synergy / interaction
Product/ service	Standard	Target group focused/ services	Modules/ bespoke	Direct, participation interaction
Price	Cost price plus	Depends on target group	Profit based on Relation/ share of wallet	Depends on relationship
Communication	Mass communication	Result focus transaction	Internet based	Internet based
Organization	Hierarchal	Matrix, business units	Customer clusters	Network organization
Digitalization	Website	Website and Web shop, limited functional support	Applied within existing processes	Being digital, networks, and interaction with customers domain approach
Cooperation	Limited	Within target group	Between suppliers and last link of the chain Limited sharing of information	Close cooperation with suppliers about customer information, functions and support (e.g. stock levels)
Commercial process	Customers are the final link in a supply chain	Customers are a link in the supply chain Building brand value an association	Direct communication with end users. Product focus	Interaction, loyalty loop needs based intensive communication driven by algorithms,

Figure 9.2 Applications of information technology in marketing, from transaction based to relationships.
Source: Molenaar (1997)

Restructuring occurs when the orientation shifts from product to customer. As a result, functions must change, but also the structure must be adapted. A hierarchical structure is giving way to a structure based on functional clusters, the cooperation between the various business functions must also be more intensive to be able to respond quickly to a change in demand or based on the interaction with customers. At Zara we see a close collaboration between sales (stores) and design to quickly translate the demand into a new collection. In internet shops, logistics, including inventory management, is particularly closely involved in sales and planning. Analysis departments are also not only focused on analyzing what has happened, but also what is expected, so that other business functions can adjust to this. In health, the information function will be especially important, while in an "edge" strategy, the sharing of property will be central. This change is of great importance for the focus of an organization. The original focus was on the product to be brought to market. Product values and transactions were dominant, as well as, for example, market share. Since the price was often determined by what was feasible in the market, profitability could be increased by a strong focus on costs. In customer orientation, the focus is much more on adding value and buying motives. What does the customer want to buy and why, should be anticipated? For one customer, this can be the quality, another the immediate availability or home delivery. Based on these buying motives, the complexity for an organization has increased. In addition, the organization can no longer suffice with efficiency, but the organization must be adapted around a customer cluster or service clusters. Interfunctional coordination between the departments is necessary to achieve this. The original departments are often split up to facilitate these clusters. For example, each cluster has its own analyses, its own website, its own stock management systems and its own business model. Because the clusters must be able to respond quickly to changes in demand and the interaction with the customer, greater leeway is needed than in the old model. There is no longer a centrally managed organization, management takes place on the basis of KPIs that are part of a process. Every process step is analyzed. This is mainly due to the dynamics in the market, which means that the end result can no longer be determined in advance, but it can be determined whether the necessary decisions have been taken that can lead to an expected result. It can also be determined whether there has been a timely response to changes in the market and the demand from buyers. This requires the knowledge of purchasing behavior as we have seen before.

From Hierarchy to Data Driven

For organizations digitalization is more than using technology in all strategic processes. In the past these decisions were based on "returns on investments." However, because of dynamic market circumstances this is not possible anymore. New technologies are adopted, new start-ups will enter the market and the market is more transparent than ever. Also, the loyalty and commitment from customers is changing, in the consumer market the loyalty is diminishing, in the business-to-business market the loyalty is a shared value by sharing processes (networking and platforming) and more a risk sharing. A company has not the luxury anymore to have a transaction-based focus but should partner with their customers. For decades, IT was used to enhance the performance of specific functions and organizational units. For a long time, companies have optimized their scale, scope and learning through greater focus and specialization, which led to the siloed structures that the vast majority of enterprises today have. But digitalization should break with these fixed structures. Hierarchy should change in dependency, all departments are linked to each other in a demand-based network, triggered from outside the company.

IT Systems for Demand-driven Organizations

Although production is still a major part of a company's activity, the trigger is not based on production or changes in product features but on need matching and product offering. The decision process will shift from a hierarchy approach through a network approach and clustering. This is a major shift and not easy because employees and especially customer contact should have the authority to make decisions. Control will be done after a decision is made, not before the decision is made. Re-architecting a company's operating model means rebuilding each business unit on a new, integrated foundation of data, analytics, and software. This challenging and time-consuming undertaking demands focus and a consistent top-down mandate to coordinate and inspire all involved.

Building a base of software, data science, and advanced analytics capabilities is an incremental process which is guided by a small team of change leaders. They have a blueprint of the steps to be taken, involve the various project leaders and make sure that it is a coordinated process.

In the past, IT was largely about keeping existing systems working, deploying software updates, protecting against cyberattacks, and running help desks. Developing operating-model software is a different game. New software is built on dynamics and agility. Response to a change in market dynamics or buying patterns should be prompt and adequate. Low coding systems like Microsoft OutSystems or Mendis are a set of software tools which work like an assembly tool for small software components.

> *Low-code* is a software development approach that requires little to no *coding* in order to build applications and processes. A low-code development platform uses visual interfaces with simple logic and drag-and-drop features instead of extensive coding languages.

This way adaptions to the system and reactions to changes are quick and prompt. It also means that the system architecture should have a centralized database or a network of connected data sources. An advanced set of connections based on API (application program interfaces) make a seamless connection possible, inside the organization as well as with outside sources.

In a data-driven world, based on machine learning, the requirements for competition have less to do with specialization and more to do with a universal set of capabilities in data sourcing, processing, analytics, and algorithm development. The competitive advantages are based on the analytics of data and the use of algorithms. These new universal capabilities are reshaping strategy, business design, marketing and even control. When everybody has the same data it is important to analyze and update the data and to react timely to changes. Industry expertise has become less important, because it is not the industry that is leading but the use of the products and needs of customers.

This is a reason why platforms and collaborations, can be dominant in a wide range of markets. Need matching based on product features is different from product selling to users. Amazon, Alibaba are competitors in various markets although they have a different background and business proposition. Regardless of markets, they use the same infrastructure and machine learning (AI) techniques to make the right match for suppliers and customers. All markets have many similar technological foundations and employ common methods and tools. Strategies are shifting away from traditional differentiation based on cost, quality, and brand equity and specialized, vertical expertise and toward advantages like business network position, the accumulation of unique data, and the deployment of sophisticated analytics. Platforms can compete on price with the existing trade because of their efficiency and direct contact with customers also, because of the optimal processes and lack of supply chain. Between the platforms the competition is based on reputation, services and customer loyalty. Platforms such as Alibaba and Amazon work in networks, they outsource functions which were normally part of activities of a company, like logistics, staffing, payment systems.

Direct Contacts and Interactions

As a result, executives in companies that were born digital have assumptions about how transactions should be structured that are completely different from those of executives in legacy companies. What's more, because digital firms' structures are evolving all the time, their managers revisit those assumptions frequently. Direct-to-consumer businesses use the customer data to optimize the service offering, communication and proposition. The direct contacts are essential to gather the right data and to analyze the data based on AI techniques. This need will be stronger when the individual needs are no longer grouped with target groups. Distribution channels, supply chains are based on a transaction model with various links and individual values. The imploding of a supply chain is needed to get the right data. The distribution channel will be triggered from customers (or last link) and no longer from the suppliers. The control of processes will shift from supplier to buyer. In that case the demand-driven approach is successful. Those tactics simply aren't available to an incumbent selling through distributors, also because the digital businesses cut out intermediaries, they can be profitable at a much lower scale.

Company leaders will have to integrate agility and innovation into their broader organizations and communicate the new ways of digital thinking while minimizing disruption to their existing businesses.

Networks

As we see in the present development of supply in the market, companies are less independent as before. The focus on core functions and core activities is needed to stay competitive, but as a result it improved the "changeability" or agility of organizations. Companies work close together with other companies with complementary skills or core competences. The effect will be discussed in the next chapter. However, this kind of cooperation is only possible when networks are linking the companies together on a functional level. A business network is a complex network of companies, working together to accomplish certain objectives. These objectives, which are strategic and operational, are adopted by business networks based on their role in the market. Although a network is a generic way of working together, for companies a structured way is needed to take fully advantage, especially when the organizational structures are adapted to the network opportunities.

These strategic choices are:

- outsourcing;
- fixed connection; or
- purpose driven.

Outsourcing is the most strategic option, activities which are not core for a company are outsourced to external companies, although the control can still be part of managing an organization. Examples of outsourcing are staffing, logistics, recruiting, maintenance or premises. Control is possible based on strict guidelines or service levels, response times or costs. It is obvious that transport companies or logistic companies like DHL or FedEx can play this role. For internet companies they are an integrated part of the business, in other cases they are the preferred partners. Fixed connections are integrated in certain business functions. In some production companies supply levels are controlled by the suppliers. A supplier will supply new stocks when the stock is under a critical level. In the car industry suppliers are connected to the planning system of the production facility to anticipate on production levels for the supply of parts.

In retail the same kind of structure can be seen in the stock control of supermarkets, main stores or web shops. Suppliers can act based on the level of sales and the minimum stock levels. This can be a direct link of systems. Connection between the systems is based on APIs as we have seen before. The API is an interface to translate data formats from one system to another system. An API (application programming interface) is an information gateway that allows the back ends of software and services to communicate with one another. The API is the reason why systems can be connected. Platforms use the APIs for connection direct with the product offering or stock level of suppliers and the other way round.

Finally, a purpose-driven network is based on occasional needs of a company. Networks of specialists like consultants, transport, news, staffing are examples. Whenever a company needs a specialist or a special service, they can link direct to the relevant network. Academics have their own network for academic papers and publications. Mostly this are subscription-based networks but can also be "transactional" based.

All these networks will make a company less independent, but also more agile and will reduce costs. Networks are the result of the progress in information technology. A network is information based, it connects information from various sources and makes it approachable and useful for other sources. The networked information economy provided varied alternative platforms for communication which have their own source, culture and users. In the network the information can be owned by the distributor, like Google and other search engines, by the factory or supplier (like Apple) or by the creator like software developers. The network is a shift from the mass media to network-based information and collaboration. This has consequences as we see in business, but also private life. Although the network is vast, we see a closer relationship with preexisting relations. More and better contact through social media like LinkedIn (business), Facebook and Instagram (private) and specialized networks topic driven. We also see an increase in contacts with companies or people who were not easily reachable in pre-network period (pre-internet). Like decision makers in companies or professionals. In private life we see new contacts with old friends or acquittances. A network is linking all contact and companies together, but at the same time loosening the hierarchical levels to a kind of added value level (Benkler, 2006, p. 359). The basic observation that internet permits the emergence of new relationships that play a significant role in their partici-pants' lives (private or company) and are anchored in online communications continues to be made. Research shows that the new online relationships develop in addition to, rather than instead of, physical face-to-face human interactions in community and family, which turn out to be alive and well.

Conclusion

Gathering data is not enough for a change of strategy, the data should be analyzed and be used for transformation to a demand-driven strategy. Data is the fundament of an organization where the profile of customers and customer behavior is lead-ing. It is the knowledge of customer behavior which is linked to product offerings. Because knowledge of customers is the driving force behind this transformation, the need of a customer is the focus, product offering should be adapted. No longer is product leading sales, but customer context. Relationships are built around ful-filling the needs and expectations of customers. This will create loyalty, repeat sales and direct relations. The organizations will add services to products and will cooperate in networks to fulfill all the needs of the customers. Data gathering is crucial for an organization to be successful.

Student's Mind

Implementation of changes goes in three steps: optimalization, innovation and disruption.

1   Define the roadmap of change for a company?
2   What will be the reaction of the market on disruption?
3   How can you add value in this transformation process for customers?
4   Can you describe the orientations in the roadmap of change?
5   Please explain the role of data in this process.

Discussion Point

If you cannot afford a transformation strategy, which options do you have left?

STAKEHOLDERS	ENHANCE MAGNITUDE	REIMAGINE ACTIVITY	SHIFT DIRECTION
Customers	Invest in the growth of your core offerings; Emphasize brand equity over price; Expand sales and service teams; Invest in customer segmentation; Monitor industry trends and customer needs; Migrate customers to a recurring revenue model	Customize service offerings; Focus on areas of unique competence; Implement pricing optimization and bundling; Consider new forms of distribution; Outsource business functions; Copy rivals or white-label their products and services	Redefine your value proposition; Enter new product/service markets
Employees	Increase training on customer success; Increase recruitment; Accelerate R&D on next generation of current offering	Realign your organizational structure; Focus on specific skill sets; Fund R&D on next generation of technology; Promote cultural adaptation	Articulate new corporate focus and purpose; Retrain to match new required job skills; Offer early retirement and/or implement downsizing
Partners (SUPPLIERS AND DISTRIBUTORS)	Enlarge partner ecosystem; Rationalize partner ecosystem; Lower sourcing costs	Offer unique/enhanced value; Outsource business functions; Drive down partner costs	Partner to reduce barriers to entry in new markets; Explore potential for vertical integration
Investors	Consider economy-of-scale merger; Assess opportunity for economy-of-scope merger	Initiate industry consolidation; Merge to acquire new capabilities; Cut costs to enhance margins	Engage in portfolio diversification; Manage for cash returns; Seek potential purchasers
Communities	Invest in community economic development; Fund employee volunteering	Enhance focus on corporate reputation; Undertake community-based branding	Loan people to community organizations; Donate facilities

Figure 9.3 Overall view of changes to demand-driven structures.

References

Benkler, Y. (2006). *The Wealth of Networks*. New Haven, CT: Yale University Press.
Molenaar, C. N. A. (1997). *New Marketing*. Deventer: Kluwer uitgeverij.
Rogers, D. L. (2016). *The Digital Transformation Playbook*. New York: Columbia University Press.

10 The New Playground for Organizations

Changes in Markets

The model (Figure 10.1) shows the evolution of using internet for business. Of course, it is most easy to use all standard facilities, like a supply chain. Also, the investment is a major decision point and finally the acceptance of customers. The first movers on internet were companies where the acceptance of customers was high, the investments controlled, and it was easy to link to existing supply facilities like distribution channels. Nothing new, only different. A second group of new entrants came from service providers, information brokers. Low investment, but they need an audience. Because of the early adaptors a growing group of users could be reached and created the market for this group of companies.

Future Developments

These first movers used existing channels, but that changed when suppliers used new cloud facilities and when companies did focus more on agility and customer loyalty. A clear example is software as a service. The software was not sold anymore as a license, with a contract for a few years, but as a flexible usage model. Especially service companies and software companies (like

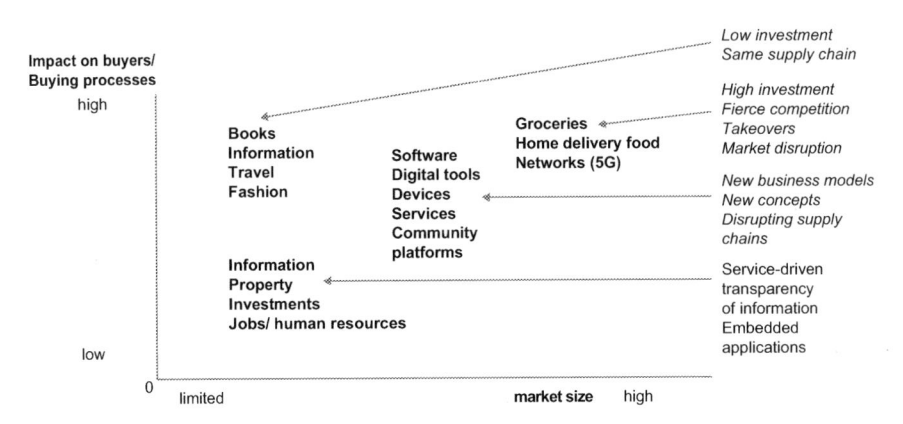

Figure 10.1 Market developments and impact on existing business.

DOI: 10.4324/9781003226161-10

Salesforce and Microsoft) where the first group changed the business model and the product concepts. The disruption in markets created a "snowball" effect to other markets. Now it was time to focus on more disruption in existing markets and to change big markets. The new companies used new digital possibilities to grow fast. The companies became focal companies in each market and put pressure on the existing companies to change accordingly: from doing digital to being digital. Next concepts like platforms, networks and service models are restructuring markets and companies and are facilitators of the demand-driven economy.

The use of networks and platform is closely linked with an integrated approach of business functions. From a demand-driven approach it is essential to decide about the ownership of the contacts and the link specifications of an API. The party that is leading in the contact has the data for more initiatives like direct communication. In the case of search engines, the business model is based on links of suppliers and connection with customers on request. The platform, like Google, is owner of the data, because they are owner of the connection to suppliers and customers. They charge suppliers for the links, advertising and ranking. A customer (buyer) does not pay for the information. The business model of Google is strongly based on adwords, advertising. In the case of selling products through a platform, the platform owns the data as well. They sell the product for a third party.

The future will be dominated by platforms and networks that form the basis of competition against traditional organizations, but also against one another. Three types of competition arise as a result:

- First, the competition between producers. The producers still compete through products or services, but these are now offered on a platform based on the needs of individual customers.
- Second, competition between platforms. Platforms may face competition from new platforms or from traditional platforms that want to expand into a new market.
- There is also competition between platforms and producers. Producers can create their own network within a platform and try to pull this network out of the platform. Platforms will have to avoid this.

From Pipeline to Platform Interactions

The classical business approach is a pipeline approach, inflexible, supply-driven and lacking actual market information. Therefore, this linear value chain is being replaced by the more interactive platform structure based on relationships. The values may be created, changed, exchanged and consumed in a variety of ways and places all made possible by the connections that the platform facilitates.

A pipeline, like the supply chain will manage each step and specially the next steps in the process. The distance between a customer and a factory is long, the

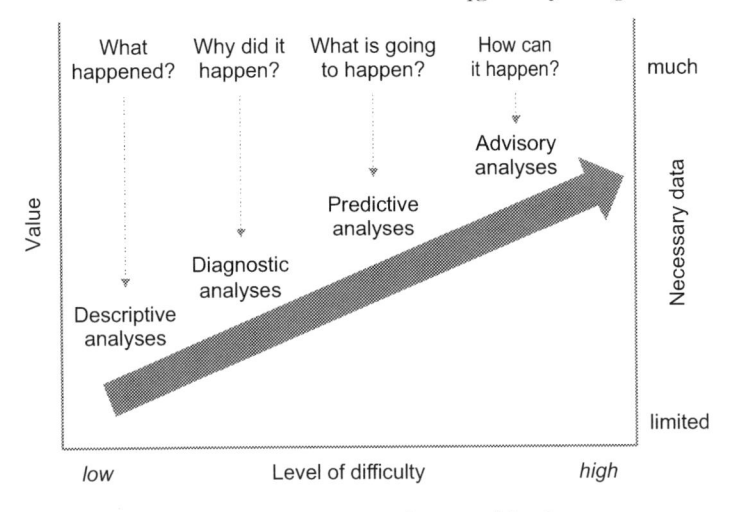

Figure 10.2 Is marketing still a competition or the use of data?

information is only shared between all the links in the chain (pipeline). The most powerful platforms are the multi-sided platforms because they get direct information from customers and will match this information with the product information of a supplier. A platform has the function of a middleman supporting two markets, the buyer's market, and the seller's market. Each market will influence each other. The more customers are interested, the more buyers will sell the articles and vice versa. This is what is called the network effect.

Network Effects

Same-Side Effects

What is the impact of one side of the market (consumers) on the other side (suppliers)? There are cross–side effects, but also an impact on the same side (suppliers on suppliers and consumers on consumers).

Organizational Effects

It's a challenge for organizations to change the culture and structure. No longer is it a matter of controlling the pipeline but is a matter of controlling a buying process. The need for data is imminent, but data is the source for machine learning. For an organization is data management, agility and prediction essential. The hierarchy of an organization will change to an outside-in structure. A change of hierarchy and culture. The main resistance from change is within a company, the people. The want to keep things as they are:

- legacy systems;
- legacy cultures; and
- legacy skill sets.

For a change to a demand-driven organization it is essential to change the culture in an organization. An internal culture should change to an external culture. A focus on production and transaction should change to a focus on customer needs and interaction. Mostly this means that processes must be re-defined, communication must change to direct communication and interaction and finally people must be trained. For this change in the organization the people are important. A skill set based on customer contact, customer needs and customer loyalty is needed. Training is a part of this change but also to get new people with these skills. It might mean a change in HRM and a change in staff. Not everybody can be trained successfully.

The main problem for a change in structure and culture are the people, from board to production. People do not like change because they like routines. Routines lead to confidence, change to uncertainty. Reluctance about the role of data, not just for analyses about the past but especially for prediction. Old competitive tools like price or design will be less important. Competition will take place about knowledge (of behavior and preferences) and about direct and relevant communication

The Incumbent Fights Back: Pipelines Becoming Platforms and Networks

Platforms are disruptive not only by displacing some of the world's biggest incumbent forms, but also by transforming familiar business processes, value creation and consumer behavior as well as altering the structure of major industries. Some of the major questions which should be asked to coordinate the change are outsourcing questions and about the impact of cloud and out-sourced service (like SaaS).

- How can we empower outside partners to create products and services that will generate new forms of value for our existing customers?
- Are there ways we can network with current competitors to produce valuable new services for customers? It is even possible to cooperate with competitors because selling will be buying based on customer preferences.
- How can the value of the goods and services we currently provide be enhanced through new data streams, interpersonal connections, and curation tools?
- Vertical integration, horizontal integration or otherwise?

The leaders of incumbent companies who understand the new business model can begin building tomorrow's platforms in a way that not only leverages their existing assets but strengthens and reinforces them.

Strategy

The swiftness of Alibaba's ascent and similar companies is largely a function of the new realities of platform competition and network cooperation: explosive networks and strong economies of scale. Alibaba and other platform companies like Uber and Airbnb have compressed the whole middle layer of retail. That way it is more efficient, the pipeline will implode, and a company has direct contact, and knowledge, of the end user. New business concepts are based on this kind of cooperation, and knowledge, between partners and will cut out the middleman. The network or platform will replace this role with data and algorithms. It is a matter of trust if people will accept this, a replacement of humans with algorithms. In a demand-driven strategy the platforms are shrewdly leveraging another enormous competitive strength of platforms, the ability to seamlessly incorporate the resources and connections of outside partners into the activities and capabilities of the platform.

The nature of competition has transformed from the classical approach that many businesspeople take for granted to a new approach where the role of the customer is more dominant. In that case the risk has changed from a risk for buyers (*caveat emptor*) to a risk for sellers (*caveat vendor*). In the past new protection laws for customers guaranteed less risk, but was still a supply, transaction approach. The new business concepts are an interaction approach where a customer will specify the needs. It is up to the seller to fulfill the needs, this is a change of power, but also the risk will change of a transaction, from buyer to seller. The present law will still protect the buyer, the business approach will strengthen this protection.

The approach of *caveat emptor* means let the buyer beware and the approach of *caveat vendor* means let the seller beware. The change is taking place because the customer is leading in the buying process in the current competitive market and all marketing efforts of a company revolve round him. The *caveat emptor* principle arises primarily from the asymmetry of information between a purchaser and a seller. The information is asymmetric because the seller tends to possess more information regarding the product than the buyer. Therefore, the buyer assumes the risk of possible defects in the purchased product.

If there is no explicit warranty regarding the product's quality, then it is the buyer's responsibility to gather all the information about the purchased product. At the same time, the seller must not misrepresent the product or provide the buyer with false information about the product. Browsing for information and giving the right search criteria are important in the buying process. Now Google is taking a major place in this process, but that is changing to the platforms and networks. Big platforms like Amazon fulfill more searches than Google, for instance, in America. Browsing is a standard feature in all modern internet concepts. Airbnb allows a person to search through options organized not only according to their own characteristics, but also by quality, number of rooms, price and mapping geolocations. A user can strike deals immediately through Airbnb without leaving the platform. This makes Airbnb far easier to use and enabled the platform to rapidly outgrow others.

The shift in approach from *caveat emptor* to *caveat vendor* has brought into the picture a new concept termed as *consumerism*, which means any movement to protect and inform the consumers against defective goods and services or unsafe products or misleading/fraudulent trade practices which are practiced by the seller. Consumerism has both positive and negative impacts on society. The positive effect brought in by consumerism is that it protects the rights and interest of the consumers by spreading awareness against unfair trade practices or any fraudulent/misleading act. However, there are certain adverse effects that the concept of consumerism has brought along in the sense that it has led to increase in demand, because of the increased awareness which is resulting in a speedy depletion of the available resources. It also has a negative impact that, with the increase in the demand, the resources are being depleted.

Peter Drucker's dictum is well known: the purpose of business is to create a customer. In a world where sustainable advantage is an illusion, a company's relationship with customers is its only lasting source of value.

- Networks remake markets, not just respond to them. Rather than re-dividing a pie of more or less static size, platform businesses often grow the pie. Examples include Amazon with publishing, Airbnb alongside the traditional hotel industry and Uber with the taxi industry.
- Platforms and networks turn businesses inside out, moving managerial influence from inside to outside the firm's boundaries.

Those two points add a dramatic layer of complexity to business competition. It creates competition on three levels:

- One platform with another, as in the music world (Apple against Sony).
- A platform competes with its partners, like Amazon within the marketplace. This is a delicate and dangerous move; it can strengthen the platform, but it can be a short-term gain.
- A third level is the competition between partners for positions within the platform eco-structure.

The shift from protecting value inside the firm to creating value outside the firm means that the crucial factor is no longer ownership but opportunity, while the main tool is no longer dictation but persuasion. The resource-based view assumes that a firm must own or control the inimitable resource. In the world of networks, the nature of the inimitable resources shifts from physical assets to access to customer-producer networks and the interaction that results. In fact, it can be better for a firm not to own physical resources, since eschewing ownership enables it to grow more quickly, and react quicker to changes in markets or customer behavior.

The new playground for organizations has an external side and an internal side. In this case external developments are leading to internal changes. In the supply pipeline concept, it was the internal efficiency that was leading and had the control over the supply chain. The change to external makes a buyer leading; the internal changes should facilitate this change. Companies who do not react quickly enough will be confronted with new players, new start-ups. The new playground is dominated by the demand of customers (BtoB and BtoC). A dominant factor for success is the knowledge of customers and buying behavior. Analyses should predict changes and initiated processes (like communication). Machine learning, artificial intelligence including deep learning are decisive about the success of a company. A company should restructure to these changes.

Conclusion

The nature of competition in this world is very different from that in the world of traditional pipeline business. The competition is no longer based on the five forces of Porter to protect vital parts of the company, but is concentrated on customers, interactions and value creating. This competition will change the market structure, market competition and will lead to new market leaders (focal companies). Too late in changing or too reluctant to adapt to market changes or use the new opportunities on an effective way will lead to failure to compete (the Nokia effect). Pipeline efficiency is not a competitive force anymore for the future. Start-ups are more flexible and more focused on creating value for customers. Interaction is the basis for the future.

Student's Mind

1   How can you overcome the reluctance to change within a company?
2   What will be the role of a focal company in this change and how can you predict a future focal company?
3   What are the main objectives for outsourcing, internal resources?
4   What are the reasons to collaborate in a network or a platform?
5   How can you create value in this new playfield?

Discussion Point

What is the moment that an existing company should change to a demand focus and a new business model?

11 Competition and Technology

Technological developments have impacted the marketplace and have specially influenced the way companies nowadays view competition. The impact of technologies has modified the way firms view their own customers, and has created a demand-driven economy. Furthermore, most companies now provide platforms which offer connectivity and a more personalized process for purchasing for each client. Companies have to maintain a close and loyal relationship with their customers, while constantly having to collaborate with their network. All in all, technology will soon become the main point that would help firms continue improving and staying ahead in the marketplace.

According to Roblek, Meško and Krapež (2016) the Fourth Industrial Revolution was presented in Germany in 2011, also known as "Industry 4.0." With that being said, this revolution is characterized by embracing the development of technologies which provide digitalization, cyber-systems and even more general automation (Roblek, Meško & Krapež, 2016). Belsky (2019) argued that the Fourth Industrial Revolution will be marked by the years in which automation will take over at least 40% of current jobs. However, the technological developments do not only lead to changes in people's jobs, but rather change the entire economy (Roblek, Meško & Krapež, 2016). Now, the marketplace has not only modified its level of competition, but as well has changed the focus on its drive. The fourth revolution is characterized by the shift from a supply-driven economy to a demand-driven economy.

Hence, the focus of the supply chain is not on cost-reduction anymore. The technological developments have created a connected community in which customers are now driven by mobile technology (KPMG, 2019). Supply chain management is now about providing differentiation, creating value and fulfillment to their customers. Companies now have to focus on the demand, on developing their products and services to the public's desire, the customization of the marketplace is now taking place and the economy is no longer focused on just changing the prices to sell, therefore, overall business models are changing.

Technological developments changed the way in which businesses operate by offering multiple beneficial possibilities to which businesses need to adapt. There are some companies which are still trying to digitalize processes but this is only an initial step of transformation. Companies as Uber, Airbnb and Bol.

DOI: 10.4324/9781003226161-11

com are taking a new approach by "being digital." These companies do not try to optimize business processes by the forces of technology and do not build software, instead they use technology as a mediator, to enable business and social interactions that are essential to create an ecosystem. These organizations have better knowledge of customer behavior and a greater possibility to match their offering with a customer's need, therefore representing a threat to existing organizations. Technologies can be applied in multiple business processes from manufacturing to delivery offering multiple possibilities to which organizations need to adapt.

The Consequences of Technological Developments

Technological developments have quickly penetrated management and manufacturing processes. During the fourth revolution, a convergence between manufacturing technologies and communication technologies can be seen, allowing easier collaboration and exchange of information within businesses and customers. The change of customers' needs and the necessity to improve technological capability pressured the marketplace to create new dynamics, and new products were introduced rapidly. Therefore, the digital transformation of manufacturing does not only change the quality of the production but also the efficiency of each process, including the supply chain. Many factors such as production planning, production control, scheduling, process and product optimization are consequences of the impact of advanced technological developments in the manufacturing of businesses.

Moreover, technological innovation, during the past couple of years, has disrupted many traditional processes in the marketplace. Companies such as Netflix have grown solely through their innovative expansion through the internet. In the current marketplace, companies have to adapt to customers' needs, and technological developments have offered a smooth way through the creation of new platforms and products for buyers that are more and more in need of customized ideas. Furthermore, businesses are able to improve their cost, delivery time and overall quality; ultimately the market can easily develop new and innovative strategies.

In the current marketplace, companies have to adapt to customers' needs, and technological developments have offered a smooth way through the creation of new platforms and products for buyers that are more and more in need of customized ideas. Disruptive technologies also become essential for certain behavior recognition and identification of the reasons for such behavior. With the use of technological tools, via data analysis and finding links between data elements, consumer behavior can be studied and predicted easily.

Relevance of Michael Porter's View on Competition in Today's World

In order to discuss the traditional approach in relation to competition, we can compare Porter's Five Forces model. In his model, Michael Porter assumes that there are five forces that determine competitiveness: *supplier power* (suppliers' ability to increase prices easily), *buyer power* (buyers' ability to decrease prices), *competitive rivalry* (the number and capability of your competitors), *threat of substitution* (customers' ability to find substitutes) and *threat of new entry* (ability to enter your market). According to Porter, there were mainly two ways in which a company would develop a strategy to compete in the market:

- Firstly, companies would aim at becoming low-cost producers, and that includes scale and operational efficiency. Therefore, many times the focus was on lowering the price of the product or service to attract more and more customers, and this strategy was often considered successful.
- The second way companies would compete in the market was by implementing a differentiation strategy, which requires the ability to develop innovative new products and services. This strategy was as well considered important, and many companies grew into successful businesses due to their creative ideas, and the digitalization helped the development of new products that helped businesses prosper in a competitive growing market (Porter, 1979).

There are a few issues with these assumptions based on the change to demand focus. First, based on Michael Porter's assumptions it is clear that competition is key. This point of view is supported by Porter's thinking that the market is considered attractive if you are one of the few businesses—the less competitors the less power they and customers have, if there are less substitutes and high barriers to entry. However, the power shift towards customers that is caused by the Fourth Industrial Revolution and the application of machine learning forces to rethink this statement:

- Customer focus and later customer behavior has become an essential element of success for businesses.
- Second, in today's world, markets and competitors are dynamic and boundaries just do not exist anymore. Competitors can bring a challenge from all over the world and from other market sectors. It means that a competitive advantage no longer comes from low cost or product differentiation, instead it is about out-thinking others, rethinking business models and experiences. This is where technological possibilities like networks and platforms are important, especially if they lie at the core of a business model.
- Third, organizations are part of an ecosystem, a value chain. A traditional linear model of suppliers is no longer relevant. By focusing on your product and core competencies the connection to reality that is changing so fast can be easily lost. Partnering now becomes essential; there may be others who can do better. Networks and collaboration become key for competitive advantage as value is created via interaction and not by the producer.

- Lastly, economies of scale are not 100% successful. In the past, to be successful, businesses were entering homogeneous markets with undifferentiated products to win in volume. Today, vision and ideas are more important. By being small, agile and smart tremendous success can still be achieved.

Therefore, based on aspects considered above Porter's model is no longer sufficient in today's world. Furthermore, it is important to note that such changes in markets are influenced by the applications of online platforms and networks.

Also, Tom Peters and Robert Waterman, authors of *In Search of Excellence* warned that competition will be different in the future (Peters & Waterman, 1982): After centuries of competing based on mass, organizations now are competing based on time. We have now new management tools to deal with such a profound change. While information technology is the undisputed engine of this transformation, nothing less than new rules will increase the odds of success, in political or economic warfare.

1   *Use of leading-edge information technology.* Merely keeping up with the Joneses in the application of information technology (IT) is not enough. One must be an IT pioneer.
2   *Radical reorganization.* Too many leap in the latest IT tools and largely overlook issues of organizational structure. Radical structural redesign must come first, or else one ends up, in the words of a respected industry consultant, "automating [your] worst mistakes." In short, most of the hierarchy found in the traditional firm must be eliminated, and the walls between functional staff must be destroyed.
3   *Replacement of adversarial relations with partnerships.* Traditional adversarial dealings, inside the firm as well as outside, eat up hours which are not available when a company is forced to compete in time. In the future, product developers, marketers, operations people, and field service groups must become allies, if speedy innovation is to be achieved.

A better approach in today's world is the value approach: or why do customers buy? This question will get an individual answer based on personal motives from an organization or a person. As we have seen before, we can detect four value drivers: functional, economic, emotional and cohesion. Based on those individual values we should develop drivers for each value proposition and define the support which is needed with data and machine learning.

The clusters are defined with machine learning by interpreting the data. Who will react to product changes, new releases (functional benefits), who will react to promotion or discounts (economic benefits), who can be influenced by vloggers, testimonial or video, new releases (emotional benefits) and finally what are the links with social media, communities (cohesion)?

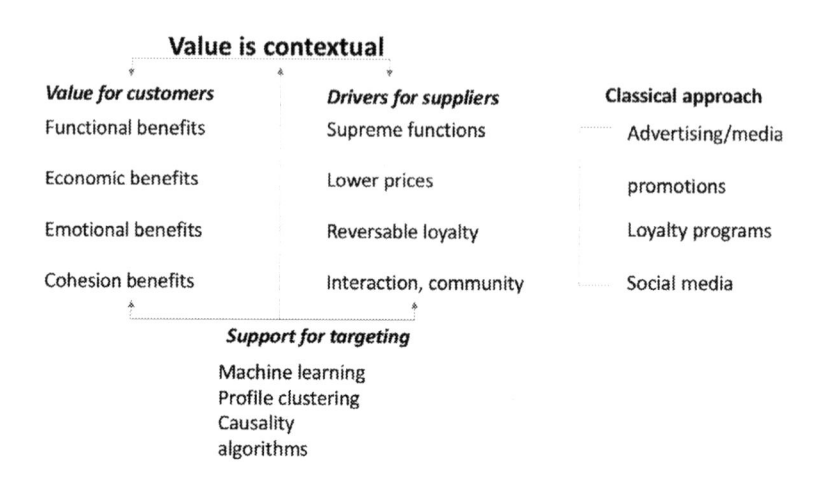

Figure 11.1 Value propositions.

Using the old media is a very broad approach of the target group. Defining the clusters with machine learning and using the profiles and algorithm will give more insight into the behavior of the customer per cluster. Not only is this a direct form of communication, but also a fine tuning within the cluster. The competition is no longer a matter of focusing on classical competition tools like price or availability but is more linked to the strategy of Peters and Waterman (1982), or Treacy and Wiersema (1995):

- Product leadership is linked to functional benefits and will fit product orientation strategies.
- Operational excellence to economic benefits.
- Customer intimacy to emotional and cohesion benefits (Treacy & Wiersema, 1995).

Peters and Waterman (1982) specified two main strategies:

- a price strategy which can be linked to economic benefits; and
- a diversity strategy which can be linked in various forms to the other values.

Competing on value is competing on customer preference and loyalty. This is a sustainable competition strategy because it will motivate customers for repeat sales. Competitors have to give added value to individual customers above the value of existing suppliers. The use and sophistication of machine learning and algorithms are decisive for the competitive advantages.

The Shift from Supply-Driven to Demand-Driven and its Impact on Competition

With the adoption of the internet a few years ago, competition between companies increased, because it was easier for customers to compare prices and quality differences online. Due to the rise of competition, companies also saw their margins drop, causing firms to lower their prices. Customers gained more power with the introduction of the internet (Figure 11.2). Therefore, competition is changing, because customer behavior is transforming more and more. As a result, a major shift from the usual to a demand-driven economy was facilitated.

Before the introduction of the internet, companies were supply oriented. They produced and sold as many products as possible without actually listening to the wishes and desires of customers. Companies first produced and designed a product or service and then they would try to find a market for the product. Companies didn't care whether these products led to the same loyalty as previous or other product designs. As long as it was a unique product, or it was the cheapest. Companies were not aware of customer preferences and that the needs in the future might be different. Between companies and customers, there was no good interaction, but then the shift from product orientation to customer orientation came, as shown in the orientation model.

When a company uses customer orientation, they first research customer needs, and then the company produces a product. A customer nowadays has a larger amount of choices due to the various opportunities to buy online from all over the world, so a firm must respond to special customer needs, especially considering that there are large sets of related products available to choose from. Thus, companies need to focus on what customers want and expect from a product so the customers will buy their product and come back because they are satisfied. Companies should start asking their customers questions such as:

- "Why would you buy this?"
- "Why would you not buy this?"
- "Who are you?"
- "What motivates you to buy a product?"
- "What are your needs?"

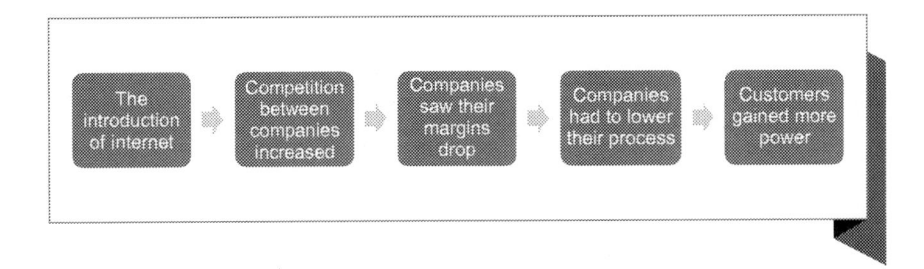

Figure 11.2 Customers gained power with the introduction of the internet.

Customer acquisition is important for organizations but customer retention is more important. Satisfaction affects customer retention, therefore, in order to stay competitive a customer-centric vision is essential and has to be applied.

The Shift in Competitive Advantage (from Resources to Ecosystems) and the Role of Data in Competition

A major shift in competitive advantage took place with a move in business models from "pipes" to "platforms." This move was a result of the internet restructuring the way in which businesses create and deliver value. In relation to the so-called "pipes," value is created upstream and consumed downstream following a linear path (like a traditional manufacturing supply chain), meaning that each product goes through a sequence of processes that add value to the end product. However, due to increased connectedness and the rise of artificial intelligence, it is not the same nowadays. Now with platforms, an infrastructure of communication is created, which allows participants to co-create and exchange value with each other. For example, Uber coordinates drivers and passengers towards economic exchanges. Platforms can facilitate remote (like Airbnb) and in-person interactions (like Tinder), and movement of resources (like Uber). Therefore, value is increased via interactions, not through a sequence of processes.

Changes in business models lead to a shift in competitive advantage. The resource-based view on competition is changing to a network view (including platforms). It means that the competitive advantage is no longer gained through ownership and organization of resources, but instead via interaction, matching resources from producers with customers. For example, being highly focused on processes, hotels own a lot of inventory, when a platform like Airbnb focuses on matching supply and demand via data processing and improvement of algorithms. Owning a lot of data and then processing and implementing it, allows for a better match of customers' needs and therefore gives a greater opportunity for success.

The role of data in this view is just tremendous. In order to be competitive it is important to use and analyze data, and take action based on the results. As previously mentioned, finding links between customers' actions via data analysis allows us to predict customer behavior. Those players who possess this knowledge will have a major competitive advantage and will easily overcome their rivals. Competitive strength is now based on multiple aspects:

- the transparency in information, communication processes prior to the sale (which allows for a better customer experience making the choice easier);
- effective customer support based on specific data (analysis of data regarding customer behavior);
- total product concept that forms trust, unequivocal touchpoint experience with an integral application of service;
- communication and interaction (quality of customer experience); and lastly,

- algorithms being a basis for communication and predictions (data collection and analysis giving better knowledge about customer and pushing better communication).

In addition, it is important to note that with the transparency data offers and with the existence of a large number of providers, companies face a new competition problem. The transaction point is no longer at the end of the supply chain. It is actually when the buying process begins. This highlights the importance of data since a very good knowledge about the customer and purchasing behavior is required. Furthermore, earlier a bond with a customer was shop/supplier based (it could be local presence), but today due to the extensive internet developments as "a fully fledged place" in the buying process, companies have to compete with each new transaction again and again. For online shops it means that the focus has to be on making everything for a great customer experience, constantly improving it and building trust so they will come back again and again—this is a new approach towards bonding with customers.

Industry Boundaries Getting Blurred: How Does it Affect Competition?

Another development on the new view on competition is that industry boundaries are getting blurred. Back in the days a company that was not defined by one industry was rare. Now with the development of technology things are different. Digitization and advancements in technology, such as Artificial Intelligence, enable us to realize synergies that were previously beyond the reach of enterprises. These new opportunities offered by digitization have incentivized companies to enter unrelated sectors and challenge the companies in those sectors. So an increasing number of industries has converged and will converge under newer and more dynamic alignments. Several developments like biotechnology, artificial intelligence, 3D printing and virtual reality will accelerate this process.

Creation of ecosystems that are able to play in multiple industries will bring a hard time for those players who are not members of digital ecosystems. Traditional companies have to compete against companies and industries that were never viewed as competitors. But what are the priorities for companies who compete in the borderless economy? First, it is important to adopt an ecosystem mindset. In particular, a view on competitors and opportunities should be broadened (becoming multisectoral). The view should define the ecosystems and industries where change will be fastest and should identify the critical new sources of value most meaningful for expanding a customer base. Questions like "What surprising, disruptive boundary shifts can we imagine—and try to get ahead of?" and "How can we turn our physical assets and long-established customer relationships into genuine consumer insights to secure what we have and stake out an advantage over our competitors—including the digital giants?" must be asked. Answering the questions, new strategic priorities should be created and existing business goals and incentives are more likely to be adjusted.

Second, data needs to be analyzed. The role of data in a network view on competition was already highlighted, therefore to compete effectively, large amounts of data need to be collected, and capabilities for storage, processing and translation of data need to be developed (Atluri et al., 2017). Furthermore, the data diversity plays an important role. It can be achieved via partnerships (even across different segments) which can enable you to create value more broadly (Atluri et al., 2017). Third, building emotional ties with customers is important. To create the ties data, content and digital engagement models are key. Data is to be used for customization of offerings; content is a tool to attract customers' attention; and digital engagement models are to be used for creation of unique customer experience (creation of a journey). In this initiative an essential question to ask is "What else can we provide with simplicity and speed in order to strengthen our customer bond?" For example, Google's launch of Gmail and Chrome was not because they already had a huge customer base and just wanted to get more revenue. It was made to maintain their customer base and expand it further. Lastly, a change in partnership paradigm is required, in particular a wide and diverse partnership base is essential. Partners need to be found regardless of geographical and industrial boundaries. What white spaces still need to be filled in and what are the mutual benefits? Moreover, a good flow of information with partners has to be ensured.

Is it Crucial for Companies to Apply Technology in Order to Retain their Competitive Strength?

Due to a lot of technological developments the last few years, more and faster new developments were made and designed. These disruptive, new technologies are influencing and complementing each other. So it's important for companies to have a strategy for creating value that is unique compared with other providers within the network. A company is ahead of its competitors, when a company continues to innovate and creates value that is unique.

But it is hard for organizations and competitors to face the rapidly evolving technology and emerging business models. It will create huge uncertainties for the future. Organizations that change their strategy from the core, to keep up with the emerging technologies, can expect a lot of resistance from their employees. But why do employees resist change? Often a decision to change in an organization is taken by the higher management and afterwards employees are poorly too little informed why a decision has been taken. To create a unity, a company has to create a context for change. How does a company cope with the resistance of employees? A company has to inform and educate employees at all levels in the company's strategy and a company has to motivate and position employees to support the strategy and the performance goals. It is also important to keep informing your employees, not just in the beginning of a change. Ask employees for their opinion. What went well? What can be done better? It is important that employees also make suggestions for improvements. If you implement a new strategy, it is important to integrate the strategy completely. It is not smart to start with a department first and after some time start with another department to implement a change in the organization. So a company must implement a new strategy in all departments at the same time. It is also important to keep in mind: organizations don't change, people do. It is the people in the organization that will make the change a success or a failure. To keep in mind: resistance is inevitable; significant change is a disruption in people's expectations about the future.

Companies that are scared or rigid to change because right now the company is making profit will be overtaken by other competitors in the end. This also applies to companies who are not sure what to do and wait too long to take steps to change. The "if I ignore it, it will go away" method is also common with companies who are scared of change. Also, with this method competitors who do change and innovate will overtake them. Besides being scared of change, companies often blindly follow their competitors in the industry. When a company blindly follows their competitors, the company is likely to result in failure. That is because this company doesn't acknowledge and embrace their own strengths and values, and because they are following another company, they do not create value. The company who started the change will gain the value.

This will lead to platforms (network based with a great application of technology and data analysis) becoming the new dominant players in the market and competing with large online shops (application of technologies and well-known players). Also, an emergence of niche players (disruptors) will take place. These market players will focus on small customer groups with specific needs, targeting a specific aspect, and will devote particular attention towards close communication.

Differences in Ways Platforms Scale in Comparison with Traditional Business Models and How it Will Affect Competition

The traditional business models, a company designs a product, the product is manufactured and is later sold to a customer, seem no longer to apply. In the traditional business model the value was produced upstream. We are shifting from traditional, linear pipelines to platforms. A platform allows external participants, consumers and producers, to exchange and co-create value with each other. A platform is therefore not a straight line or a pipe, but an open, decentralized infrastructure of all different external partners. The motion from straight pipelines to platforms is caused by three different shifts.

- The first shift is the focus from consumers to producers. In the old days the producer created the value for the consumer. In a platform everyone in the network, producer and consumer, creates value together.
- The second shift is the shift from resources to ecosystems. Pipeline companies competed on resources and market shares. However, in the world of platforms there is no such thing as resources. Everything is about adding

value in the ecosystem of producers and consumers through using and collecting data.

- The last shift is the shift from processes to interactions. Creating value on its own as a company is no longer the way of producing. Value is created by resources through interactions in the whole ecosystem.

These three shifts influence building and maintaining competitive advantages. We are still in the beginning of the shifts from pipes to platforms, some industries have adopted the platform model more than other industries. Although some companies and governments see platforms as a threat, they will be growing in the coming years. Platforms rely on networks, if there are no players in the network, then no value can be exchanged. This is the network effect, very important for a successful platform. Platforms and ecosystems also rely on data, the more data you collect as a platform, the more you know about your customers. If you know your customers well, you can also better understand, satisfy them and co-create more value. Algorithms are the decision makers in an ecosystem. Algorithms will increasingly take over managerial tasks such as decision-making. By using so much data, real-time customization, producing something based on one consumer's preferences, is possible. The last difference with pipes is that the hierarchy in a platform becomes flat and decentralized. Good and fast contact is needed in an ecosystem and this is not possible with a hierarchical structure. Every part in the ecosystem must be able to communicate with each other in order to exchange value.

What Should a Company Do to Keep up with Competition and to Stay Relevant?

A company should not keep track of who is a competitor. Neither should a company look how to compete against a competitor. A company should look at whether there is a chance for co-action and co-creating with competitors. A collaboration will create value in a network instead of lower your profits, as Michael Porter claimed. The old way of adding value in the chain was collaboration within the supply chain, this was a linear growing process. Nowadays, there is a network with components who are connected to each other. A platform is a connected world with multiple sides, adding value in the middle. A platform's growing process is exponential because users in the network influence all other users. A platform is based on the network effect. The network effect is based on allowing everyone to join the network and all components in the network give value to each other.

Moreover, a firm as an isolated organization will disappear in the future. However, the question still remains: What are the best options for a company with a traditional strategy and with the will to change?

- The first option is to develop a new concept themselves. You can think of developing a platform themselves.

- The second option is to join a platform that already exists.
- The last option is to focus on other added value they can provide as a niche player. In this way, they can challenge other platforms with a specialization.

When a company does not choose one of these options, it is doomed to fail as an organization. The choice right now is: adapt to the possibilities of new technologies or fail.

Student's Mind

1   How can you compete on values and not on price?
2   What is the main focus of competition in the future?
3   How can data be a competitive tool?
4   Can algorithms be a decisive factor in competition?
5   Should a company focus on existing product/markets or is a different strategy better?

Discussion Point

Explain the competitive strategy of Amazon.com.

References

Atluri, V. et al. (2017). Competing in a World of Sectors without Borders. Retrieved from www.mckinsey.com/business-functions/mckinsey-analytics/our-insights/comp eting-in-a-world-of-sectors-without-borders

Belsky, L. (2019). Where Online Learning Goes Next. *HBR*, November 26.

KPMG. (2019). *The Road to Everywhere: The Future of Supply Chain*. London: KPMG. Retrieved from https://assets.kpmg/content/dam/kpmg/xx/pdf/2019/11/future-of-supply-chain-the-road-to-everywhere.pdf

Peters, T. J. & Waterman, R. H., Jr. (1982). *In Search of Excellence: Lessons from America's Best-Run Companies*. New York: Harper Business.

Porter, M. (1979). How Competitive Forces Shape Strategy. Retrieved from https://hbr.org/1979/03/how-competitive-forces-shape-strategy

Roblek, V., Meško, M. & Krapež, A. (2016). A Complex View of Industry 4.0. *Sage Open*, 6(2). Retrieved from https://journals.sagepub.com/doi/10.1177/2158244016653987

Treacy, M. & Wiersema, F. (1995). *The Discipline of Market Leaders*. Reading, MA: Addison-Wesley.

12 The Road Ahead

But what is the advantage for an existing organization to change from supply-driven to demand-driven? Networks and platforms have no boundaries, neither physical nor virtual. The new technology, artificial intelligence, has the power to make combinations that were not possible before and on the user side the smartphone and the computer are a new way of communication for buyers. New development techniques, the APIs, the apps, and cloud computing, ensure that access for the user is simple and that the necessary software is already present. It is just a matter of using the possibilities on the best possible way. As a result, the focus is on the integration of the various programs and using them in the best interest of buyers.

The networks combine various suppliers and buyers, the platform is directly accessible everywhere thanks to the application of cloud computing. This is the case for business applications, but also for buyers and sellers (multi-sided platforms). This can be seen by Uber, where you can order a taxi locally in many countries, while the software is centrally located on a host (anywhere in the world). All applications are managed and controlled from the US. The commission also goes directly to Uber for payments for services. Rolling out around the world is easy. Just search for car owners, who want to drive as a taxi and connect them to the platform. Its simplicity ensures rapid acceptance from both providers and users. The flexibility for the user and the car owner is also an advantage. You will be charged for the use.

Important Changes

Customer Behavior

Customers are better informed than ever before. As somebody once said: "nowadays there is no reason anymore to be stupid, all answers are available on internet."

Based on this knowledge customers (consumers and companies) will use this knowledge to be more dominant in a buying process. Transparency of markets will support this empowerment of buyers. Consumers are more aware of the world they live in or the world they will leave to their children. Issues like security, environment, child labor, poverty and power play will be more

DOI: 10.4324/9781003226161-12

important in the final discussion. Part of this is the new legislation on labor, child protection, environment, companies, privacy and customer protection. All these rules and legislation will empower the customer and will lead to change in markets and companies.

Internationalization

Because of internet, mobility and international companies will change the scope of suppliers and consumers. Language will no longer be a problem for anybody. English will be the standard language for at least some time. Internet is just a communication network between computers, people, companies and devices. Everybody is part of this worldwide communication network but will use it how they want. Because of all the available information and functions consumers will be more individual than ever before. Machine learning will make clusters of similar behavior if it lasts. And recalculate whenever needed.

Consolidation

The business world is really entangled in partnerships and networks. Companies will focus on their added values and will specialize based on values, profit pools, skills and partnerships. This will be international networks replacing the existing, analogue, supply chains. A supply chain is a chain of independent companies each with a different function. In a network all companies are linked (and depend) together based on a value chain approach. The total network is the value chain where every participant will fulfill a function, the total network is an independent entity. See it as a necklace of beads. In a supply chain every bead is independent and can be part of everything. In a network we talk about an integrated necklace. The beads are no longer independent but linked to each other and just fulfilling a small part of the total necklace. These companies are dependent on the total collaboration in a network. Specialization and curation are inevitable. In every market there will be a dominant network, taking the place of a focal company. Networks will compete with networks, like platforms will compete with platforms. There will only be room for very specialized companies or local players with high impact in their market.

Platforms/Networks

As a part of a network, we can see all kinds of platforms. A platform has a specific function and will link all stakeholders, B2B and B2C, with a common interest. Platforms can be single sided, by combining similar stakeholders like people with the same interest, background, or purpose. Also, companies with a similar focus. Examples of consumers are the platforms for sport, health, alumni, immigrants. For companies platforms of professional like physiotherapist, car dealers, same location. In all cases it is a matter of sharing and collaboration. Find what you have in common and work together. This way a platform is a part of a value network or is the value network. Examples are Booking.com, Uber.com, Airbnb.com.

Added Value of Collaborations

Start-ups have no past and no fixed resources, so they can quickly build or join a network. This is the great advantage of internet applications, as we see with Google and Priceline. Other existing organizations do not have this advantage and must make a choice. That is not all, they have also a business model and an earning model based on a supply of goods or services, not based on individual demand matching or collaboration on common interest or common purpose. A choice between starting with a new business separate from the existing organization, where a choice can be made for your own management model or to join an existing network or platform. Existing organizations are almost always organized hierarchically, with the advantage of control and management, but the disadvantage of slow decision-making and slow information flows. It is precisely the existing systems, structures and organizational form (including culture) that are obstacles to the development of a platform and to join a network, unless this can become part of the existing products or services. This involves an integrated concept with its own structure with connections to external parties via the so-called APIs (interfaces). This has been the choice of Telecom companies, as well as Apple or Amazon.com. In both cases, the application is integrated within the range in such a way that its own proposition (sale of telephones or other products) is strengthened.

For organizations with many committed resources and often a lot of investments, platform applications are used to generate additional sales or attract additional customers. As a result, these companies also want to adjust their business model. Smartphone manufacturers such as Samsung and Xiaomi want to become less dependent on the sales of smartphones and more dependent on the profits of a platform. This is also the case with Apple. This information is included in the interaction and communication with the visitors. But visitors can also go to relevant websites. The core of the platform is the relationship between the visitor and desired products; therefore, a platform should focus on their competitive edge and should be dominant in markets.

The relationship between providers and customers in a network/platform will lead to changes, especially for manufacturers. The supply chain will implode, and the functions will converge in the platform. There is a direct link between buyers and providers via a network/platform. Knowledge of this process is available through the platform, so that it is also possible to respond much more directly to individual needs. When considering sales channels, the choice of a platform will be disruptive to existing channels. If you can sell directly through a channel, perhaps with local sales outlets, a different revenue model is needed and the relationship with shops, resellers, will change immediately. A power struggle will result based on customer knowledge, marketing power.

Organizations change more slowly than technology. Martec's law of disruption, named after marketing technologist Scott Brinker, shows that companies are developing less quickly than technology does. The exponential growth that technology is experiencing is a direct derivative of Moore's Law, which predicts that the capacity of computers will double every year and a half at the same cost. Andrew McAfee (professor at MIT) and others also talk about this doubling of technological possibilities.

On the field of technology major changes will take place. Technology by producing goods, efficiency in many forms, customized and bespoke. Technology in the products to detect weak spots, wear and tear, navigating, tracking and tracing just to mention a few possibilities. But relevant for the topic of this book are the development in the supply chain and the contacts with customers.

Technology and the Buying Process

Developments like augmented reality and virtual reality are taking a major part in the customer buying process. The distinctions between VR and AR come down to the devices they require and the experience itself: AR uses a real-world setting while VR is completely virtual. VR requires a headset device, but AR can be accessed with a smartphone. AR enhances both the virtual and real world while VR only enhances a fictional reality.

Augmented reality overlays digital content and information onto the physical world as if they're actually there with you, in your own space. AR opens up new ways for your devices to be helpful throughout your day by letting you experience digital content in the same way you experience the world. It lets you search things visually, simply by pointing your camera at them. It can put answers right where your questions are by overlaying visual, immersive content on top of your real world. Facebook introduced META as a new virtual world, the social medium of the future in 2021.

While AR superimposes digital information on the physical world, VR replaces physical reality with a computer-generated environment. Though VR is used mostly for entertainment applications, it can also replicate physical settings for training purposes. It is especially useful when the settings involved are hazardous or remote. Or, if the machinery required for training is not available, VR can immerse technicians in a virtual environment using holograms of the equipment. So when needed, VR adds a fourth capability, simulate, to AR's core capabilities of visualize, instruct and interact.

All the major developments are based on data, we have reached the end of the analogue era and have entered in the digital world. All major changes are based on data, digital and technology application (and adoption). Machine learning and artificial intelligence will be behind all these digital applications.

Chips will become more powerful and ethical boundaries will be discussed more fiercely, still in a human body it will become eventually more accepted.

In the first place because the chips can stimulate certain functions (like heart problems), can detect malfunction of organs, and can replace some body functions, like movements. Also, chips will be used to compensate for function losses because of losing activities like the case with spinal cord injuries. Other not medical function will be a point of discussing, but will also be used, more like tracking and tracing, possible kidnapping danger or otherwise, diet control or food control, or identification. What happens with humans can also happen with animals and goods. To detect a lost smartphone is an example, to check if an animal is registered or if the owner has paid taxes. This can also be the case of humans. A chip in the body to get access to premises is happening already. All in all, the application of technology is moving fast, and we haven't seen anything yet.

More Changes in the Buying Process

Mobility

To make the world more transparent mobile devices will be supported by fast networks like 5G networks. Huge amounts of data can be transferred in a minimum of time which opens possibilities for support functions (traffic control), but also for functions like streaming and virtual reality. Soon direct connections will be important. It will support an integration between real time and virtual time, between human behavior and virtual support, During the corona lockdowns we have experienced the fast adoption of new technology like "video reality" with Zoom and Microsoft Teams, but also the impact on online shopping. The inclusion of AR and VR will make this an even more real experience and will replace old shopping habits.

New Storage and Developments Techniques

All this data, data transport and data stores will require big data stores. We see Microsoft, Google, Amazon as an example building big data storage. All over the world the storage centers will support the data transport and data stores. Cloud computing, as storage tool, is supported by local access through mobile phones. A new infrastructure is in place to fulfill the needs of users and to satisfy the needs of suppliers. These storage rooms are of vital importance for the acceptance and for the further growth of all digital applications. These rooms need, however, power, electricity, and cooling. Cooling can be obtained from location close by the sea, but electricity might be a challenger for the future, especially as part of the environmental discussions.

Developments and application will also change as we have seen in the transformation from a supply-driven economy to a demand-driven economy. Key features as connectivity, communication and coordination should be linked. Each application should add value to the total context. This is a new model for software developers. Interfaces on every point in the process should link to added features. These application programing interfaces (APIs) define the data streams and curate the data needed. This way the overall or leading program can use data or functions from other programs.

Competition, the Fight for End Users

To be able to trace and interpret these changes the application of new technological possibilities is required. There is simply no effective response without customer data and purchase data. This does not concern aggregated data, but rather personal, individual data. Without the use of this data, which is generated with internet-based applications, the necessary change cannot be implemented, and companies will remain in a so-called paralyzed zone. This is a dangerous situation. Companies postpone change, while the competition integrates new applications and defines the strategy based on customer behavior and digital opportunities. New entrants make use of this and ensure a structural change in markets. The change is dominated with new networks and platforms, which bring together supply and demand, and direct the marketing process (both supply and demand). An example of this was Amazon.com, but nowadays Uber, Airbnb, Netflix, Spotify and Alibaba are important disruptors. Sneaking into a market through a low-price strategy, and then changing the market (growth hacking). The new service UberEats Takeaway does not charge delivery costs for the time being and allows you to follow the bicycle delivery driver live on a map.

The Adaptation of Organizations

The first change occurs when external parties take over functions from existing organizations. At first glance, this is a good development, because it means that costs can be saved, and an organization can focus more on its core tasks. But this also means that company functions are "outsourced." This is okay if these are support functions, such as cleaning offices or managing a fleet. However, if this function is going to maintain the relationship with the customer, like with reservation systems or call centers, it can affect the competitive position of the existing organization. This is the case when current applications and possibilities become less relevant. During this change process, old systems must be replaced, whereby there is a discontinuity of the systems, but also of existing processes and routines. These adjustments and the speed of adoption are decisive for competitiveness. In the hotel industry, for example, the choice for outsourcing came from the fear of investing too much in these new IT systems. In addition to adapting the systems, investments also had to be made in the existing proposition (product), which meant that a choice had to be made which investment had priority. It was logical that technology (reservations) was outsourced. The investment in your own reservation system is expensive, as is management. With the rapid development of technology, depreciation will also weigh on the results proportionally. This means that organizations that do the technology in-house, in addition to the operational costs, also must deal with rapid innovations. A short amortization period and corresponding costs are the result. By "outsourcing" the reservation system, a hotel does not need its own system, it does not always have to adapt the system to new developments, and it also limits the "committed capacity." because of this. The power of platform strategy (or network strategy) is better to apply all resources to the core activities. The application of cloud computing, with mainly "variable" costs, for example per booking, is a facility for this.

Steps to a customer-based offering mean the last link will ultimately take control of the entire process, based on needs and purchase data. This is an example of the changes which will take place, a disruption of the structures and the supply chain. This gives more control over motives, sales information and customer preferences. An alignment between these three factors leads to a mutual adjustment and a fast turnaround time, enabling a rapid response to changes at the customer and in the market. Physical processes and physical adjustments take longer than virtual adjustments.

The Overall Concept Must Be Considered (Contextual)

Does the customer only need a physical product or a set of values? Products consist of several characteristics: the physical element, a service element and a perception element. They form the basis on which a product is purchased. It is about the value set (value unit). This is more than just a physical product. By starting from the entire product concept—physical part, service part, perception and usefulness—flexibility can arise based on personal preference, even though the product can only be physically adapted slowly. Curated content, a selection of products based on a customer's detected needs, is an example of this. The changes in organizations that respond to changes in markets and customer buying behavior have taken place in several areas: in distribution, in interaction and information provision, in collaboration in the organization, in customer and supplier contacts, in the relationship with customers. These areas and functions will be integrated in a collaborating concept like a platform or a network. If the total needs of a customer on a specific domain is known a supplier can offer all relevant products and services (in this network view). A need for a set of pans is part of the domain cooking for instance, running shoes in the domain running or even sport. This is a contextual approach. If a company has the trust of the customer, a wider range of product or services can be offered.

From Searching to Browsing

Although it is still early days, a new trend is appearing in China. Until now all web shops and websites had a search button. Some of the popular sites even use the software of Google to guide visitors direct to the right page or right products. This just shows the functional part of shopping which aligns with the supply focus, as we have seen. However, some major changes have taken place over the last few years, accelerated by the lockdowns of 2020 and 2021. Internet became a major way of shopping and social contacts. The social possibilities became more and more important, gaming, social media sites, entertainment, information, and videos, just to mention a few important activities. In customer behavior it was a change from functional to social and a mix from social to functional. Social media sites became important for advertising, but also offered links to products and websites for direct shopping. Google offers advertisers a direct link to key words so search and shopping is integrated. The search on Google was a direct link to the web shop. Data was gathered from your web shop but not shared with Google. Google analytics will give more insight in profiles of visitors, number, geographic, age groups, bounces, but not on personal search data. However, there is a growing need for customer data and buying data.

Browsing Platforms

Browsing data are important, therefore a website should ask more questions before linking to products. This way browsing is a part of the search process, but the data adds value to the customers and is part of the clustering, as we have seen with machine learning. To apply this on the website a special browsing module should be integrated, asking questions, and will lead to more specific questions before a product offering based on product comparison is shown. The visitor will go now to the desired product. This way more insight in motives and considerations can be analyzed and later similar clusters can be formed based on behavior. This is needed to align this with algorithms and direct communication based on cluster profiles (see Chapter 5 on RFM methodology).

Besides the changes in existing websites, where the fundament will stay in place based on supply and transactions, new internet application can also be based on the demand-driven approach, based on browsing. This is exactly the new trend which is seen in China. Browsing platforms are directly integrated with machine learning tools. Instead of searching, just products are shown based on the profile of customers, past behavior, and similar behavior of other customers in the same cluster. It is just like a moving belt with product (or services); the visitor will click on a product, but can also add this with more information or similar products. The biggest company is Pinduoduo, a company just as big as JD.com and Alibaba. Pinduoduo Inc. is the largest agriculture-focused technology platform in China. It has created a platform that connects farmers and distributors with consumers directly through its interactive shopping experience. In 2019, nearly 600,000 merchants sold farm produce through Pinduoduo (Hariharan & Dardenne, 2020). Users visit Pinduoduo without any specific intent, much like visiting a real-world shopping mall. In a shopping mall, the time that a consumer spends at the mall directly correlates with the amount he or she buys. As such, Pinduoduo has gamified the experience to maximize the amount of time a user spends on the app irrespective of whether they make a purchase or not. The primary features/experiences that have incentivized sharing and usage are Daily Check-Ins, Price Cuts, Card Programs, and Mini Games. Social commerce does not just mean connecting user accounts to Facebook. It means investing in creating physical world experiences online, specifically bringing the fun of shopping offline to online platforms.

Pinduoduo further incentivizes social sharing and bulk purchases by rewarding loyal users with free products, cash and other perks. This often creates "viral" effects that drive up purchasing activity. The interface is more similar to a Facebook newsfeed than an Amazon-like digital storefront. While Team Purchase was the main reason for Pinduoduo's rapid growth, a significant enabler of Pinduoduo's virality was the widespread use of WeChat as a platform in China. Tencent (WeChat's owner) is a large investor in Pinduoduo, and as a result was happy to let Pinduoduo grow on top of their ecosystem. Integrating the browsing feature in a website is a future development which can be important for collecting data and therefore as competitive business strategy, demand-driven. Platforms based on browsing can integrate machine learning, clusters based on behavior and social features to get a closer relationship with customers, as we have seen above. This kind of online proposition can be the fundament of the demand-driven future.

Conclusion

It is important for an organization to determine the changes based on the current focus and strategy and the community or demand focus. It will need a change of every part of a company to be successful. The orientations determine the application of the internet, from supply-driven, with a product focus, to demand-driven, with a "need" focus. The dynamic orientation model indicates the different orientations of an organization and the application of the internet. By starting from these buying motives, the complexity for an organization has increased. In addition, the organization can no longer survive with efficiency, but the organization must adapt around customer clusters or service clusters. Inter-functional coordination between the departments is necessary to achieve this.

Browsing will generate more data of the interaction process before a transaction. The integration between browsing and machine learning is an important fundament of the demand-driven economy. The future has started, but organizations and management still must adapt.

Student's Mind

1   What will be the major trends for the near future?
2   What will be the major restrictions for applying the trends?
3   What are the reasons for adoption (customers) and acceptance (suppliers)?
4   How will international developments interfere with local constraints?
5   What are the major values for change?

Discussion Point

Will the future be dominated by technology or by human behavior?

Reference

Hariharan, A. & Dardenne, N. (2020). Pinduoduo and the Rise of Social E-Commerce. Retrieved from www.ycombinator.com/library/2z-pinduoduo-and-the-rise-of-social-e-commerce

13 Practical Research

Product as a Service in Practice

A growing number of businesses are adopting new business models, including some industries that one might not expect. From the Gaming industry, Airlines to the Car industry and online media, there are some important changes taking place as part of the transformation from supply-driven to demand-driven. In the following practical research, the car industry is being analyzed, regarding the subscription-model of Volvo, "Care by Volvo."

Alternative Consumption Models in the Automobile Industry

Car ownership is not a necessity in the same way as it was in the past; ownership was especially important in the last century, but now access is more important. On top of this there is an increased urbanization and younger people opt to live in metropolitan areas with plenty of alternatives to car uses (access). This growing demand for having car access and not ownership led companies to become more demand-driven in their business models and to meet that specific demand by developing alternative consumption models.

The alternatives for access lead to different concepts like Uber, lease contracts or hiring cars, sharing urban cars and pay per hour, taxis, or other forms of transport.

Not only Zipcar, which was founded in 2000 and provides access to their vehicles on demand for $7 per month and an hourly rate for each individual ride, but also Hertz and Enterprise have introduced subscription car services. In addition, automotive OEMs are testing the demand-driven subscription approach. Audi, BMW, Cadillac, Jaguar Land Rover, Mercedes-Benz and Volvo have integrated this new approach into their business model.

These developments in the car industry point out that the shift towards a demand-driven economy needs to be integrated in one's strategy. This development from an ownership to a subscription-based business model can help legacy businesses to adapt to the realities of shifting consumer habits. Since consumers will not buy as many cars as they did in the past, companies change their business models and start to engage with consumers in a way that works for them.

DOI: 10.4324/9781003226161-13

Figure 13.1 summarizes alternative consumption models in the automobile sector and distinguishes between the traditional consumption model (ownership and leasing/long-term rental) and the non-traditional model (pay-per-use).

Introduction and Value Proposition

"Care by Volvo" is a single brand and all-inclusive car subscription model where they sell the solution of mobility without the hassle of owning a car. This concept started in Sweden in 2017 but has extended to other markets such as the USA, United Kingdom, The Netherlands, Germany and Norway with the aspiration to become a global online business. Care by Volvo is marketed as an offer that is simple, convenient, safe and carefree with no surprises. The concept is illustrated with the slogan "By not owning things, you're not owned by things." This service goes above and beyond traditional leasing and includes insurance coverage, maintenance and more for one monthly payment (around US$700 per month, depending on the car model). In essence, Care by Volvo offers an easier and a more flexible, personalized alternative to traditional car ownership and traditional car leasing. It provides three main value propositions:

- First, it's all-inclusive, meaning that the subscription includes all excess costs and services that would be necessary for the consumer to sort out themselves.
- Second, Volvo offers additional value to their consumers by making the process incredibly simple and convenient. All subscription services are pre-negotiated, and consumers can complete the application process online, select their preferred Volvo model and delivery is scheduled within two weeks. There is even a home delivery option available.

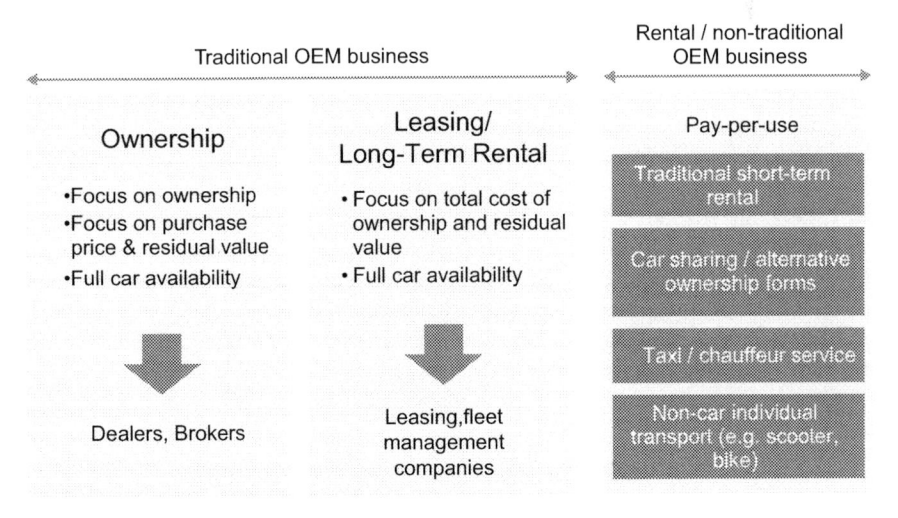

Figure 13.1 Alternative consumption models.

- Third, the subscription is very flexible, providing the possibility to upgrade or change models to fit customers' needs as well as cancel if no longer required (Kjellberg & Lagerkvist, 2018, pp. 46–52).

The Demand-Driven Nature of Care by Volvo

As defined in the 2019 annual report, the Volvo Car Group purpose is "Freedom to Move." Their company purpose is one that is fundamentally demand-driven in the sense that it centers around the customer's need for mobility and they develop products to fulfill this need. As stated in the 2019 annual report, "Everything we do starts and ends with our company purpose—providing Freedom to move in a personal, sustainable and safe way" resulting in a strategy that at its core is demand-driven. As such, being people-centric is one of their core strategic principles and they believe that this is essential to build a sustainable business as well as bring out the best in both employees and consumers. In essence, Volvo has shifted from a product-centered company to one that focuses on value creation through offering demand-driven solutions to a consumer's need for mobility. This has opened the possibility for them to extend their business with the addition of subscription business models in addition to traditional ones.

The introduction of Care by Volvo as a subscription model represents a significant shift to a demand-driven mindset that strives to develop the service end of their business to nurture direct consumer relationships and develop into a direct consumer business. In the development of Care by Volvo, emerging trends such as the shift of being able to compete on a basis of customer experience and adding value on the service end of their business as well as the rise of alternative consumption models were analyzed. With Care by Volvo, Volvo is broadening their consumer relationships aiming to capture a greater share of the value chain by expanding into new markets and consumer segments. Volvo essentially created a dynamic demand landscape that analyzed and mapped consumer demand changes in the realms of convenient mobility, broad-scale mobility, seamless integration, and urbanization.

Consequently, they recognized that there is a large untapped demand profit pool of individual consumers who want to be mobile but expect on-demand convenient, personalized services. They recognized that access is an area that needs development in the automobile industry which has traditionally focused on ownership. Therefore, Care by Volvo was born to extend and transform their business into one that is demand-driven and can offer each demand pool a unique offer that caters to their specific needs (Volvo Car Group, 2019, p. 51). Also, the value propositions of Care by Volvo recognized the unique needs of this demand profit pool and created a comprehensive service that adds value above and beyond traditional ownership and leasing leading to a competitive advantage.

In addition to creating a package based on the demands of a potential profitable demand pool, Care by Volvo also makes use of an integrated demand chain model through real-time communication from Volvo manufacturers to retail partners. The Volvo car company developed the concept and is in the process of transitioning into a distribution system that includes direct consumer relations. Presently, they are still relying on Volvo retailers as their primary route to market. Facilitating real-time communication between their retail network globally plays a key role (regardless of how Volvo cars are accessed) in the transition to an omni-channel distribution system with direct consumer relations, as retail is their main consumer touchpoint handling the delivery, maintenance of the cars as well as serving the consumers (Volvo Car Group, 2019, p. 51; Volvo Car Group, 2018, p. 26). The intellectual capital created is used by manufacturers to continue developing products and concepts that offer the most value to the end consumers who are serviced by the retailers. Additionally, by working in collaboration with their retailer network they can enhance their other consumer touchpoints such as their online buying platform and customize the experience of owning or using a Volvo (Volvo Car Group, 2019, p. 51).

Analyzing the Impact of Care by Volvo

On a business level, Care by Volvo has had an impact by increasing the amount of consistent income flowing into the Volvo car group. When launched in the USA, the projected first-year sales of Care by Volvo subscriptions sold in the first four months of the service (Finlay, 2020).

Since Volvo Care's launch the revenues from subscription, leasing and rental business have grown from 0.9% to 1.5% in 2019 and this is expected to increase continually as people shift away from ownership to more flexible rental or subscription options (Volvo Car Group, 2018, p. 110; Volvo Car Group, 2019, p. 82).

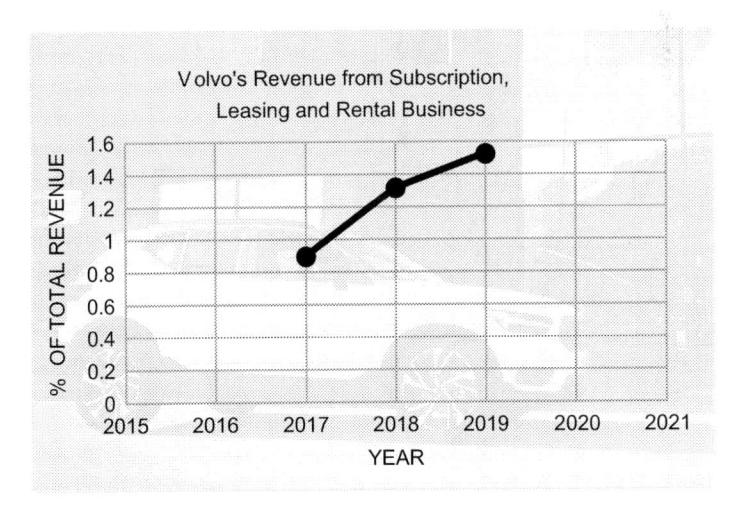

Figure 13.2 Volvo's revenue from subscription, leasing and rental business.
Source: created by author based on Volvo Car Group (2018, p. 110) and Volvo Car Group (2019, p. 82)

Beyond this, the impact of Care by Volvo can be seen in an analysis of how this new subscription model impacts customer relationships by looking at how Volvo Care has impacted customer conversion, retention and acquisition.

Care by Volvo value propositions are above and beyond what has traditionally been offered in the industry. As stated by spokesperson Jim Nichols, over 95% of Care by Volvo subscribers are first time Volvo users. This statistic shows the success of the Care by Volvo service as it is converting both first time car buyers and "conquest" buyers (those who presently own vehicles from other brands). This program is also attracting individuals who are on average ten years younger than the average buyer. This conversion coupled with their focus on adding value and creating a unique customer experience leads into customer retention and a long-term competitive advantage.

In terms of customer acquisition, Care by Volvo makes use of online channels for all steps in the process allowing people to subscribe by using the app or online making it as easy and simple as possible. In addition to this many digital advertising campaigns are run to showcase the value of Care by Volvo for consumers. Additionally, in the USA and UK, Care by Volvo gives individuals the opportunity to subscribe risk-free for a month to entice individuals to sign up and try a thin unconventional unfamiliar alternative to owning or leasing (Automotive World, 2020).

Volvo has recognized that in the demand-driven economy customer retention is the name of the game. Subscription models in essence are a good customer retention strategy as they promote consumers using a product out of habit and individuals get used to all the benefits of a subscription model. Care by Volvo aims to create high barriers to leaving the service in the sense that they aim to create emotional barriers by offering superior experience than their competitors and having consumers get used to this higher level of care and the benefit of having an all-inclusive hassle-free experience (Kjellberg & Lagerkvist, 2018, p. 49).

Challenges

Despite the successes and potential for future success of Care by Volvo in the demand-driven economy there are still many challenges faced by this program. The main issue faced by Care by Volvo is the issue that consumers do not understand the difference between leasing and the added value that their subscription service provides (Kjellberg & Lagerkvist, 2018, p. 47).

Additionally, the Care by Volvo team has faced pushback from management because Care by Volvo and the addition of e-commerce platforms represent a switch to a direct consumer business which is not traditional in the automobile industry (Volvo Car Group, 2019, p. 69). Before Care by Volvo, the company had never had direct connection nor direct contracts with their end consumers and operated through their traditional supply chain (Kjellberg & Lagerkvist, 2018, p. 48). As such, the Care by Volvo team in Sweden are pushing for this shift to direct business as it allows for more intimate connection with the customers as well as using this insight to drive other areas in their value chain (Kjellberg & Lagerkvist, 2018, p. 47). This agile addition of subscription-based business models can be considered a risk as this is not common in the automobile industry and has never been attempted by Volvo before (Volvo Car Group, 2019, p. 69). Volvo understands that customer expectations are changing quickly as new market offerings emerge and expects that interest in alternative forms of accessing cars and transportation will increase in the upcoming years. Care by Volvo is an attempt at letting demand lead their business as well as strengthening their relationship with their customers (Volvo Car Group, 2019, p. 69).

Another big challenge with the transition to a direct consumer business is dealerships' pushback as well as franchise legislation. Car dealerships have responded negatively to the growing popularity of the subscription model where the manufacturers sell directly to the end consumer as they are effectively cut out of the supply chain. Consequently, particularly in the United States, car dealerships are building political organizations to protect their revenue streams (Finlay, 2020). This culminated in the cancellation of Care by Volvo 1.0 in California as the California's Department of Motor Vehicles found that Volvo's subscription plan violates state franchise law. Their main issue was that the subscription model undercuts dealers on price as opposed to leasing or selling the same car (Finlay, 2020).

As stated previously, Volvo dealerships are the company's primary route to market, therefore it is in their interest to arrange that it caters to the needs of dealerships while continuing with Care by Volvo. In this transition, Volvo aims to update its retail strategy to adapt to the changes in consumer demands and to facilitate collaboration with their global dealership network (Volvo Car Group, 2019 p. 69). Additionally, they will work more collaboratively with their retailers by allowing them to select the car from their retailers' inventory as well as designing a strategy to re-sell the Volvos that are returned after the two-year subscription is over ultimately re-integrating the dealerships in the supply chain (Finlay, 2020).

Other issues faced by Care by Volvo are partially attributed to the program's success. In the USA, Volvo was not anticipating the level of demand resulting in a lack of supply (in both the subscription business model and for their traditional dealerships) of the specific models used by Care by Volvo. Additionally, this has resulted in long waiting lists for individuals who expected their car within two weeks of subscribing. This unanticipated success has ultimately undermined their value proposition of being simple, convenient and easy, as this has caused significant frustration for end-consumers. Additionally, the speed of the launch is also a complication as the necessary infrastructure such as training dealerships, and having enough care by Volvo representatives has not been developed yet resulting in further customer dissatisfaction.

Long-Term Ambitions

Despite Care by Volvo being a new and innovative way for Volvo to shift their business to one that is demand-driven, there is still a long way to go before their services are optimized as well as accepted as an easier alternative to owning or leasing a car. Care by Volvo is a step in the right direction for Volvo as this aligns with their overall strategy of becoming a "global mobility provider" (Volvo Car Group, 2019, p. 11) while also acknowledging the trends of consumers shifting away from ownership to alternative consumption models.

Care by Volvo aims to grow their subscription business to become a leader in the growing car subscription industry. By doing this, they will benefit from increased stable flows of income as well as increased customer retention. Additionally, by engaging in direct consumer business they will be able to develop a deeper competitively advantaged understanding of demand and will be able to use this information beyond the Care by Volvo program and use this information to create even more value in terms of both changing their products to suit the changing needs of consumers as well as add value above and beyond their competitors in terms of customer experience across all digital and physical touchpoints (Volvo Car Group, 2019, p. 69). As such, by growing and improving the Care by Volvo program they will be able to extend the knowledge they gain to all areas of their business transforming them into a business that is fit for success in the demand-driven economy.

Care by Volvo also must work on improving the understanding of consumers as to why their program is different to owning or leasing cars. To do this, they need a strong marketing campaign stressing their value propositions and the creation of a platform where Care by Volvo participants can come together and share their experiences (Kjellberg & Lagerkvist, 2018, p. 136). They could also focus on adding more value on the service end of their business with other add-ons such as free car washes, refueling services, parking payment solutions as well as possible in car deliveries (Kjellberg & Lagerkvist, 2018, p. 137). In addition to the above, Care by Volvo needs to improve their collaboration with dealerships and effectively train Care by Volvo personnel as this will help improve consumers' understanding of the value of Care by Volvo as well as help retain individuals by offering an experience that does not stop once the individual receives their car. This entails a strong service delivery failure strategy that helps maintain consumer satisfaction and possibly a digital platform where consumers can connect with each other as well as trained Care by Volvo personnel to handle their issues and queries.

Another ambition of Care by Volvo is to collaborate with dealerships to provide an area to resell the cars after they have been returned. By retaining ownership of the cars, Volvo creates an opportunity where they can resell the cars and achieve an even higher ROI for each individual car. This system has not been developed yet but is in the initial stages of development across the markets in which Care by Volvo is present (Kjellberg & Lagerkvist, 2018, p. 48).

As aforementioned, the transaction to online platforms has become increasingly crucial after the surge of coronavirus. One sector that enormously experienced this shift is the food industry, especially restaurants. Not only did this shift exponentially increase during the pandemic, but this drastic growth is being witnessed for the past five years. This increased popularity of delivery platforms has captured significant attention, leading to in-depth studies of this emerging digital world. Analyses report that, when taking a closer look at the food platforms, it is possible to identify three different types of food delivery business models: the order-only model, the order and delivery model, and the fully integrated model, where the delivery company is responsible for the whole journey of the meal. This also includes the initial food preparation. Regardless of which type of business model is being leveraged, a common food delivery business model canvas has been drawn, shedding light on how this type of platforms function and what is prioritized. As food delivery platforms are multi-sided, the value proposition includes all the different parties involved such as customers, drivers and delivery persons.

Conclusion

Customers represent a key factor: reliability and non-stop customer support and service are crucial. One of the key activities and resources is the use of algorithms which is the key to finding customer preferences and providing recommendations. Therefore, food delivery platforms can be defined as demand-driven platforms. This type of platform focuses on indulging consumers' demand for products by providing them with tailored solutions. It is not a matter of bombarding consumers with innumerable options that they might not care about. The aim is to create a comeback flow by giving customers exactly what they asked for.

Student's Mind

1   Why is a subscription model more attractive for Volvo than a transaction model?
2   Why will a customer prefer to choose Care by Volvo rather than just buying a Volvo?
3   What will the impact be on the business model of Volvo?
4   Why are the dealers reluctant for this approach?
5   How will machine learning fit in the model?

Discussion Point

How will marketing change if more companies choose a similar model as Volvo?

References

Automotive World. (2020). Volvo Car Launches New Care by Volvo Subscription Service in the UK. *Automotive World*, September 2. Retrieved from www.automoti veworld.com/news-releases/volvo-cars-launches-new-care-by-volvo-subscrip tion-service-in-the-uk/

Finlay, S. (2020) Auto Dealers Successfully Challenge Volvo's Subscription Plan. Retrieved from www.wardsauto.com/dealers/auto-dealers-successfully-challenge-volvo-s-subscription-plan

Kjellberg, R. & Lagerkvist, E. (2018). Servitization in the Car Industry: A Case Study of the Concept Care by Volvo. Retrieved from https://gupea.ub.gu.se/bitstream/2077/57247/1/gupea_2077_57247_1.pdf

Volvo Car Group. (2018). Annual Report 2018. Retrieved from https://investors.volvocars.com/annualreport2018

Volvo Car Group. (2019). Annual Report 2019. Retrieved from https://investors.volvocars.com/annualreport2019

14 Business Models and Comparison

2020 (the year of the lockdowns because of corona) has been revealed as an extremely crucial year in terms of digital transformation and business innovation. As a matter of fact, the vast majority of businesses have been forced to step out of their comfort zone and find ways to adapt to a slightly different world. A world that more than ever is relying on the proximity and developments of the digital world. As a consequence, now, more than ever, it is imperative for businesses to seriously start innovating by not only giving birth to small start-ups that would eventually end up being successful in the Silicon Valley.

Imagining an Optimal Business Model Canvas

It was more than ever necessary for digital transformation by making drastic changes in the business model. Three aspects are required to be implemented for businesses not to fall back but thrive in this new era.

- The first one revolves around working on supply chain transparency and flexibility. Transparency is fundamental as it fosters trust across customers in this period of uncertainty, whereas flexibility benefits the retailers themselves which may happen to experience moments of scarcity, such as the toilet paper shortage experienced during the first month of quarantine. Therefore, having a plan B or even enough stock to overcome these obstacles is vital.
- The second aspect is data security. The Zoom scandal should have taught us that, whenever a digital platform faces leaks of personal data, users do not hesitate to try to destroy that platform's reputation. It happened with Zoom during quarantine, where the mere doubt that the platform was making use of personal data in a way that was not cited in the terms and conditions agreement sparked terror among millions of students, teachers and smart workers. Inevitably, the last element concerns remote working and automation.
- Considering the forecasted exponential increase in remote working due to the pandemic, it has become extremely important for businesses to grant flexibility and diversity in the ways this working mode is implemented.

DOI: 10.4324/9781003226161-14

- Finally, the automation aspect speaks for itself: investments in the techno-logical sector are predicted to be highly beneficial for the future.

UberEats and Just Eats

The UberEats Business Model

UberEats is a three-sided marketplace connecting a driver, a restaurant owner and a customer, with UberEats platform at the center. The three-sided marketplace moves around three players: restaurants pay commission on the orders to UberEats; customers pay the small delivery charges, and at times, cancellation fee; drivers earn through making reliable deliveries on time.

The competition on the home delivery market of food is a fierce competition. It is not only a fight for restaurants/partners but also a fight for customers. UberEats and Just Eat Takeaway.com are two main players in the market.

With global governments continually enforcing semi-lockdowns that see restaurants and bars being the most affected sector, people are increasingly relying on food delivery. Considering the UberEats and Just Eat business models and their comparison, it is possible to draft a hypothetical optimal busi-ness model canvas. This would include elements of both the incredibly successful platforms, underlined both in the similarities and differences comparison, in addition to important post-quarantine modifications.

Transparency and flexibility fall within the value proposition segment. Providing transparency about the supply chain, including the order delivery and the people involved in it, must represent the backbone of the food delivery platform. Transparency leads to trust, which, in turn, makes the platform reliable. Placing a food order the customer can track it, to know who oversees it, how far away the restaurant is located and will be informed of any disruptions. Furthermore, flexibility with the orders can benefit both the stakeholders, meaning the users and the restaurants, and the platform itself. Having a back-up plan in case of unsuccessful delivery not only would save the platform reputation, but would also make the customer satisfied, and help the restaurants having customers buying their food.

The second important aspect is granting data security, which would be placed within the key activities and customer relationship segments. Although users are increasingly aware of the fact that, whenever an order is placed, personal data gets transferred to the platform and, possibly, also to restaurants. Clear boundaries about who has access to the data must be explicitly set. If the platform retrieves personal data to make accurate suggestions and predictions, access to data is a risk that most users are not afraid to take. However, if data becomes available to external parties, for instance political parties or organizations outside the food domain, users would inevitably leave that platform.

Consequently, data security and clarity are crucial among food delivery platforms as well. Information technology allows companies to free their mind about aspects that human interference makes complicated, slower and inefficient (Gupta, 2018). Food delivery platforms still heavily rely on drivers and riders. Why not replace a percentage of these employees with drones or other technological tools that would guarantee a smoother delivery? Amazon has already kicked it off, and delivering a phone charger is not much different than delivering a burger.

The new value proposition segment would include transparency, flexibility, high-quality advertising and algorithms, convenience and openness and easy payment procedure. The selection of these specific elements stems from the fact that all of them are crucial in the digital era. For instance, high-quality algorithms are the key to success nowadays: users get increasingly involved with the platform if they notice that their favorite sushi place provides them with occasional discounts. On top of this, an easy payment procedure fosters trust and indulges customers' necessity to save time.

A smooth transaction avoids making customers associate negative thoughts with the payment moment. No one likes paying online. At least a smooth transaction is quick and does not rub it in. The optimal customer relationship sector would include promo codes, social media and email marketing, on top of granting data security. Although social media could create advertising fatigue, it is a proper way to nurture the relationship with existing customers and expand the consumers' base. Nurturing this relationship via email and social media marketing contributes to adding costs for the platform, together with the delivery workers and their partial potential automation. In addition to costs, leveraging social media marketing entails the management of social media as channels, together with monitoring the app and the website.

Costs must be balanced out by a solid revenue stream, which would consist of commissions to key partners, meaning affiliate websites and blogs, restaurants and drivers, non-standard delivery fees and in-platform advertisements. Moreover, this customer relationship segment assumes a target audience that uses social media and in-phone apps on a daily basis. That is why the customer segment is covered by university students, young professionals and high/middle-class families or, more generally, by people who do not have enough time to cook themselves but would like a complete meal. This target audience is easy to reach and persuade thanks to social media and emails. When it comes to touch upon granting data security and clarity, the key activities segment comes into play as well. As a matter of fact, this sector is filled in by data security and supply chain monitoring, including placing, picking and delivering orders. Eventually, there is the key resources segment, which involves customers, delivery operators and the restaurant owners.

The ideal business model has to grant data security to its customers, which is an extremely delicate and important aspect in today's business. Moreover, it needs to be transparent with the customers—a fundamental aspect to gain customer trust. Flexibility is also needed in order to adapt to the changes in the market. Transparency and flexibility need to represent the backbone of the business model canvas, meaning the core features of the value proposition. Lastly, a fundamental aspect that has to be increasingly implemented is technological developments, such as the automation of the processes for a smoother delivery. Implementing all these aspects will enhance the customer experience and their relationship with the platform, ensuring the return of the consumer to the platform. Particularly in times of uncertainty, such as this post-Covid-19 era, customer trust and tight relationships ensure an ever-working platform, which is unlikely to face bankruptcy.

A six-point value proposition distinguishes the platform from its competitors:

- First, the company promises to deliver within 30 minutes in most of the cities.
- Second, the company has a standard delivery fee which ensures that all orders are fulfilled irrespective of the order value, hence no concept of minimum order.
- The third point is one of the most valuable assets to the company. As there are several active Uber users across the globe, these users can also be potential customers for UberEats.
- The top-class algorithm that the company developed organized three major factors for the platform: order management, order allocation and order dispatch.
- Another crucial value proposition is the global presence. Although they may face local competitors in every market, their global dominance will be hard to beat.
- Last but not the least, they have cars/drivers for Uber, the same vehicles and people can be used for UberEats leading to a better and effective utilization of resources.

However, this business model does not mention the convenience and user-friendliness of the platform due to tailored restaurant recommendations, order tracking, customizable delivery details and other advanced search filters. The customer segment comprises an individual who wishes to order food, wants the food to be delivered on their doorstep, people who don't have the time to cook and who do not wish to go to the eatery to buy things. These individuals can be working professionals and families. The other segment, suppliers, are the food restaurants. The company forms good relationships with its customers by providing promo codes and coupons to gain discounts on their orders. For instance, from a personal experience, when ordering KFC, received a discount of 55% by using a promo code that UberEats provided. There's a customer support chat, rating, review and feedback system to connect with the consumers about their experience with the food delivery process. One can even track the order or use social media platforms to stay connected.

If UberEats does not have any minimum amount and gives discounts to consumers, then how do they make money? There are three ways in which the company generates revenue in its ecosystem:

1   Standard delivery fee or convenience fee: a flat delivery fee is charged from its customers regardless of the price of the order.

2 Recurring revenue share from restaurant partners: the company takes a cut of 15% to 40% on every order from the restaurant partners and decides the percentage of commission.

3 Marketing and advertising fee from restaurant partners: UberEats offer customer-oriented brand campaigns, social posts and email marketing to help the restaurant partners attract customers and reach out to a larger customer base.

The cost structure is mostly on marketing, technology, delivery workers and discounts for the customers. However, it also has a cost-effective system due to certain factors like lesser customer acquisition cost, shared network of drivers and riders and savings on logistics costs. Customer acquisition cost is less as most of its users are through cross-promotion on the Uber app. The drivers are shared from Uber, which eases the trouble of setting up a delivery network from the start. Lastly, multiple food orders on the same route can be delivered in a single delivery run, therefore logistical costs are saved.

The Just Eat Takeaway.com Business Model

Just Eat Takeaway.com's core business model connects consumers with restaurants, enabling the consumer to order and pay for a meal through their websites or apps, which is then delivered to the consumer or collected by them in person (Figure 14.1). While most participating restaurants deliver the food themselves, they are expanding their own logistics offering, giving restaurants access to new sales opportunities where they use their courier network to deliver their food. In

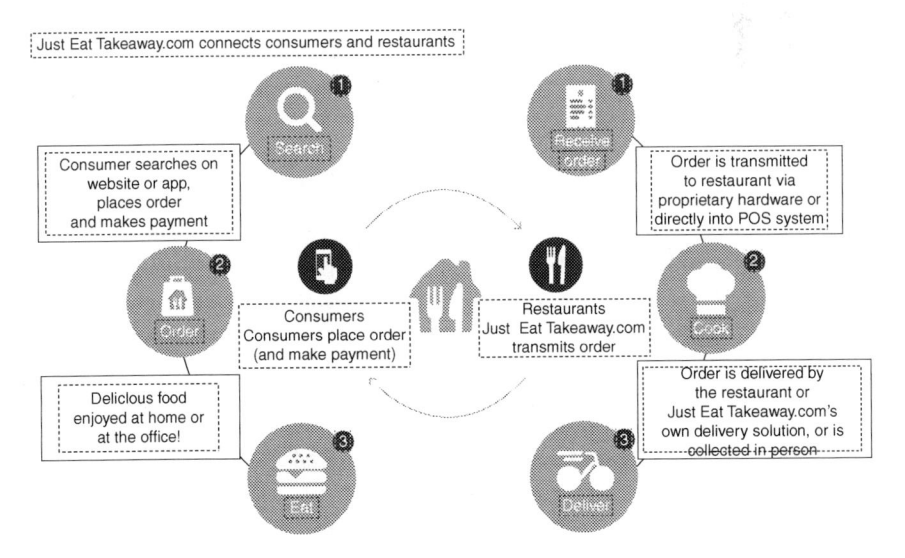

Figure 14.1 The process of Just Eat Takeaway.com.

some cases, they can also use the courier service of Just Eat Takeaway.com (started in 2016). On average this happens in 8% of the orders.

For *consumers*, their marketplace provides a simple way to order and pay for food, and Just Eat Takeaway.com aims to offer the best user experience by providing a large and varied selection of cuisines, broad restaurant choice, an easy-to-use and engaging product interface, seamless payment processes and transparent order-tracking features.

For *restaurants*, Just Eat Takeaway.com offers access to a wider consumer-base and provides publicity at a relatively low cost, allowing partners to broaden their reach beyond local marketing and generate incremental orders.

The business is primarily a business-to-consumer (B2C) operation, but Just Eat Takeaway.com has also invested in solutions to serve the corporate market, including Takeaway Pay, 10bis and City Pantry. These business-to-business (B2B) services allow corporate customers to offer their employees (partially) subsidized food orders, assigning budgets to employees to order food through the Just Eat Takeaway.com platforms. Their B2B services remove complicated expense processes, with companies receiving one invoice at the end of each month, which they can integrate with HR and accounting systems. In this way, Just Eat Takeaway.com offers an alternative to the company canteen, providing significantly greater choice to employees in an economical way.

They derive their revenue principally from the commissions they charge restaurants based on the gross merchandise value (GMV) of the food ordered through their marketplace. GMV is a term used in online retailing to indicate a total sales monetary-value for merchandise sold through a particular market-place over a certain time frame, and it includes any fees or other deductions which a seller might calculate. To a lesser extent, revenue is derived from other services such as online payment services, sales of merchandise and packaging, and promoted placement. In addition, they also derive revenue from delivery fees charged to consumers on orders for which Just Eat Takeaway.com is responsible for the delivery.

The business model benefits from powerful network effects, reinforcing growth in orders, restaurants and consumers (Figure 14.2).

As the number of consumers increases, more orders and higher GMV are generated, attracting more restaurants to their marketplace, which further enhances and diversifies the offering and in turn attracts more consumers. This typically provides a strong tailwind to growth for market leaders. In addition, network effects drive operating leverage, with revenue growth typically not requiring a linear increase in marketing or overhead costs, thereby leading to improved operating margins in the long run.

The value propositions of Just Eat focuses on the convenience and openness for its customers. They are a leading online meal delivery market across Europe, hence they have a regional presence. A wide range of options is provided for the consumers in terms of cuisines, local restaurants and even the way they want to pay for their order. They can pay in cash or via iDeal, PayPal, MasterCard, American Express and Visa. The company also offers deals and

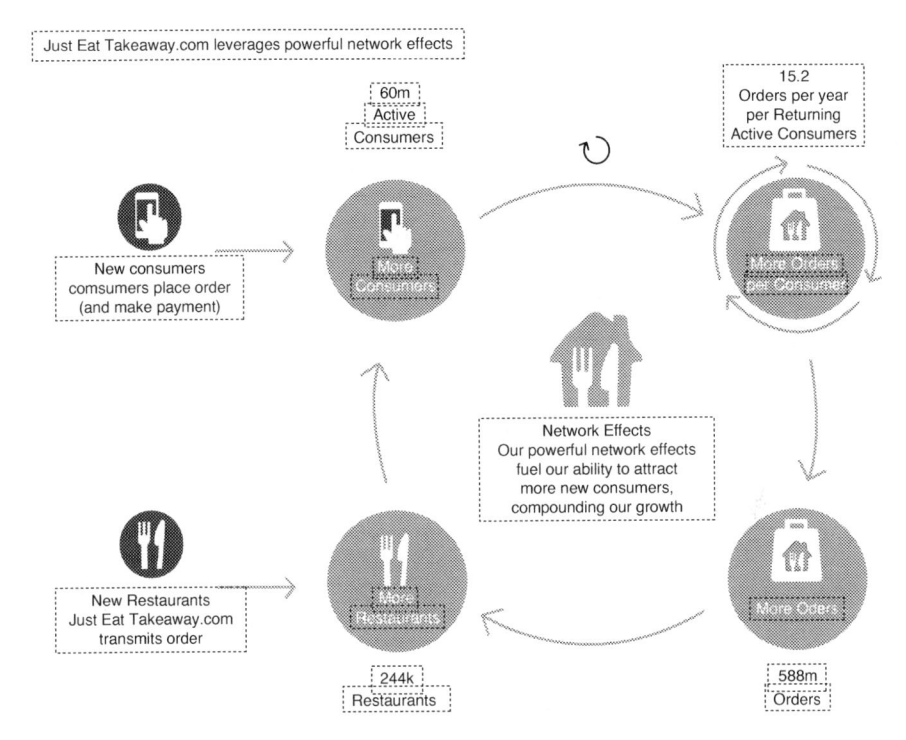

Figure 14.2 Network effects of Just Eat Takeaway.com.
Source: Just Eat Takeaway.com annual report

discounts for the consumers when ordering. Although their cost structure involves marketing, one of their main value propositions is their advertising capabilities. Just Eat Takeaway.com proposes to increase the sales of the restaurants by advertising their menus and focuses on improving their visibility on Google. The customer segment involves people who do not have the time, capacity or habit to cook for themselves and who wish to order food and get it delivered to where they are located. This service typically attracts university students, working families and young professionals. Customer relationships are based on user support like reviews after each order, sending emails on updates of where the order is, guides for ordering and payment processes, and FAQs. To build a stronger relationship, customers can directly contact Just Eat Takeaway.com through online contact forms if they have any complaints, suggestions or inquiries. They also have social media accounts allowing customers to interact with them directly.

The company's key partners include the restaurants and fast-food providers. For instance, partners with small businesses that do not have their own online ordering system as well as companies like Dominos that has its own website.

McDonald's, Wok 24, 91 spices and Marco Polo are among the few restaurant companies that Just Eat has partnered with in The Netherlands. It also has affiliates for marketing programs like promoting and generating sales on other websites, blogs and social media services. Online ordering gateways, its innovation, IT foundation and its faculty are the key resources.

Finally, as mentioned earlier, marketing is one of their main cost structures with the upkeep of the platform and app. Moreover, the administration of its eatery organization and the salaries for the Just Eat delivery drivers are a few of the other expenses in its business model. Most of the times the restaurants send their own drivers to deliver the order. They charge a commission to its key partners (restaurants) on all orders, which automatically deducts before keeping the profits into their accounts. The company receives a 13% commission on every meal ordered through their platform. They charge a non-standard delivery fee as well.

Similarities between the Two Business Models

Both Just Eat Takeaway.com and UberEats include similarities in their business model. From the above analysis, it can be seen that the value propositions that both the companies propose are almost similar as they both focus on comforting and giving the best food delivery services from ordering to payment to home delivery to their customers. They both have a top-class algorithm that helps, gives recommendations to their customers and predicts what the customer would want. From the start of clicking on the platform link till the payment procedure, both companies make sure that the platform is easy to use and not complicated. In terms of customer relationships, both try to build a strong bond with their customers through their email marketing, social media marketing and support services from their platform and application. For instance, UberEats constantly sends emails to its customers about promo codes and discounts along with reviews from their past orders. Similarly, Just Eat sends messages and emails to the customers regarding promotions and discounts, latest updates on the orders, interesting information regarding their newest features and review emails. These strategies make sure that the customers stay connected with the brand and enjoy a top-notch service by the two platforms. Both companies are demand-driven and target similar customers. Their key partners are also similar as its drivers, a variety of restaurants, affiliate websites and blogs. These are some of the similarities that the two companies encompass. Despite these, there are multiple differences that the two business models hold.

Differences between the Two Business Models

In addition to specifying the similarities, an analysis of the differences contributes to the uniqueness of both businesses. These differences are the basis for competitive advantage. The first major difference is the way in which the two platforms operate: Just Eat Takeaway.com offers a platform in which customers are able to order online from selected restaurants. This platform allows orders to be placed; however, it is the restaurant itself that has to provide the delivery. Nonetheless, it is important to highlight that, even if Just Eat Takeaway.com mainly provides the delivery services, it is common that the restaurant delivers the orders as well. On the other hand, UberEats represents a platform that allows restaurants to sell their meals online and, at the same time, it also enables restaurants to arrange the delivery themselves.

Another difference includes the customers segment, or more precisely where they can place the order from. In fact, Just Eat Takeaway.com delivers almost everywhere: in both cities and smaller towns; while UberEats currently delivers worldwide but only in big cities, to make sure it remains economically feasible for the company, and to ensure a high quality of the food once delivered. Furthermore, the management of the employees works in a different way. For instance, Just Eat Takeaway.com directly employs its riders who are paid on an hourly wage, while on UberEats riders are self-employed contractors and are paid based on the number of deliveries completed. Although, this model is under pressure in Europe due to labor regulations

Additionally, the two companies operate in different ways when making deliveries. UberEats focuses mainly on the efficiency of the delivery, therefore they hand over orders as fast as possible. As a matter of fact, they promise to deliver within 30 minutes, and with no minimum order requirements as seen in the description of the business model of UberEats above. In other words, customers can choose their favorite snack worth €4 and place the order without having to buy themselves a complete meal, which would suffice to reach the minimum order value of €10 or €15. However, a standard delivery fee is charged. On the other hand, in order to make the delivery service free, Just Eat Takeaway.com adds a minimum order value that the customer has to pay in order to receive the delivery service. However, if the distance of the restaurant to the delivery address is long, the platform does charge a delivery fee to the customer. Lastly, unlike UberEats, Just Eat Takeaway.com does not have an existing customer base as mentioned in the description earlier. Hence, it makes it harder for the platform to reach global presence like UberEats.

It is important to underline that we live in an extremely fast world, thus the market is continuously changing and adapting and so are these platforms. Therefore, the differences that are pointed out in this segment are significant.

Nike+

Another example is Nike (see also Chapter 6). Traditionally they build their business through a combination of innovative products, intensive brand building through multimedia platforms and efficient operations. As the possibilities of the new digital technology emerged, Nike quickly capitalized on all three areas. Nike transformed its customer experience by introducing new selling processes and connecting athletes worldwide and its operations with new design and manufacturing methods. Nike did not start by strategizing on its business model, but rather looked at ways it could provide even more value to its connected customers. Nike decided to weave its technology and information together into a new business model, Nike+.

Nike+ includes multiple connected components: a shoe, sensor, an internet platform, and a device like iPod, iPhone, Xbox, a GPS watch, or a fuel band. The fuel band uses geo-tracking, following a person throughout the day giving users real-time updates on how many calories they have burned, the number of steps and providing real motivation for athletes. Runners can also share their performance and routes with their friends (just like Strava) on Twitter and Facebook. Nike of course get valuable data about users, their products and the community. Nike has changed its business model from providing only apparel to providing new hardware, technology, rich data and useful add-on service for its customers. Nike is now attracting external partners to continually enhance the service on the Nike+ platform. Nike has increased its market share and developed new revenue streams (profit pools) with a range of add-on products and services. It understood the nature of its customers' needs for engagement and asked, "How do we provide more value?" In this way Nike engineered a coherent digital platform that interconnects its products and services to the benefit of the athletes.

Booking.com

Booking Holdings (BKNG) is the world leader in online travel and related services, provided to customers and partners in over 220 countries and territories through six primary consumer-facing brands: Booking.com, priceline, agoda.com, Rentalcars.com, Kayak and OpenTable. The mission of Booking Holdings is to make it easier for everyone to experience the world.

Founded in 1996 in Amsterdam, Booking.com has grown from a small Dutch start-up to one of the world's leading digital travel companies. Booking.com's mission is to make it easier for everyone to experience the world. By investing in the technology that helps take the friction out of travel, Booking.com seamlessly connects millions of travelers with memorable experiences, a range of transportation options and incredible places to stay—from homes to hotels and much more. As one of the world's largest travel marketplaces for both established brands and entrepreneurs of all sizes, Booking.com enables properties all over the world to reach a global audience and grow their businesses. Booking.com is available in 44 languages and dialects and offers more than 28 million total reported accommodation listings, including more than 6.5 million listings alone of homes, apartments and other unique places to stay.

The agency business model is the premium business model of Booking.com.

Booking.com works with a commission-based model, meaning that properties that choose to list on the site pay a set percentage on each reservation made through their platform that ends up with a paying, staying guest at their property. The global commission rate average is 15%, among the lowest in the industry, and can vary slightly depending on the location.

Innovation tactics has specified the value proposition for Booking.com. In this case it is obvious that Booking.com is also servicing two markets: the bookings for temporary accommodation (consumers) and the owners of accommodations (suppliers). Finally, Booking.com has also build their own brand value. Therefore Booking.com is a platform/network fitting the demand-driven economy.

Booking.com generates most of its revenue through the agency model where each stayed reservation incurs a commission (they also generate some ad, merchant and other revenues, but these are a very small percentage). Here are some examples where Booking.com and the other subsidiaries of the Priceline Group use the above business models:

- Reservation of accommodation, rental cars, etc. generate commissions and fall into the agency business model.
- Priceline's "name your own price" and package deals fall under the merchant business model.
- Their meta search engine Kayak.com earns advertising revenues on a cost per click pricing model.
- OpenTable earns commissions but also subscription services for their reservation management system.
- Travel insurance fees, which for now I am not going to elaborate further on.
- Revenues generated by Booking.com's BookingSuite accommodation marketing and business analytics services.

Value proposition to travelers

1 **Great prices:** Booking.com has contracts in place with the properties that choose to list on its platform. One of the standard clauses refers to rate parity, which means that a hotel should offer the same price on the same (type of) room on their own web pages. Without such a rule, users could compare and find a hotel on Booking.com, but then complete the booking on the hotel's pages. Despite some changes in this space, Booking.com is still able to offer competitive prices on those hotels it most prominently features.
2 **Amount of choice:** Booking.com has now over 28 million listings places on their platform and a large amount of filtering options that make it easier for the user to find what they are after. Moreover, Booking.com helps consumers to make value choices.
3 **Reduction of risk:** the star rating and reviews generated (over 218 million reviews to date) by other users reduce the risk of being disappointed. Booking.com features reviews only from those who have booked through them and stayed at the property. This system effectively prevents manipulation, a problem well known on many other platforms.

4   **Call centers:** many people still want to talk to a human prior to committing a considerable amount of money. Two-thirds of Booking.com's employees are in the customer service areas for this reason.
5   **Useful app:** the traveler's journey does not end with the booking. Booking.com's app has useful content prior to the booking but increasingly also travel guide functionality in their app. Also, bookings through apps have multiplied from 2015 onward and are expected to stay in the double-digit growth space.
6   **Useful travel content:** useful content that accompanies the traveler's micro moments.

Value proposition to hotels

Hotels have a love-hate relationship with the OTAs (networks,platforms). While most of their bookings come through other channels, OTAs remain crucial to get as close to being fully booked as possible. (Some of the most important KPIs in the hotel industry are average daily rates and revenue per available room. For the purposes of this analysis, note that "fully booked" means maximizing these KPIs.)

1   **Incremental revenue:** the key value proposition is that Booking.com helps to fill otherwise empty-staying rooms. Hotel rooms are like perishable goods. If they are not booked on a night the revenue for that room that night is irrecoverably gone. With hotels being high fixed cost assets, this loses the room's contribution to the high fixed cost base.
2   **Ability to react:** Booking.com allows hotels to implement their revenue management strategy by providing the ability to flexibly decide/change which rooms they offer through Booking.com on which nights and its rates. This allows hotels to drive additional business on a short fuse, to put up special promotions, and dynamically adjust commission for soft periods to rank higher.
3   **Global reach:** Booking.com helps hotels to reach global markets and potential customers that by themselves they would not reach. Achieving global reach in a meaningful way (i.e. high conversion rates) requires investments that may be underestimated. Booking.com have localized content, payment options, apps, etc. They also translate the hotel content into the local language (40 languages done by a localization team) and are present on the relevant advertising channels. The Priceline Group have acquired local online travel agencies who have captured a meaningful local market share and built a recognized brand. They have offices in many countries an online presence in over 220 countries, feed their mobile apps and keep all the content consistent.
4   **Risk reduction:** fees are structured in a way that there is no upfront payment and no payment whatsoever unless there is a booking. Unlike in online marketing, there is no risk of paying money for advertising for no return. Cost-per-click models that I have described previously come with the risk of no or low returns.

5   **Drive additional traffic to the hotel's website ("billboard effect"):** one prominent study came to the conclusion that there is a considerable amount of travelers who research on the OTAs, like Booking.com, but then book on the respective hotel's website. Thus, the OTA pays for the customer acquisition cost (CAC) but generates no revenue for themselves. This effect is called "billboard effect." More recently, other studies have questioned that this effect (still) exists. It is ultimately hard to measure due to the hundreds of micro moments over which the customer journey unfolds. But there are two things I am very certain of:

- Being present on an OTA with good ratings will have positive effects.
- Bookings will take place where the customer gets additional benefits (loyalty benefits, perks, freebies) at the same price, be it on the hotel page or on the OTA pages.

6   **Market intelligence:** Booking.com shares market intelligence, booking forecasts for given locations as well as how the hotel is performing on the Booking.com platform in relation to competition.

Lessons from platforms

The era after the Covid-19 lockdown is a revival food delivery platform; however, it is important to remember that the market is in constant evolution, therefore the business models must be updated continuously to be able to keep up with its continuous changes. Moreover, both UberEats and Just Eat are platforms that did not face significant issues during the pandemic, considering their high popularity also pre-coronavirus.

It is evident that there is a shift to a demand-driven economy and businesses need to address this shift by reimagining their business and changing their strategy. It is important to keep in mind that to remain competitive, businesses need to build upon what customers want, rather than what the suppliers already have. Hence, businesses do not change their strategy simply by chance, but systematically address the changes towards a demand-driven economy. Also, being demand-driven means to have a deeper understanding of consumers and to leverage the information to change the way in which business functions across all areas of the value chain while remaining agile in this fast-paced new landscape. The results show that the journey of becoming demand-driven requires an entire shift in the business model.

Conclusion

A key finding is that companies need to implement a digital leadership strategy because this is the most essential ingredient for succeeding in the demand-driven economy. This means that machine learning should be applied to continuously gather information about people and market developments to implement these insights into the strategy. In addition, the results show that if a company wants to transform its business it needs to make use of specific tools and models. The tool demand profit pooling is useful to understand how a business creates value to individuals who have similar motivations for buying a product. Also, companies should integrate a demand chain model that enables a real-time communication between the manufacturer, the distribution channel, and the media so that a holistic approach to customer acquisition, retention and conversion can be developed. Becoming demand-driven is possible by implementing a product-as-a-service model (like the subscription-based model). Results show that this access not ownership-oriented model has several benefits, both for the company and the consumer. The practical research of the subscription-based "Care by Volvo" model underlined the possibility for a legacy business to adapt to the realities of shifting consumer habits (Chan, 2017). However, it must be taken into consideration that a shift in mindset and strategy cannot be under-estimated and takes a long time to be deeply and sustainably implemented.

Student's Mind

1   What are the steps to become demand-driven?
2   What are the values for suppliers and what for buyers?
3   Is it possible to be demand-driven without machine learning tools?
4   How can you compete based on a demand-driven strategy?
5   Which parties will oppose this kind of transformation?

Discussion Point

A demand-driven approach is a total change of focus, the organizations, and the values of a company. Why should a company start this change and what happens if they do not?

References

Chan, M. (2017). Care by Volvo leasing service launched in Europe. Retrieved from https://paultan.org/2017/09/27/care-by-volvo-leasing-service-launched-in-europe/
Gupta, S. (2018). *Driving Digital Strategy: A Guide to Reimagining Your Business*. Boston, MA: Harvard Business Review Press.

Index

Note: Page locators in *italic* refer to figures.

Printed in the United States
by Baker & Taylor Publisher Services